seven aunts

Also by Staci Lola Drouillard
Published by the University of Minnesota Press

*Walking the Old Road: A People's History of Chippewa City
and the Grand Marais Anishinaabe*

seven aunts

Staci Lola Drouillard

University of Minnesota Press
Minneapolis
London

Published by the University of Minnesota Press
111 Third Avenue South, Suite 290
Minneapolis, MN 55401-2520
http://www.upress.umn.edu

ISBN 978-1-5179-1285-7 (pb)

Library of Congress record available at https://lccn.loc.gov/2021062307.

Printed in Canada on acid-free paper

The University of Minnesota is an equal-opportunity educator and employer.

28 27 26 25 24 23 22   10 9 8 7 6 5 4 3 2 1

For my mother,
Joyce Alice Burge Drouillard,
who taught us how to swim

Contents

My Aunties

I'VE SPENT A LOT OF TIME feeling invisible. In school, knowing the answer to a question but too afraid to raise my hand. Being profiled as a shy girl, a tall girl, a chubby girl, a girl who always has her nose in a book, a person who doesn't quite fit into a neatly shaped box. As an adult I've felt ignored at important meetings, been talked over by others, and carelessly overlooked—as if I weren't standing inside the room at all. I know that a lot of people can relate to feeling dismissed or invisible, which is a complicated state of being. And I know some might say this perception is somehow our fault, or that it originates inside us or is something we put on, like a camouflage coat. But in truth, women, people of color, those who live in poverty, people who identify as gender nonbinary, and nonconformists of all shapes and sizes know very well when we are being discounted. This prompts the question: why are some people's lives and histories held up like shining stars, while other people's lives and histories are kept in the dark, like an amaryllis bulb wintered away in a pot of dirt and deprived of sunlight?

This book is about the hidden lives of women. Those who rarely speak out of turn and those who shout their truths to the sky, even though no one is paying attention. The women who will never grace the cover of a magazine because of a scar they have carried with them since they were a baby or because they pulled out all their own eyelashes, as the case may be. These are the women who will never have a street or road named after them, like I wish each of my aunties had.

If I had my choice there would be Faye's Way, Lila Lane, Doreen Drive, Gloria Boulevard, the Betty Memorial Highway, Carol Cove, and the Diane Scenic Byway. Because the truth is that our grandmothers, mothers, and aunties have all committed great acts of heroism, devotion, and self-sacrifice so that the people they love might have a chance at being seen one day. And, like the lives of these women, the collective hurts that accompany their lived experiences are many, which, like the women themselves, are often hidden in plain sight. If I am being completely honest, some of my aunts were invisible even to me, until I started collecting stories and writing about their lives. But when you begin to see, there is no way to unsee. It's all there in Technicolor. If my seven aunties were part of a quilt, they would be unusually shaped patches, boast a diversity of patterns, and be bound together with multiple colors of thread. This quilt would have blood-stains on it, from childbirth and the pain of dying. It would have dirt ground into it, from being dragged through the farm fields of Warba in northern Minnesota, and tattered rips in the fabric, from being caught on the scratchy branches of a black spruce tree on the North Shore of Lake Superior. There would be watermarks from an ocean of salty tears, and embroidered flowers in brightly colored floss—sunflowers, pussy willows, marsh marigolds, and thorny, wild roses.

To honor these women, I am shouting out, stitching together, reciting, rhyming, quietly stirring, and at times delicately whispering these real stories about seven women who matter a lot. The truth is that without each of them our extended family would have crumbled into pieces, like a cake made without eggs. It is also true that without each other, their shared lives as sisters, wives, and mothers would have been much mightier struggles than they already were. The things all these women share in common with girls born into large, impoverished, midwestern families are the things they carry with them, far beyond the edge of the woods and many, many miles past the nearest neighbor's fields. Their identity as girls—and later as wives, mothers, aunties, and grandmothers—places them as heroines at the center of the world stage, in a society that tries persistently to keep them hidden away in the wings. And so, this book is a testament to an extended family of culturally overlooked women who were born between the Great Depression and the start of World War II. It's the story of women and girls from a long time ago, and the story of girls and women today. It feels good to make them the shining stars of the show because that's how I imagine all of them.

On these seven roadways named for seven aunties are a multitude of houses. Some are single-family units tucked inside low-income apartment buildings and some are big isolated farmhouses with horses and three-legged German shepherds. My seven aunties all set up housekeeping in a number of places—from Weyauwega and Milwaukee in east central Wisconsin, to the northern Minnesota towns of Warba, Skunk Hollow, Taconite Harbor, Duluth, and Grand Marais. Some of them moved very far away for a time, and many of them tried to fit into the big cities of Minneapolis, St. Paul, and Chicago. In the end, all of them eventually came back home to the North Shore of Lake Superior.

My aunt Lila once told me that she loved me "no matter what." I write about each of my seven aunties with this kind of unconditional love in my heart, just like Aunt Lila taught me to do. All seven of my aunties belong to me unconditionally, and I to them. Each woman's story is vital to tell—not because they were famous astronauts, inventors, politicians, or war heroes, but because they had the courage to live in this world at all. And that, for me, is enough.

Faye

ILIKE TO IMAGINE that my aunties' stories are
like separate rooms inside two different houses.
There are seven rooms for seven aunts—four on
my mother's side and three on my dad's. Each of my auntie's rooms
has at least one door, and they all have windows to let the light in.
Some rooms are filled with collectibles—ceramic chickens, flowered
English teacups, picture frames made from quills and birchbark.
Some have hidden closets, or stairs leading to places you've never
been before. If these rooms represent the stories of our relatives,
then the houses that shelter them contain the collective histories of
our extended families. These are the really old parts of each building
that contain the foundational elements of our families. Some of these
houses are sturdily built, support many levels, and can accommodate a
multitude of rooms in every shape and size. Some houses are shoddily
built, with leaky roofs, cracked foundations, and squeaky staircases.
The condition and longevity of these symbolic homes have very little
to do with financial wealth and everything to do with how well the
rooms and living spaces are maintained and cared for as time passes
from one generation to the next. Because once the carpenter ants or
dry rot sets in, it's much too late to save what's left of the house.

The Burge house of stories has five rooms for five sisters, two
rooms for two brothers, plus a shared one for Grandma Freda and
Grandpa Bill. The house looks like any midwestern-style farmhouse
from the 1940s, but this one has a foundation built of cinder blocks
from Germany, Canada, and Wisconsin. The cement walls that hold

up the building's dugout basement have water stains that go halfway up to the main floor—a reminder of the night their actual homestead was completely flooded in a torrential rainstorm, on the very first day they moved from Lawrence Lake to a potato farm a mile outside Warba, Minnesota, on the Mesabi Iron Range (also known in Minnesota as the "Range," *mesaabe* being the Ojibwe word for "giant").

All eight of the rooms in the Burge house are in various stages of occupancy, like an apartment on moving day, with partially filled boxes and furniture covered with dust covers. The only exception is the one that belongs to my mother, Joyce Alice Burge, the youngest Burge daughter. My mother's room is packed full, decorated with all the things that make her a mother to me and my younger sister, Dawn, and her room is next to the rooms of her older sisters: Faye, Lila, Betty, and Carol. As sisters, each of them has helped add furniture, curtains, clothing, good food, and warmth to my mother's story, and they have all enriched my story too. They belong to us and we belong to them. But there are still so many boxes left to unpack. Staring at the four doors that will lead me into the lives of my aunts, I start with the oldest, Faye, whose room is almost totally empty, at least to me. There are a few old photos on the wall and a rickety wooden table on which someone has left behind a kid's Lone Ranger mask, the kind you would have seen in an old Sears, Roebuck catalog from the 1950s.

For all the years Faye was my aunt, there are only a few small moments of clarity in an otherwise out-of-focus home movie. These small bits are mostly snapshots of her and do not tell a reliable story about who she really was and what her life was like. Within the room of her story, there are quite a few closets that need to be opened and explored, along with a number of shuttered windows that need to be dusted off and opened to the daylight. This is not to say that Faye was a bad housekeeper or lived her life in the dark—neither is true. But the simple act of opening the shutters is a bit like welcoming in the past— something that takes a little bit of bravery, a little bit of tenderness, and at times, a good dose of careful consideration. This is something Aunt Faye would have understood very well.

I remember that Aunt Faye was never quick with her words and always seemed to be formulating her thoughts ahead of time, as if she was trying to conserve the time and energy it would take to speak her mind. She was soft, like a comfortable place to rest, and I can see her most clearly wearing floaty, utilitarian nightgowns well into the day, her large bosom serving as a sturdy shelf for the rows of lace and delicate pin pleats on the front of her gown. These nighties were almost always soft pastel blue or pale yellow. They draped loosely over her shoulders and tumbled toward the floor—her body hidden underneath, a plump parsnip tapering down to slender and delicate ankles. I have a vague memory of her feet, which were always covered in new, white cotton socks and wedged into slippers that matched the color of her nightgown that day. Trying to extract a person's essence from these tiny bits is like trying to experience the sensation of weightlessness on the moon through the lens of a telescope, firmly planted on earth, 238,900 miles away.

Faye was a curly-haired brunette with a bow-shaped mouth and dark-brown eyes. She was of average height for most women and carried the burden of extra weight from the time she was a young girl. Aunt Faye was not someone who likely would draw anyone's attention based on the way she looked or the way she dressed. In photographs, she is familiar to me, because she has the dark eyes of my mother and grandmother, and her face is full and shaped like a heart, just like mine. But that photographic image of a dark-haired Faye is not within my experience of knowing her. Her hair had turned wispy and white by the time I was first able to spend time with her when I was two or three years old. And if she ever wore anything but cotton nighties, I'm not really sure what that would have been. Although I won't ever really know what motivated Auntie Faye to stay in her nightgown all day, I do know that she was as kind and tenderhearted to me as she was erased by a world that, in profound ways, dismissed and disparaged her. Anyone who really knew Faye loved her for who she was and admired her as a gentle and protective part of the Burge family. But here's the thing—when family secrets and hidden truths are shuttered away and protected at all costs, someone always has to pay the price. This is something that is hard for me to reconcile when I think of Auntie Faye's life and how we remember her.

My mother enjoys telling the story of how Aunt Faye visited us in Grand Marais when I was a little girl and she sat with me for hours reading and rereading my favorite picture book, *Holiday for Edith and* the Bears, by Dare Wright. It's the story of a lonely doll named Edith who goes on a lovely vacation to the sea with her teddy bear friends. On a beautiful sunny day, they convene in a convertible, have a picnic, drive to the ocean, and wade into the surf, a blond-haired doll and her two fluffy, teddy bear companions. I remember absorbing every glossy, black-and-white picture with all my senses. Aunt Faye had a thin yet husky voice and an easy, restrained laugh, because she suffered from asthma her whole life. Every minute of every day she had to struggle for air—she spent her life unable to breathe. Her raspy voice is what sticks with me the most. She would read a few pages to me, laugh, wheeze, and then take a big puff of her atomizer. When I would ask her to read more, she would start the book from the beginning, laugh, wheeze, and take another puff. It's as if she was containing an enormous belly laugh but didn't have enough wind left in her body to let it out, so her giggles bubbled up and out of her throat in a dry, strung-out cacophony. Perhaps just reading out loud was laborious for her, but she loved me, so she wheezed, laughed, and coughed her way through the story of Edith and the bears, over and over again.

****

Faye lived in California for most of my life, which was not as far away as the moon but felt that way to a kid from northern Minnesota. We only visited the West Coast one time when we were kids, and it was to see her younger sister, my aunt Carol, who lived in Los Angeles. It was 1980 and the people I knew really didn't fly on planes back then— especially moms with little kids who barely had enough money for a weekly grocery run. So, the only way for us to get there was to pile into our wood-paneled station wagon, with my little sister, Dawn, my cousin Cindy, and me crammed together in the back seat. Mom was driving because her sister Betty never drove that much, so Aunt Betty stayed on the passenger side for all 2,186 miles. We drove out to California that one winter, just us women and girls. I was twelve going on thirteen. Terrycloth was a new fashion trend, and Mom had bought me a brand-new orange-and-white striped shorts set to wear as soon as we put the northern winter behind us. Door to door, it takes over thirty hours to drive from northern Minnesota to Southern California. With three kids, a layover in Arizona to pick up white-haired Grandma

Freda Burge, and two nicotine-addicted mothers who had to stop for cigarettes and empty the Country Squire's deep ashtray every few hundred miles, it actually took five days to get there.

When we left Grand Marais, on the North Shore of Lake Superior, we drove out of a late-March blizzard and tooled our way cross-country, pausing for a few days to pick up Grandma Freda at her and Grandpa's double-wide trailer in Tucson. There would be a lot of firsts during this trip—shopping at a Walmart, experiencing pickled jalapeño peppers swimming in a cup of melted nacho cheese, seeing a cactus in real life. When we drove through the white sands of Yuma I made the discovery that sand could drift just like snow. It was similar to Edith and the two teddy bears' packing up and going to the beach, except our moms were chain-smoking Kent III 100s, with Grandma complaining periodically from the back seat about how the smoke was making her eyes water. Grandma Freda always wore Roses, Roses cologne, which had dutifully gone to war against the wretched smell of hot cigarette smoke, with battle lines drawn somewhere between Tucson and Joshua Tree National Monument (now a national park).

It's important to point out that on road trips back then, there were no cell phones with GPS to help you navigate the big cities, avoid traffic jams, or find the closest fast food. So, until we got to Tucson it was Stuckey's, Stuckey's, or Stuckey's—your choice. And Mom still jokes about big city traffic jams and how "If that nice man in Kansas City hadn't let us in, we'd still be sitting there." This trip was meant to be a reunion of three of the five Burge sisters, and after it was over, it would cement in my mind how all the Burge aunties fit together to form a puzzle—or sometimes didn't fit, as was the case with Aunt Faye, the oldest daughter of Bill and Freda Burge.

* * * * * *

In order to understand Auntie Faye and the complexities of her life, especially as they relate to her strong desire to be a wife and mother, we need to dig into the really old parts of the Burge family house— the stones, bricks, and mortar that form the foundation of the Burge extended family history.

It's true that Auntie Faye's metaphorical room in the Burge family house belonged to her as the oldest girl, but before Faye was born, Bill and Freda had two sons—George and Mark. Only one of these boys made it to adulthood, a fact of family history that had an impact on everyone, especially Grandma Freda. According to my mom, Grandma Freda never tried to hide the fact that she had lost a newborn baby, and she talked a lot about how she and Grandpa Bill, or "Billie" as she affectionately called him, had to bury the little boy's body in the family plot in Weyauwega, Wisconsin. It pains me to think of Grandma's sorrow and confusion caused by carrying a baby to full term, only having enough time on earth to cradle his hollow little body in her arms, christen him "Mark," and kiss him goodbye. Grandma was very "otherworldly" in some ways, and all her grandchildren knew she strongly believed in a place called heaven, which she talked about a lot. There are many roses there, their thorny stalks covered with silky, ruffled flowers in every color. In Grandma's heaven there are dressers loaded with creams, rouges, and decorative tins of talcum powder to ensure that the denizens of heaven always had "their faces on." God and Jesus lived there, too, and it's a good thing, because Grandma Freda was forced to relinquish her second baby to this imagined, unearthly place, and her little son would need the loving light of her strong, Christian spirits.

Growing a big family at that time in our shared American story was an expectation placed on young couples, especially farm country families, where there were always too many chores and not enough hands to do the work. Farmer's wives watched their own mothers raise ten or eleven children, and that same expectation would be made of them. This was definitely the case with the Burge family, with Freda watching her own mother raise a brood of kids, and Faye, watching and learning the same thing from Freda. There was no access to family planning options or birth control back then, and to even think about corking the bottle of motherhood until you had a chance to discover yourself, go to college, or build a career, was considered a sinful affront to nature and an assault on the very definition of American womanhood. I've come to think of this deeply ingrained expectation to have babies as a kind of "morbidity of motherhood," which is my own invented phrase to describe how far women in my family were willing to go to fulfill the expectations placed on them by others in society—including their own mothers, sisters, teachers, pastors, and themselves. Because there are elements of mental and physical neediness to this feminine, twentieth-century ailment, as well as the strict requirement that a woman's body be physiologically sound enough to bear children for ten years or more, the morbidity of motherhood contains an all-consuming quest to marry a man and have many, many children as quickly as the woman's body will allow. This malady affected all the Burge aunties to varying degrees. Symptoms include an insatiable desire to have children, melancholy over the inability to bear offspring, and the deep-seated belief that a woman's value is proportional to the number of children she has. My imaginary dictionary entry would look like this: **mor·bid·i·ty of moth·er·hood.** Noun: 1. condition of being sickened physically by the need to be a mother. 2. mental affliction affecting women whose only desire is to bear children; i.e., if you are not a mother, your life has no meaning. Use: "Young Faye suffered the anguish caused by the morbidity of motherhood, which posits that only women with children have value." Also: "Therapy can substantially reduce motherhood morbidity in women who have too many children or, conversely, not enough children."

In other words, a woman can't win if she is cursed with the morbidity of motherhood.

* * * * * * *

Bearing lots of children was to be expected of Grandma Freda, but I wonder what kind of expectation was put on her as a young woman and wife when it was time to grieve the loss of her second son and then move on to the next baby? Within the morbidity-of-motherhood mindset, was she just expected to let him go and try again? Is losing a baby at the age of twenty-three similar to losing a piece of your own body that you will never get back? Did Grandma Freda's body have time to rest before she was pregnant with Faye, her third child? And who did she turn to for help while the blackness of mourning an infant baby touched down inside her head and roiled around like a late spring tornado. Part of the answer is that she would have had help from her mother, Pauline, who was never very far away. And this gives me some comfort.

Great-grandma Pauline (Polena) Wangerin was born in Baden,

Germany, in 1860. She came to America on a ship from Hamburg when she was five years old. Her father was Johann Christian Friedrich Wangerin, and her mother was Wilhelmine (Streichel) Wangerin, whose father was German and mother Czechoslovakian. Sadly, Polena's mother, Wilhelmine, died when she was forty-five, leaving behind a family of young children, including Polena, who was just ten years old. The survivors among the Wangerin family followed in the path of many other German immigrants who moved through the port of New York and settled in the Milwaukee area. By the time Polena was in her twenties, her name had been Americanized to "Pauline." When she was twenty-two, Pauline got her deeply European roots tangled up with the German roots of a man named Otto Stelter, who was six years older than she. The couple were married on August 15, 1882, in Milwaukee.

Otto was also born in Germany in 1854. His father's name was Gottlieb Stelter II, and his mother was Anna Christina (Langen) Stelter. He was ten years old when he and his family arrived in New York in 1865. Both the Stelters and the Wangerins were part of the first and second waves of Germans to settle in Wisconsin, the heartland of the Midwest. (This was before World War II, of course, so any stigma attached to being of German descent came much later. Based on what I've learned about some of my Stelter and Burge relatives, that stigma was well deserved in some cases, but now's not quite the time to tell that part of their story.) So, as part of those first two waves of immigrants, many German families chose to live in Wisconsin because of the cheap, available farmland. Great-grandpa's family, the Stelters, originally settled in Bloomfield, a small farm town near the border of Wisconsin and Illinois. The closest city is Milwaukee, a place many German immigrants chose as their adopted hometown because of the growing wheat and agricultural shipping industry—the economic boom that can be credited to the surrounding fertile growing conditions and the city's location on Lake Michigan. At that time, Milwaukee was also known as *die deutsche Athen*, or "the German Athens." And, true to form, Grandma Freda always had a crock of shredded cabbage specked with caraway seeds fermenting on the counter in their farmhouse kitchen to serve alongside sausages or schnitzel.

As a young man, Great-grandpa Stelter worked as a *Braumeister* in Milwaukee, where he met Great-grandma Pauline somewhere in the bowels of that industrial town, which was built, in part, on bottles of beer. The people of Milwaukee love their German-style lagers so much they even named their baseball team the Brewers—after these inventive people who knew how to coax bubbles out of a vat of Lake Michigan water, malted grains, Wisconsin-grown hop flowers, and sugar. Women would not have been allowed in the same room as men in taverns in the late 1800s—but they did work in Wisconsin beer factories, washing, filling, and capping bottles—so I imagine a scenario in which the young brewer Otto Stelter, smelling of yesterday's sharp hops and fermentation, meets a German-speaking young lady while attending church with their respective families at one of the German-founded Lutheran churches that were built close to the Milwaukee River. I choose this wholesome approach to history because of what's known about the Stelters, churchgoing traditionalists who worked very hard during the week and worshipped just as hard every Sunday.

****

The Stelters raised their children on the farm in Bloomfield. That's where my Grandma Freda was born in August 1903. We still have her Christian confirmation certificate, torn and yellowed, which is printed in German and dated April 1, 1917. It was stowed away in an old wooden box that came from my grandma's house and, after she passed on, was kept at Aunt Lila's house and ended up in my mom's care. This chest of family treasures is now perched next to my writing desk and is full of old letters and documents from the life story of the Burges as well as some errant trinkets, like a pale blue silhouette pendant, and one of Grandpa Burge's scuffed and dented metal name tags from one of his many jobs. Grandma's full name is printed on the certificate in old-fashioned calligraphy: *Frieda Helene Wilhelmine Stelter*. I don't know exactly when her name was shortened to Freda, but the missing *i* and the choice to use only an *e* instead are intriguing. Just more proof that there was no one quite like her. Grandma Freda was the youngest of eleven, but two of her older siblings died when they were infants, dual traumas that undoubtedly took a toll on her mother, Pauline, just as it would later take a toll on Freda when she had to face the birth and subsequent death of her own baby boy.

When she was sixteen, two years after her church confirmation, Grandma Freda's family sold their working farm in Bloomfield and moved north, to the river town of Weyauwega, Wisconsin. The Stelters were not quite middle class, but they did have enough money and resources to live well in a town that had a developed downtown area studded with four-story buildings. A product of the railroad boom, the village served as an active rail intersection between Milwaukee and all points west. A town of about 1,800 people in the water-rich river country of Wisconsin, Weyauwega is named for the Menominee "chief" Weyauwega who lived in a settlement on the banks of White Lake. Steeped in the tradition of rooting out Indigenous people to make way for European-style farming and religion, Weyauwega unabashedly touts a history of desecration as part of their welcome wagon. According to the area Chamber of Commerce, a key piece of Chief Weyauwega was stolen from his final resting place, and "thanks to the efforts of Dr. Bliss of Royalton, Wisconsin," the chief's skull "now resides in the Smithsonian Institute in Washington, D.C." The name Weyauwega is said to be Menominee for "here we rest," which may be true for some of my Stelter relatives, but is decidedly not true for Chief Weyauwega. Digging into the history of tillable ground in Wisconsin is likely to expose a whole different aspect of putting down roots in America. But for the Stelters of Bloomfield, and now Weyauwega, the Midwest was a place where almost any farm family could move about freely, unencumbered by a historical sense of social responsibility to the places where they fished and planted their gardens. If the soil could grow potatoes and carrots, there was no need to dig any farther.

Weyauwega is where Grandma Freda finished high school. Grandma's other siblings were already spread out across the country at that time. Her oldest brother, Oscar, and sister Clara were living in Bloomer, Wisconsin. Otto Jr. resided in Chippewa Falls, Walter in Milwaukee, and her brother Martin moved the farthest away, to New York City. Martin always played a big part in Freda's life, and he is an important part of her story (no doubt his room is adjacent to hers in the Stelter family house of stories). Their relationship would save her more than a few times, when the rest of the world, including her husband, had let her down. Martin remained single his whole life, and my mother and my uncle Pete openly acknowledge now that their uncle Martin was gay. Both also confirmed that no one in the family ever talked about the fact that Martin preferred the company of men. It was just never acknowledged or intruded upon in any way. In spite of that, Grandma Freda never cut ties to her brother, and it is because of Martin that the Burge family would ultimately all come to live in northern Minnesota. This is a part of the family story that will have to be told a few different ways, by a few different aunts.

* * * * * * *

My grandfather William Burge was born and raised in Winnipeg, Manitoba, and crossed the Canada–U.S. border as an illegal immigrant around the age of fifteen. There is no paperwork to support this because he intentionally left the Burge home and sneaked into America. As a young man, Grandpa lived on his own and worked his way around the Midwest. He did odd construction and farming jobs, and according to Aunt Betty, while Grandpa was a transient worker in New York City, he was operating a tractor out on an open field and was struck by lightning. He lived with a raised, hidden scar somewhere on his skin, which was precisely the opposite of where the bolt of electricity entered his body. It is statistically rare to survive a lightning strike that actually surges through your body, and so by the time he was just twenty years old, Grandpa Bill had already proved that his time here on earth was either divinely sanctioned or that he was incredibly unlucky. It was perhaps this intimate encounter with a colossal force of nature that helped prepare him for a full life with the human equivalent of cloud-to-ground lightning—a heavenly charged beauty by the name of Freda Stelter. Like that godly smack on the head, the diminutive, dark-haired Freda swept six-foot-three William off his feet. Grandma was twenty when she met Bill Burge in Bloomer, Wisconsin. They were married in nearby Eau Claire on May 10, 1924.

At that time, Grandma Freda was working as a beauty operator in Bloomer, and though she had a full client list, she didn't make enough money to sustain the two of them. Her new husband worked as a laborer and heavy equipment operator, the construction jobs were often short term, and Grandpa would get laid off as soon as the work was finished. So, by the fall of 1924, just five months after their wedding, the newlyweds were already separated by location—she back in Eau Claire with her sister and family, and he doing his best to make a living for the two of them by working construction in Cudahy, a suburb of Milwaukee. Separated by farmland, but not by love, the young couple experienced tough times, and a letter Grandma wrote to Grandpa just after they were married alludes to the dire state of their finances: "So, you still figure on going to Akron, have you had an answer already? How do you manage to live so cheaply? You must be a better house keeper than I. But darling do not starve yourself."

During this period, Grandma would write to him every day, but he was very slow to send a letter back, making his young bride beside herself with worry and insecurity. In one letter she asked him outright why she had not heard from him, and Grandpa was forced to admit why he was unable to reply sooner. He wrote to her twice that week, explaining, "I don't know when we were ever so hard up before Freda. Haven't even enough to buy postage stamps so that's why you didn't get a letter sooner—but don't tell anyone we are that poor will you?"

And then a few days later he shared better news: "I'll tell you why I didn't write to you before. I didn't have stamps but got a big pay last nite, $4.60 my first nites work, but guess I'll make better in the future."

There are many woebegone letters from one lover to the other from late in 1924 through 1925. To her he is "Daddie"; to him she is his "Skookenpoof." In this letter she wrote to her Billie during the summer of 1924, life at the Stelter home in Eau Claire is one of lighthearted bounty: "We had fish for supper and kuchen. I am going to send you some Monday. Did you receive the candy? Darling I am so glad you are going to write to me every day, as your letters make me so happy. I am going to write to you too . . . Dad bought a large basket of grapes today. Now he is going to make wine. And he has got some more real beer down cellar. He went fishing yesterday and caught fifty-one. Isn't that some catch?"

My mother told me that Grandma Burge loved living in Wisconsin because of its plentiful farmland, apple orchards, and good fishing. A plucky farm girl who was at home in a garden or on the river fishing with her father, Freda knew how to live off the land.

By November 1924, a lonesome and heartsick Freda tried to entice her husband, Bill, to leave his job in Milwaukee and join her in preparing for a new addition to their family. At the time, she was four months pregnant with their first baby. "Dad brought a big batch of sunfish. Yum, yum they sure were good. I wish you could have had some too. Darling I miss you too, I would be glad if you would catch the train here. Ida [her sister] said if you would come, she wouldn't let you go back. She said they would help you start a business of your own. Wouldn't that be wonderful! I sewed a little dress for Ray [her nephew] yesterday, he looks so cute in it. Ida and I are going down this morning and get some more goods and we are going to sew again. Darling, later I am going to sew some baby clothes for our little darling."

It's not clear why Grandpa Burge decided against leaving his job to try to make a go of life in Weyauwega, but Freda's letter did not convince him to make a change. And so, the pair would be rejoined and living under the same roof, prior to the arrival of George, their first son, born in April 1925 at a hospital in Cudahy. I would very much like to know the contents of a letter sent to them by Freda's father, Otto Stelter. It's dated May 9, 1925. The return address is simply "from Otto Stelter, Weyauwega, Wis." The four-page letter is written all in German with a sharp pencil, in tidy cursive. I imagine that the letter included her father's well wishes, along with some money to help support their burgeoning family. Or perhaps the gift was to be used by his daughter as traveling money, for when it was time to bring her baby boy home to meet his grandparents. And that's exactly what happened. When George was a tiny baby, Grandma left her husband in Cudahy and went back to her mother's house in Weyauwega. My mom shared what her sisters had told me about Great-grandma Stelter's role in raising her grandchildren, which is vitally important to Aunt Faye's story as well as the stories of her sisters. As my mother described, "Each time a baby was born, my mother went to her mother's house and then Grandma Stelter took care of each baby."

****

William and Freda had eight children in relatively rapid succession, beginning with Uncle George in 1925 and ending with my mom, Joyce Alice Burge, who was born in Morrison, Illinois, in 1938. In order they are George, Mark, Faye, Lila, Ray (Pete), Betty, Carol, and Joyce. As Aunt Betty said, "I don't think any of us were born in the same place." The years when Grandma went from being pregnant to giving birth and being pregnant again were a very mobile time for Grandpa—sometimes his family followed him, and sometimes they stayed in Weyauwega, close to Freda's parents. It is in Weyauwega that their second son, Mark, was born and is buried.

For Freda, here's where the morbidity of motherhood takes over. In order to fill the well of sadness that Grandma must have been feeling at the loss of Mark, she rested her body and mind for one year and then she and Grandpa got their family back on track. I imagine it was Freda's mother who whispered to her about the beautiful gift of children, and how important it was to have something joyful to look forward to. I would also imagine, given the staunchly Christian values instilled in the Stelter family, it would have been her older sisters as well as her mother who reminded her that a houseful of children is blessed in the eyes of God. And Freda herself undoubtedly knew that making plenty of healthy children would be good for the well-being of her marriage, even with the emotional and physical pain that goes along with it. In another one of his letters when she was pregnant with their first son, George, Grandpa tenderly tells her how important children are to his family plan: "How are you feeling now sweetheart—do you still have those awful pains? I do hope they have gone away by now dearest . . . Oh Freda dearest you don't know how I really do love you and I do so want to make you happy and have a nice home for us and our little one but I haven't done much in that line yet have I dearest? But you still believe, don't you? Oh, my darling how we'll love it won't we. I don't know what I'd have done if you didn't like children. I know I'd have been real miserable."

My mother told me that after she read the flurry of love letters between her parents, Bill and Freda, she realized for the first time that they had actually loved each other. The bond of their young love would have been a help to Freda, because the two of them would have had to wade through the muck and sadness together, like plodding through a muddy field after that late spring tornado had its way with the farm. They made it through the crisis because they had each other, as well as the help of Freda's mother and father. The Stelters were people who apparently had a lot to give, at a time when their daughter really needed it, because she was about to have a daughter of her very own.

In 1928 Freda and Bill welcomed their third child into the world, a daughter named Faye, who was brought into the world with love and held inside the safety of her mother, Freda's, heart. And with the arrival of each new baby, a new hope was formed in the minds of Freda and Bill, who were still very young but had already experienced the ache and disappointment of a cruel and punishing world. And while George, by all accounts was a sturdy and healthy boy, Faye was not sturdy or particularly healthy. From the day she was born, she was plagued with medical problems, including chronic asthma. *Asthma*, it turns out, is the Greek word for "wind," named after the way it causes its victims to struggle for air. Faye was born in this fragile state at a time when medical care was a luxury, and the family was still blowing across the farm fields of Wisconsin, like dry coughs extruded from the lungs of a very sick little girl.

* * * * * * *

His early days as *Braumeister* finally caught up with Great-grandpa Otto Stelter, and he died of cirrhosis of the liver in 1929, when Faye was just one year old. Every other year after that, Grandma Freda continued to take her babies home to be cared for by her mother, Pauline, regardless of where Bill was working, or if the family was living with him at the time. This pattern of taking the babies home was so fully formed that Great-grandma Pauline had a hand in raising all my Burge aunts and uncles. The oldest kids have very fond memories of her, saying that their Grandma Stelter was always a kind and loving person in their lives, who seemed to treat each one of them as her own, very special grandchild. Her commitment to nurturing the children in her life may very well be attributed to her own history, but it also speaks to her character and capacity for love. In Freda's case, it may also have had a lot to do with the reality of the Burge family's financial situation, which continued to get in the way of Freda and Bill's desire to provide a suitable home for the growing brood of Burge children. When they were broke, the Stelters were always there to help.

According to Aunt Lila, who was born in Weyauwega in 1930, even when he was working full-time Grandpa never made enough money to buy a house of their own. She remembers her mother working part-time as a beautician or having to wait tables in a café to make a little money on the side. Both Aunt Lila and Aunt Betty remember that their dad was almost always away at work, with very little of his time spent at home. From 1925, when Uncle George was born, to 1938, when my mom, the youngest of the Burges joined the world, the family was forced to move from house to house in and around Wisconsin, Iowa, and Illinois, which is where they were living when my mom was born. The fact that she was born in Morrison, Illinois, seems very strange, since we have absolutely no connection to the land or the people there. Due to the rootlessness of the Burge family, there is quite a bit of confusion about my mom's birthday and how she came into the world in a hospital in Illinois. Her birth certificate lists a date before Christmas, but Grandma Freda swore that she was born after Christmas. Not knowing your actual birthday is collateral damage for being the last of eight kids, born to parents who were barely able to scrape by and seemingly always in a state of transitional chaos.

Grandpa Burge had secured a temporary job in a small Iowa town, just across the Mississippi River from Morrison, and it was not an option to leave Freda home alone with six going on seven children, who ranged in age from newborn to thirteen. At that time, men and older boys did not take care of the kids—that was a job for women and girls. It was something that would have been required of them, and Aunt Faye, by the time she was ten years old, had already learned how to feed, clothe, bathe, and nurture her littlest sisters and brother. By the time her littlest sister, Joyce, was one year old, Grandpa's job in Iowa had dried up and the Burges moved back to Weyauwega to be close to Great-grandma Stelter, who was now an old woman and in very poor health.

The care of babies was likely considered a magical cure-all for Great-grandma Pauline, at least in the mind of her daughter Freda. At eighty years old, Pauline was suffering from a grave illness when the family returned to Weyauwega. Pauline's fretting and worried daughter Freda earnestly believed that "my mother will be o.k. if I just bring this beautiful baby in to see her." And so, she brought Joyce into her mother's bedroom, in the hopes that a dark-haired, apple-cheeked toddler would be able to save her diseased grandmother from certain death. In the Burge family, the morbidity of motherhood crisscrosses every generation. It carries with it the grandiose expectation of prolific mothering, which, at its root, is based in blind faith that the preponderance of children will save the mother, and by inheritance, will also save the grandmother. Those afflicted with the condition tend to take the magical view that children are bursting with a life force so bright that they have the ability to steal mortality right out from under the nose of death. But in spite of Grandma Freda's wishful thinking, the magic wasn't strong enough that day, and Pauline died soon after. The story of Great-grandma's death was remembered and then passed down to my mother from Aunt Faye, who would have been twelve years old when Great-grandma Pauline died in 1940. Faye was there to watch her little sister being whisked into her grandmother's arms in an attempt to save her life.

The perceived magic of babies and the importance of bringing children into the world very much influenced the next three generations of Stelter and Burge women. The ability to conceive a baby, or not, was one of the defining characteristics of all the Burge aunts. It started with Great-grandma Pauline, who had eleven children, and then moved like oxygen through Grandma Freda and flowed into all of the Burge daughters: Faye, Lila, Betty, Carol, and my mother, Joyce. Each one of them would experience motherhood in different ways and all with equal measures of joy, heartache, loss, and grief. For some of the Burge aunts, the expectation placed on motherhood was an overwhelming thing—especially when the babies came early and fast, as they did for Aunt Lila and Aunt Carol. But for the other three Burge sisters, who all struggled to conceive a baby, society cursed them with a different kind of expectation, one that overtook their bodies and minds with that same kind of morbidity of motherhood—where great expectation is the primary disease and having a baby is the only cure.

This kind of disorder—an all-consuming mental and physical condition—very much hobbled Aunt Faye, who was raised within a matriarchy of mothers who did their duty to bring children into the world at all costs. That was their fate and their purpose, and family was everything. To make matters worse for her, Faye was a natural at taking care of people and had a lot of love to give. She had a very tender heart, having grown up mothering her younger siblings, and perhaps she saw no other fate for herself than to be a mother to children of her own one day. By the time she was a young girl, Faye's role in the family was clear. In a letter Grandma Freda wrote to grandpa around the time Faye was about eight years old, she told him: "Faye is so much better and she is such a comfort to me, I will miss her when she goes back to school. George seems so cranky and upset. I try hard to be a good mother and wife but know I have failed at times."

Typically, Grandpa was away working at the time, leaving Grandma to care for five, soon to be six young children in Weyauwega. At the tender age of eight, Faye's role as a surrogate mother and caretaker for her younger siblings was already set, like a bowl of lime Jell-O placed at the center of the table on Easter Sunday.

****

The degree to which Aunt Faye took care of others is always the first thing that came up when I asked my other aunts about her. Her sister Betty said, "She was my mother, my sister . . . I felt like I could tell her anything. She was very special to me." Faye became a soft place for people to land, because home, in the case of many families, is where the mothering is. Motherhood in all forms becomes the root of the tree, the footings of our family buildings and the connective tissue between what we see in the mirror and what we can't see underneath our skin. Motherhood also serves as a sort of ephemeral touchstone—a place of home in an atmosphere of impermanence; especially with the Burges who moved from place to place, like hops flowers blowing in the breeze. And in Faye's case, her physical self was the embodiment of effervescent motherhood, right down to the way she took up space in the world.

I once made a painting of Aunt Faye based on an old family photo in which she is posing with a gaggle of Burge cousins in Minneapolis. She is standing directly behind the group of children who are spread out in front of her: two boys, two girls, and two dogs. The girls are in their Easter dresses, and the boys are wearing clean new clothes, as if they are just back from church. Each girl carries a dainty white Easter basket overflowing with artificial Easter grass. Faye is looking down on the backs of their heads, her body softly absorbing the children's and canines' bodies until they appear conjoined, like one, round planet. There is a sweet smile on her face, and an air of patience about her, as if she is willing to stand there all day if necessary. She is not the mother of these children; they belong to Uncle George and Aunt Elna, and yet Faye's generous arms wrap protectively around each and every one of them—the kids allowing her to herd them together and swaddle them with her affections, like a mother goose guarding her newly hatched goslings inside soft and feathered wings.

The Burge family geese and their great migratory trajectory from here to there and back again was soon about to change. When Great-grandma Stelter died in 1940, Grandma Freda inherited a sum of money that would be able to carry her family from Weyauwega to Lawrence Lake just north of Grand Rapids, Minnesota. The move was also spurred by Grandpa getting hired to work for a nearby iron mine as a crane operator. Grandpa, being rich with children but impoverished of financial options, applied for a job at a mining operation in Grand Rapids that was hiring men from all over the Midwest to work in the open pit mines. His experience as a heavy equipment operator would be in great demand, because on the Mesabi Iron Range, the depth of the pits and tunnels had no limits, and for every truckload of rock tailings, there would be another truckload of raw iron ore destined for the mills across Lake Superior. For the first time in his life, Grandpa had a job that was seemingly long term, without the threat of looming layoffs or insignificant pay.

After he secured the job, they packed up their belongings in Wisconsin and made the move to Lawrence Lake. According to Uncle Pete, the log cabin they first rented "was right on the lake shore. Ma liked to fish, and she and the kids would go fishing and catch dinner." He also said that he used to row her around in an old wooden boat, and together they would catch northern and walleye. He was about

seven years old when they moved in, but he clearly remembers the very
first night in the cabin when they woke up in the middle of the night
to furious itching and scratching. It turns out that the whole place
was infested with bedbugs. In a frenzy, Freda ordered all the children
outside and proceeded to spray the whole cabin, inside and out, with
undiluted gasoline. Pete remembers that "my dad used to get so mad
at her. I can see her yet, spraying gas all around the floor with that old
sprayer." By the time the Burges lived at Lawrence Lake, George, Faye,
Lila, and Pete were all old enough to go to school and learn the ways
of life in the north woods. Aunt Carol was only four at the time, and
my mother, Joyce, was also very young and has no memory of living
there. The family's stint at Lawrence Lake lasted only a few years, and
then, leaving the boat and rustic cabin behind, the family uprooted
once again, this time at the prospect of finally settling down for good.
The inheritance that Grandma got from her mother was enough to
buy a decent chunk of land close to the mines where Grandpa worked
almost every day. Thanks to Great-grandma Pauline, Freda was finally
able to create the beginnings of her own farm, which is something she
had always wished for.

And so, when my mother was just two, the Burge family settled
on a partially developed farm in the middle of the woods, one mile
outside Warba, a tiny town located on the Range in northern Minnesota. Warba is finally where the Burge family took off their traveling
shoes and ran after the American dream of owning land, with the
hope of gaining some of the privileges that went along with having a
place to put your things. At least, that was Grandma's intention when
she spent all her inheritance money to move from one wooded, buggy
place to another. As Aunt Faye once said while she was all grown
up and living in Minneapolis, "It's like the Minneapolis mosquitoes
know that I'm heading to Warba . . . They all jump in the car with me
and head north to meet their friends."

****

Warba has its own story of being a transitory town. It began as a logging
site known as Dickson's Spur, named for a timberman who worked
as a logger cutting down the massive forests of virgin white pine in
the 1890s. Once incorporated as a town, the name changed to Verna,

and it was located next to the village of Feeley (also known as Feeley's Spur), named for the sawmill owner (you guessed it) Thomas J. Feeley. The town grew large enough to have its own post office, which was established in 1901. To avoid confusion, the U.S. Post Office Department decided that "Feeley" was too close to "Foley," and a contest to rename the village was held. A man named A. A. Hall won; he chose the Ojibwe-inspired name "Waarbasibi," which was shortened to the unrecognizable "Warba." After the name change, the Great Northern Railway, which operated a line through the town, changed the depot name from Verna to Warba. The two towns merged into one junction, which became known for posterity as Warba.

Curiously, the Burge hometowns of Warba and Weyauwega both claim to be havens of leisure. *Waarbasibi*, the Ojibwemowin word co-opted by Hall, is inaccurately said to mean a "resting place" for the *waabishkaa waabizii*, or white swan. And though there is a nearby town named Swan River, neither *waarbasibi* nor a close translation for "resting place" is a linguistically good fit in the Ojibwe language.[1] On a map of the area, however, the Ojibwe burial mounds along the Floodwood River are clearly referenced,[2] which could be a more direct explanation for why the area is known as a place of repose. And while it sounds grand to live in a place of leisurely relaxation, the reality is that the people of Warba worked themselves to the bone, either on farms or in the mines. What is also true is that when you look at an aerial photograph of Warba, it's a tiny place that measures approximately five blocks by three blocks. From above, the buildings, roads, and anything else solid show up as sun-bleached shapes against the gray emptiness of the surrounding fields and farmlands.

We visited Warba only one time when we were kids. This was many years past any taconite boom, and to me, "downtown" Warba felt a lot like an abandoned movie set—a kind of hollow Hollywood version of a meat-and-potatoes Willa Cather prairie town. The day we visited, we rambled in our car down the main street, taking in the wooden facades and empty gas stations. I remember feeling sort of melancholy, thinking of how this was once considered the hometown of the Burge family. It's always been difficult to think of my mom and all the Burge relatives in such an empty place. As we rolled past the pavement and onto the gravel roads just at the end of the main street, we drove through stands of thick trees broken up by clearings in the forest—plots of land carved out of the landscape where farmers who came from elsewhere tried their best to coax garden produce out of the dirt. A tough enterprise for anyone given that the soil is best suited to sustain the roots of native pine trees and vast expanses of swamp brush, not grow potatoes. It seems Warba has always been a place where the woods outnumber the fields and the wood ticks and mosquitoes outnumber the people, just like Aunt Faye used to say.

When I asked my mother if she liked living in Warba when she was a little girl she said, "Not when I look back . . . not at all. We were farm, kind of trash." She says this in a softly angry way, mimicking the same tone as the people who put that idea in her head seventy years ago. She repeats it back to me in a voice that echoes her unreliable narrators from the past—the ones who would have whispered it behind her back but well within earshot. I can see her standing inside an old-timey shop where one could buy everything from bags of grain and feed corn to delicate charm bracelets tiny enough to fit a young girl's wrist: small enough even for Mom, who I imagine is about six years old. She's wearing a pair of denim coveralls handed down from her brother Pete. They are rolled up at the ankles, exposing her bare feet on the wooden floor of the shop, her pretty little face framed by dark, curly ringlets that cover her ears and fall down past the base of her neck. She is waiting for her older sister Faye, who has walked the mile to town with her smallest sister in tow to pick up the family grocery order. While Faye waits her turn at the counter, little Joyce's dark brown eyes are focused on the shelves next to the register where these tiny charm bracelets are on display along with a sprawling array of penny candy. Two women who are also there to shop examine the little barefoot girl from tip to toe, the way that certain women will always do—you know the ones.

"It's one of those Burge children," the Warba wife would whisper loudly to her stodgy friend perusing the bolts of fabric right next to her. "Just poor farm trash. What a shame."

It seems that despite Grandpa's efforts to keep his children clothed and fed, the number of feet that needed shoes compared with the number of hours in a workday kept the family in a continual state of poverty. My mother remembers there was also a liquor store downtown, just across the street from an auto garage, where her oldest sister, Faye's, first husband, Bob, once worked until things went very sour for him, and then for Faye. And there was Fats' Café, named for the owner because that's what everyone called him "Fats." She told me that any time she got a penny she'd walk into that café and get a piece of candy. She admitted that one time she didn't have a penny so she made a plan to go in and steal some purple Charms, her favorite. Once she got inside the café she got scared and couldn't bring herself to reach out and take something that she couldn't pay for. Leaving empty-handed, Mom would have to wait for someone else to buy her sweets. A lot of times that person was Faye, who was ten years older and had her own jobs as a teenager and later as a young woman. When I asked my mother about her oldest sister, she echoed the words of her sister Betty: "She was like a mother to me. She had a big influence on my life. And every time she came home to Warba on the bus, she brought us things. She was a good sister. She would bring candy, and we never got any candy ever."

In spite of Faye's loving generosity, my mother's very first memory of her is somewhat terrible, watching helplessly as she suffered through a violent asthma attack, coughing, spitting, and gagging into a metal bucket. When I asked my mom what Aunt Faye was like when they were growing up, she described her as being "very, very emotional. She got upset easily. And she always had an atomizer in her pocket in case she had an asthma attack."

* * * * * * *

Life in Warba was very formative for everyone, and though the family didn't quite fit in with the Warba establishment, the work of planting, weeding, and harvesting the farm required all hands on deck and created a sense of stability for the family for the very first time. Each of my aunts told me at one time or another that Grandma Freda always craved the ability to live in one place and not move around. What she knew the best was farm life, growing her own food, nurturing lilac and rose bushes, and understanding just how important it was to have your own chickens and at least one cow. The art of knowing how to coax milk out of a cow's udder every day was invaluable, especially when you had a big, hungry family. So, when the Burges settled in Warba, one of the first matters of business was to dig the field of potatoes that had been planted by the previous owner.

The farm, according to Uncle Pete, "was first owned by Ed Nelson, an old Norwegian." Nelson had already planted all ten acres with potatoes prior to when the Burges moved in, and so when they arrived, they had to pick every single hill of someone else's patch. Uncle Pete recalled that his sister Betty helped out on the farm, but his older brother George was going to school then, and his sister Lila "was kind of boy crazy" and not much help. He said, "We put all the potatoes in the root cellar and sold some . . . I can still smell rotten potatoes!" Farming is something the family did together for the most part. The older kids helped Grandma and Grandpa plant the garden each spring and worked to maintain the garden throughout the summer. The exceptions were Joyce, the youngest sister, and Faye, the oldest sister, who was sick a lot and didn't have to work outside. Uncle Pete remembers doing "a lot" of garden work, something he still grumbles about, even though he was eighty-seven years old when I asked him about growing up on the Warba farm.

While the younger kids were going to school in town, Faye had already dropped out, and by the time my mom was eight, her eldest sister had already left home to take a job at a children's home in Minneapolis. She did not know a soul in Minneapolis at the time, and so you could say that it was a very brave thing for her to do—to leave home at seventeen and move to the big city. As the oldest daughter, there would have been an expectation placed on Faye to set a path for her sisters. It was just after the end of World War II, and the prevailing American priorities were for women to relinquish their wartime jobs to returning servicemen and get to work building American families one baby at a time.

I can't really speculate what Faye's opinion was on the role of women at the time, and I don't think anyone else really knew either. Aunt Betty claims that Faye was always full of secrets. She never told any of her sisters much about her life or what she thought about things. Betty does remember that Faye had no experience with men at all when she left home. She never dated anyone when she was attending high school, and though she enjoyed working on crafts and art projects, she never really applied herself wholeheartedly to a hobby or expended much energy on getting to know her classmates. I suspect it's because she was very shy, and wasn't used to adding her perspective to conversations without being asked to join in. For me, it's easy to see why she didn't want to be the center of attention or even draw attention to herself. After all, she was prone to asthma attacks that could strike at any moment, which was frightening for others and humiliating for Faye. And because she struggled with her weight and was always several sizes larger than her sisters, the inverse happens inside the societally warped mind which tells us (women) that the more space you take up, the less entitled you are to take up extra space with talking. And so no one knows what the shy voices that lived inside young Faye had to say, or what she was feeling when she set off for Minneapolis to find her life.

She drove away from the farm in an old car Grandpa Burge had gotten for her. She had rarely driven outside the Grand Rapids area and somewhere between Duluth and Minneapolis she got lost, made a series of wrong turns, and began to panic. And with that panic came the dreaded wind—that brutal shortness of breath that, exacerbated by asthma, caused her to have a full-blown, panic-induced attack while behind the wheel of a car. Her erratic driving drew the attention of the police, who dutifully pulled her over. With no money in her purse for a motel, and scared out of her mind to continue driving, the police were forced to call Bill Burge back in Warba and ask him to come rescue his daughter.

This incident sticks out as a particularly formative moment for Faye, who had set out with the best of intentions, but proved to everyone (at least in her mind) that she wasn't strong enough or smart enough to leave home on her own. This was in stark contrast to her older brother, George, who did graduate from high school and went on to college. Because this was in 1945, the number of women attending college was much lower than that of men, and in fact, many prominent colleges didn't allow women to attend at all, including Harvard Medical School, which admitted female students for the first time in 1945. I imagine Grandpa Burge was grumpy with her, having to leave his job, spend the extra money on gas, perhaps blame himself for giving her a car she wasn't ready to handle, and have the extra worry that his oldest daughter wasn't equipped to make her own way in the world. But he loved Faye, so perhaps he took it all in stride. As my Grandma Burge would say, "aw quat tee saw," which is her exasperated German expression for "oh for heaven's sake!" At least, that's my guess at what she would have said when the phone rang and the police informed Grandpa that Faye was lost and stranded on the side of the road.

Eventually Aunt Faye did make it (by bus) to Minneapolis, where she settled into her early life working with children at Lutheran Social Service, a foster home for children. She had no credentials on paper for this job, but she had been caring for babies and young siblings for most of her life, so taking care of kids was a vocation she had always excelled at. Both my mom and Aunt Betty remember Faye coming back to visit the farm and bringing bags of candy and other treats for her younger siblings. And sometimes she brought more than candy home. As my mom said, "She was always bringing some baby back to the farm" from the foster home where she worked. It's not clear if she was trying these babies on to see if they would fit, or if she was following in the tradition of her own mother and bringing the babies home for everyone to see, in order to make everyone happy. Because these weren't her actual babies, Faye had nothing to lose in bringing them back to the farm. Aunt Betty remembers that some of these little kids weren't white like the Burges and 99 percent of the other families on the Iron Range were. At that time, around 1946 or so, bringing children of color home to rural Minnesota would have been considered scandalous in a number of households, but Aunt Faye was never fazed by that. And if Grandma Burge was ever bothered by it, she didn't let it show. My mom remembers that Faye "would often bring kids home to Warba. She just loved them. And Mom would just take them in. Sometimes they were kids from Lutheran Social Service where she worked or her wayward friends and their kids. One time one of Faye's friends brought bedbugs into the house and we had to take all of the bedding apart. Back then they used DDT for that kind of thing. Faye was always trying to rescue people."

It seems Grandma Burge just couldn't get away from the bane of bedbugs, no matter how she tried. And it's not clear whether DDT was a big improvement over spraying straight gas all over the house—but that's just what she decided to do that day. And each time Faye would bring home a new friend who was in trouble, or a baby that needed a home, Grandma would take Faye and her entourage in, bedbugs be damned.

Faye didn't just try to save strangers; she would often try to rescue her younger sisters, who were still back home in Warba and were often left to their own devices. In fact, it was Aunt Faye who bought Aunt Betty her first toothbrush, and it was Faye who took Betty to the eye doctor when it was determined that she had failed first grade because she couldn't see the chalkboard. When I asked Aunt Betty why her parents didn't take her to the doctor, she said, "probably because they didn't have money for glasses." Faye was, according to Betty, "my mother, my sister. I felt like I could tell her anything. She was very special to me. She was the one who told me about getting my period. And she was the one who told me when I needed to wear a bra, and she went out and bought one for me."

According to Betty, Faye worked for Lutheran Social Service in Minneapolis for a short time, but for reasons that aren't particularly clear Faye lost her job and ended up in the hospital, suffering from what Betty called "a mental breakdown." Somehow Grandpa Burge was able to retrieve her from Minneapolis and bring her back to Warba. No one could remember exactly why Faye had to go into the hospital. But for a young woman of eighteen who had never lived very far away from home, had no experience with being alone, and struggled with each breath, life was probably pretty overwhelming for her. Back in Warba, there was very little work for women at the time, and so my mom guessed that Faye may have taken a job as a babysitter when she came home, since that was always her truest calling.

****

It was just a little while after her return to the farm that Faye brought her first boyfriend home to meet everyone, something that left quite an impression on her sisters Betty, Carol, and Joyce, who were still at home. The man's name was Bob Palmer, and he was a veteran of World War II. He and Faye had met each other in Warba, although no one really recalls where that might have been. During his tenure in the army, Bob had been exposed to the kind of bombs that were filled with poisonous chemicals designed to kill a lot of people at once. Over time, exposure to the bad air of war had changed his physiology from the inside out, and he developed type 2 diabetes and other health issues that affected his ability to work or do physical labor. And so, as a young man, he was placed on disability and unable to be employed for anything strenuous or physically demanding. The two of them had a whirlwind courtship, and not long after the family met Bob, Faye announced that she and Bob were engaged to be married.

For Faye's story it's important to know how the sisters remember the sequence of events leading up to the wedding, which was to take place at the farm with the whole family in attendance. When I asked my mom about the details of Faye's wedding, it seems that her main impression was that Grandma Freda took great pains to see that Faye lost weight before she got married. It was an intention that she laid bare in front of Faye, and all of Faye's little sisters, as a way of asserting what a woman's priorities were when it came to love and marriage. This cruel approach to her own daughter's wedding comes as a bit of a shock to me, since my memories of Grandma Burge are anything but severe or restrictive. In fact, she used to let me eat my weight in Nutter Butter cookies when I was a teenager. Considering that Freda was the mother of seven children—five of them girls, her focus on Faye's weight would set the stage for every Burge auntie's fight against fat.

And here's where the morbidity of motherhood gets compounded with another Burge affliction—using food as medicine to treat what ails you. It seems that big, festive dinners, eating as much bread and butter (or Nutter Butters) as you wished, and quieting bad feelings by eating pie in the middle of the night are things that were learned in the Burge homestead, right along with how to milk a cow. It is something that was ingested by the Burge brothers and sisters and in turn, stuffed into all of the Burge cousins like jelly-filled Bismarcks. It seems to me that Aunt Faye learned this lesson very well and was now being punished for taking it to heart. Sadly, Faye's wedding was not prioritized as a celebration of happiness or love, but was instead a referendum on Faye's weight and Freda's assertion that she "wanted Faye to be thin for her wedding day." Considering that Faye was "heavy" even when she was a baby, this particular achievement was almost certainly destined to fail, and may have instead haunted her for the rest of her life. So, Faye starved herself in an attempt to fit into a wedding dress that was purposely a few sizes too small, in an attempt to please her mother, who would likely say that she just wanted Faye to be happy. And being happy, according to Grandma Freda, was being thin for one's husband.

Ultimately, Faye did successfully squeeze into that dress and when it came time for her "big day," Freda and the younger girls helped decorate the house with freshly cut greenery, candles, and festive ribbons. It was Christmastime and so there was a lighted tree and, of course, an angel food cake, kuchen, roasted meats, and the family favorite: mashed potatoes and gravy. A wonderfully cruel wedding feast to christen the event with love and glad tidings for the newlyweds. I'm sure everyone ate their fill, except for Auntie Faye, who from that point onward, would develop a secret habit of eating at night, after everyone was asleep.

The newlywed Palmers moved to Minneapolis for a time, but after a series of disappointments and financial strains, Faye and Bob ended up moving back to Warba, where he got a job as clerk at the liquor store. Unlike other young brides of that era, Faye had not yet announced that she was going to have a baby, even though that was her strongest desire. My mom was about eight or nine, and she remembers visiting the Palmers at their house in Warba. "Faye was always good to me," she said. "Anytime I would cry she would be right there. She had more influence on me than my mother did. She had brown eyes, a beautiful face, and dark curly hair. Bob had spent some time in California and so he was interesting. He had seen some of the world. He was always nice to me—he liked me, and I think he didn't really have any other kids in his life." Mom also shared her thoughts about how Faye came to be so focused on children and motherhood: "She was pushed into being a caretaker her whole life, but she was one anyway and she got pushed into it more as our family grew."

As a girl who watched five more children born into the family and experienced secondhand the difficulties of raising such a large family during the Great Depression, Faye was always expected to serve as a surrogate mother to her siblings and was never given a choice. When Grandpa was away at work and Grandma was upstairs nursing yet another new baby, Faye had to take care of the ones who needed to be fed, loved, and looked after. She was fully prepared to be a mother, and she longed to have children—not only because of the expectation but also because of her expansive capacity to love. And though she and her new husband likely tried to conceive a baby, ultimately Faye was unable to get pregnant. The magic and power of being able to bring a baby home to her own mother missed Faye completely, and no one, except maybe her sister Lila, knew why. This is the turning point in Faye's story where fresh hope dries up like a vernal pool in spring. The brave Faye, the one who tried her best to make it on her own, would become entangled in scandal and heartbreak, and would never be free of someone else's mess.

****

Not long after their wedding, the owner of the liquor store where Bob Palmer worked made an accusation that Bob had been stealing money under the counter. There was some hush-hush around the Burge farm about whether Bob actually did it—the fact that there was even a question shows that Freda and Bill knew very little about their eldest daughter's husband. If guilt is a motivator, then perhaps Bob was indeed in trouble, because he and Faye abruptly left Warba for Minneapolis, putting themselves many, many miles away from small-town gossip and accusations. My mom was still young, around eight years old, but she remembers staying all summer with Faye and Bob in Minneapolis and also the following year when they moved to Milwaukee. She said, "In the city we had fun. We'd go swimming in the lakes, we'd go to Grant Park and Lake Michigan. Faye didn't work, but Bob did. I would have rather been home in Warba with Ma, but they sent me to live with Faye."

Grandma Freda isn't here to explain why she sent her youngest daughter all the way to Milwaukee for a whole summer. It's not my place to speculate the reasons why, but I'm going to give Grandma the benefit of the doubt here. Perhaps things at the farm weren't as rosy as Grandma's Roses, Roses cologne was. And maybe she felt that Faye's emotional well-being hinged on having a little child in her care, since she was not blessed with children of her own. Perhaps she acted with a kind of misplaced morbidity of motherhood—a desperate attempt to fill her daughter's empty crib with a baby—even if that baby belonged to Grandma and not to Faye. After all, Faye's value as a person—as a woman—teetered on her ability to have children. And maybe Grandma Freda was trying to save her eldest daughter from that perceived failure by lending Faye her youngest daughter. In any case, Joyce, the littlest child, was once again being used as a balm for the sickness and sadness of others—a cure-all with a sweet face, curly, dark hair, and youthful magic. This is, of course, an unfair burden to place on any kid, especially when all Joyce wanted was love and stability from her own mother and to be home with her sisters Betty and Carol.

When Joyce had to go back to Warba to go to school, it left a big hole in Faye and Bob's lives. And so, knowing something about the way the foster system worked, she and Bob decided to be foster parents. For a time, their houses in Minneapolis and then Milwaukee were a revolving door of kids, some coming to stay for a short while, and others moving in for many months at a time. Bob, in spite of his health issues, continued to work odd jobs, and Faye stayed home and cared for whatever unclaimed children needed her the most. Around 1948–49 Faye and Bob took in two blond brothers, whose first names were Jimmy and Johnny. Faye had finally found her family and she threw her entire life into the loving care of these two orphaned boys. Here's a letter Faye wrote to "Mom and Daddy" back in Warba:

FRIDAY A.M.

Gosh, don't you ever write to anybody? Seems ages since I've heard from anyone. Just got Bob off to work and Jimmy is getting ready for school, what a poke. He's doing real good in school this year. I guess it paid to hold him back last year. Nothing has happened here. Same old thing as usual, except we started going to church again. Bob and I are going to take confirmation classes starting next Thurs. evening. Don't know what made Bob decide, but I'm not questioning it. We're going to that church where you and Esther and I went when you were here. I never got confirmed after all the times I started, so better get it done this time. Have been trying to do some sewing but you know me—takes me a month just to think about it.

Would like to do some figurine painting again, always get the urge about this time of year. Did you get the stuff I sent to Lila? Will you tell her to keep the maternity dresses when she's done if there's anything left because I think Martha's going to need them again. Don't know for sure. They weren't too good. But she can wear them around the house. Bob took his civil service test got a score of 91%, shocked me, I didn't figure he was that smart. But haven't heard any more about work, I guess it takes a couple of months. One of the guys said they probably wouldn't hire till Jan. 1st. He likes his hardware store job real well and they have given him a few extra hours this past few weeks and he gets a 10 cent/hour raise so we make out o.k. At least he's happy working there. That means more than the money—he's at least in a good humor sometimes. Also haven't heard anything further from our social worker, so can't make any definite plans till we hear from her. Couldn't hardly leave these kids. Every night they pray to move to Minn. and get a cat, and a dog and a puppy. They figure everyone there has a dog or cat, I guess. Still haven't gotten to the Dr. had to cancel my last appointment—my next one is for Oct. 25th. Where are Lila and Lee now, did they get a nice place or what are they doing? Tell her to write once in a while. Better sign off and have "The Lone Ranger" take this to the mail box. Johnny's all decked up mask and all—write soon.

Our love to all—Bob, Faye & Boys

I love this letter because Auntie Faye was happy when she wrote it. And even though she hints that her marriage to Bob isn't perfect, her voice as a mother to Jimmy and Johnny comes through with pride and a sense of completion. According to Aunt Betty, Faye and Bob were formally adopting Jimmy and Johnny, a process that required regular check-ins with a state-appointed child welfare worker. The Palmers were foster parents to the two boys for a few years while they tried to work through the state adoption process. Faye stayed home and took care of the two boys and Bob continued to work odd jobs. But as he got older, his diabetes worsened and his health deteriorated to the point that he required regular shots of insulin. The damage done to his body by the chemicals he ingested during the war eventually overtook him. Bob's death left Faye alone with two foster sons who had already been through a lot and desperately needed the continuity of a mother's love and a stable home.

* * * * * * *

The Wisconsin laws concerning adoption and the care of children in the early 1950s tilted heavily toward the nuclear family. The statutes did not specifically deny a widow the right to adopt a child, but in a similar case from 1954, a widowed mother was first denied permission to adopt a young boy that was in her care as a foster child when her husband died unexpectedly. According to the ruling the standard was that "the refusal to consent was predicated on the department's policy or rule that there must be an adoptive father and mother living at the time the written consent is given and the order for adoption is entered."[3] Even though Faye had fostered Jimmy and Johnny for a number of years, Social Services in Milwaukee decided that Faye, as a widow with severe health problems, was unfit to be the boys' adoptive mother. I imagine Auntie Faye felt this was the ultimate failure.

Aunt Betty and Aunt Carol, along with Carol's little son, Ricky, were living together in Chicago when Bob died. His family was in Minneapolis, and it was decided that his funeral would also be moved to Minnesota. All the Burges made plans to attend. After the funeral, Betty and Carol went to Milwaukee to stay with Faye to help her through the loss of her husband and sort out her finances, now that the breadwinner of the family was gone. Thankfully, her two sisters were still there in Milwaukee when social workers employed by the state showed up at Faye's door. They told Faye that the state had reviewed their adoption case, but it could not be approved because the Department of Child Welfare had determined that she was unable to sufficiently care for the two boys. The social workers ordered Faye to surrender them to the state. As Aunt Betty put it, Faye "completely lost it." She spent one night in a mental hospital in Milwaukee in a state of complete physical and mental breakdown.

Having now seen and felt the impact of the morbidity of motherhood on Faye's life, it's not hard to understand why her ability to function was forever changed the day they took her kids away from her. In a family that believed babies could cure everything, Faye was forced to suffer the emotional pain of losing two children, and losing children is the family's equivalent of losing hope. It is something that would affect all her decisions (or indecisions) for the rest of her life. When she was released from the mental hospital, her younger sister Carol, "pretty much took care of her," according to Aunt Betty. Betty also explained: "Faye had Bob's Social Security and that's what she lived on for many years after he died. She was really smart. Really intelligent, but she could never stay well enough for long enough to get her life together. We all drove back to Warba after her breakdown and then Dad, who always loved her, took her in, and they all lived together—Carol, Faye, little Ricky and your grandpa and grandma Burge."

After a period of recovery on the farm, Carol, Ricky, and Faye moved back to Milwaukee. Carol, at that time a single mother, worked full-time to pay their bills while Faye stayed home and took care of Ricky. In Milwaukee, Faye got mixed up with a man named Bud Hauge. They moved in together almost right away, but Bud never had any intention of being faithful to Faye. It's almost as if he wanted to live off Faye's dead husband's money and really didn't care about her at all. Soon after they moved in together, Bud got another woman pregnant. Aunt Betty didn't know much about who the woman was, and Aunt Lila may have known the whole story, but she is not here to tell Faye's side of it. I wish she were, since Lila would have been able to tell me more about Bud, who by all family accounts, was a self-serving mess of a man. Bud had gotten himself stuck between the devil and disgrace, because the woman who was pregnant with his child was not able to take responsibility for the baby. I don't know the birth mother's reasoning here, and it would be a misstep to speculate why. With a baby on the way, Bud was forced to come clean to Faye, telling her that she was about to be a mother—it just wasn't a baby she had given birth to.

****

Had the story of Faye started here, most people may have guessed wrong about what she decided to do the day her boyfriend ended up bringing home another woman's baby. But remember, the morbidity of motherhood was strong in Faye—stronger than reason, stronger than any emotional degradation placed on her by a man. That, combined with the loss of Jimmy and Johnny, put Faye in the resolute position of taking a new baby girl into her life, and loving it so much it wouldn't matter how the child got into her arms. And so, Bud and Faye brought the baby home and named her Jeannie.

The fate of Faye and Bud's relationship was written in mud the day he got another woman pregnant. My cousin Lilean, Aunt Lila's daughter, remembers her mother telling her about the day Bud closed the door on Faye and his baby daughter for the first time: "It was like he went to the store for a loaf of bread and never came back. Auntie Faye's sisters even tried to contact the FBI to report a missing person."

In fact, Lilean said their family was driving one time and passed a man walking down the shoulder of the road. Aunt Lila yelled, "Stop the car, that looks like Bud Hauge!" And Uncle Leroy said, "That's the last thing I would ever do, is stop the car, if it was him!" I think Uncle Leroy knew Lila would likely kneecap the man should they randomly come across him on the road someday.

It was 1957 and at the time, Lila, Betty, and my mother, Joyce, were all living in Grand Marais. My mother and dad (Francis, also known as "Pooty") were newlyweds, and Aunt Betty, who was going through her own transition, lived with my parents for a summer until she met her husband, Lloyd. It was right around this time that my parents decided to move to Phoenix, Arizona, where they spent two winters. My mother recalls that Faye came out to Phoenix with Jeannie and stayed with them that first winter: "We played three-handed pinochle every day. I worked all the time and Pooty fell in love with Jeannie who was two or three, and we all showered her with love and attention. When summer came, Poot helped Faye pick out an old Ford in Phoenix, which she drove back to the Warba farm, where she and Jeannie stayed for a while."

It's fun to picture Auntie Faye driving the open road in a robin's egg blue Ford with shiny chrome hubcaps. A car that belonged to her (and only her), with a baby girl in the back seat who also belonged to her (and only her). In a film version of her life, this is the part where the little family of two drives off into the sunset—no choking asthma attacks, no more nervous breakdowns, and no more calls to the farm asking Grandpa Burge to come rescue her. But the sky in that sunny version of Faye's life was about to turn a terrible green, like the color of the clouds right before straight-line winds topple everything in sight.

Faye drove that car all the way to Grand Marais and moved in with Betty and Lloyd for a time. And then Bud reappeared in Grand Marais, pleading with Faye to take him back, which she did. According to Aunt Betty, "They lived in Carlson Cabins for a while. I don't think he even worked. He lived off of Faye's Social Security." But true to form, Bud didn't last long on the North Shore and soon disappeared for good. Lilean remembers that Faye's sisters took Bud's departure personally: "He haunted the family in a way—they wanted to avenge their sister's trauma and abandonment. And they were always talking in code because there were always kids around, but I knew what they were saying."

* * * * * * *

Aunt Carol was also married at that time, and she had moved from Milwaukee to Minneapolis with her husband, Earl, and their three young sons. Faye and Jeannie ended up leaving the farm and moved in with Carol and her family. According to Aunt Betty, Faye "always ended up living with them, or not very far away." And while living in Minneapolis, she met a relation of Earl's named George Lindley. According to Aunt Betty, "That's . . . where it all started." Lindley took an interest in Faye, and even though Carol tried to tell her he was, to quote Betty, "a puke," Faye's desperate need to be a mother and a wife hijacked her decision-making process. Or maybe she just loved him. And love complicates everything. She had already learned the terrible lesson that strangers could, at any time, step in and take her children away from her. Perhaps Faye thought this man would be a reliable way to keep her and her little girl safe, because having a bad male role model was better than having none at all. Ultimately, no one will ever know why Faye ended up with Lindley as her next live-in boyfriend, who on the best of days, drank straight booze all day, and on the worst of days, did things to innocent people that are unforgivable.

George Lindley was a terrible man. I want to believe Aunt Faye knew better, but when confronted by the truth, she decided to ignore it. To this day, my mother wonders why her sister chose to stay. Why did she protect him and not the truth? Was it because Faye was so physically and mentally unhealthy, she felt she had no choice? Was it fear of living alone that kept her from speaking up? Was Faye so afraid of losing Jeannie, like she had lost Jimmy and Johnny, that she was willing to look the other way? And what good is the devil-take-all sanctity of the American nuclear family when the devil himself is sitting at the kitchen table pouring himself a fourth glass of whiskey? I hope to find answers to some of these questions when I start sweeping through the dark corners and under the beds of my other aunties' rooms.

My mom's analysis is that later in her life, Faye became reliant on her sister Carol—a codependency that began in inverse at the Warba farm, with Faye taking care of Carol, and ending with Carol stepping in to take care of her oldest sister. When Carol and Earl moved to Phoenix and then to Los Angeles, Faye went with them, as did Jeannie, who was now growing up. Faye and her daughter next moved to Northern California, along with the monster George Lindley, who was somehow always able to stay within close range of Faye. Abusive relationships are even more codependent than dysfunctional sisterly relationships, and Faye, under heavy duress, chose Lindley over her sister's influence and over her daughter's safety. Faye often sent Jeannie to live with Aunt Carol in Los Angeles, and Jeannie was in Los Angeles when we went on our road trip to visit our California relatives. My sister remembers Jeannie playing her favorite song for us, which was Rod Stewart's "Da Ya Think I'm Sexy?" This made quite an impression on Dawn, who was pretty little and just learning about words and ideas like being "sexy."

During our trip out west, we spent all our time at Aunt Carol's house in Los Angeles and got to know our cousins Ronny, Brian, and Jeannie, but we never saw Auntie Faye. In retrospect, it's somewhat odd that she never made the trip down to Los Angeles to visit with her three sisters, two of whom had driven all the way from Minnesota. But now it's as clear as the drifting white sands of Yuma why she wasn't there for the sisterly reunion. There would have been too many questions that desperately needed to be asked, and too many answers Aunt Faye was not prepared to deliver. It wasn't until after Faye died that my mom learned the truth about how very far Faye had fallen in her quest to be loved and be a mother.

My mom shared that throughout those very dark times, Faye and Carol remained good friends and protected each other as best they could. But there was a falling out after Grandma Burge died of cancer in Banning, California, in 1988. Faye and Carol both stayed with Grandma when she was sick and dying, and some misunderstanding during that time caused a rift between them. As my mom put it, "Whatever happened, Carol never felt the same way about Faye after that."

* * * * * * *

Auntie Faye died of colon cancer about a year after Grandma died. She was only sixty-one years old. My mom was scrubbing the floor at our house on Eighth Avenue the day before her oldest sister left this world: "She called and I just strongly felt that I should talk to her. So, we talked on the phone that day as long as she wanted to talk. She said she was afraid. There was no one there to take care of her. Jeannie was in some kind of trouble and Faye was very worried about her. And she died the next day. Faye was in a strange state of mind because she told me that she thought she could get cancer from others—like when Bob Palmer had gotten sick from fighting in the war. She thought cancer could be passed along like Agent Orange."

There's a lot about Faye's story that scares me. A woman I barely knew but whom I recognize in myself. Brown eyes, a gentle way of speaking, shy on the inside, but with a lot to give the world. She lived her life huffing for air and struggling to find someone, anyone, who would make her feel complete. As a little kid sitting in her lap, listening to her read my favorite story about Edith and the bears, I remember only kindness. I can still hear her raspy laugh and her voice, far away on the phone, asking me how school was going, and telling me that "your mom tells me how good you are doing in school . . . she is so proud of you. I know she is."

If entering the world at all takes courage, then leaving behind a world of pain and trauma, without being able to make amends before you go, must be terrifying. When Aunt Betty was revealing her thoughts to me about her oldest sister, she offered up a string of truths, as she saw and felt them, having grown up with Faye as her own surrogate mother: "She had a lot of life. She had a good sense of humor. She was very intelligent. But she was her own worst enemy. She picked people that would destroy her. Your self-worth is not good when you keep picking people who treat you like shit. She lived a life of pain . . . she had her kids taken away. She suffered an inability to care for herself. But you know, for a while she had Bob Palmer, who truly loved her, and life with Bob was boring, but they had Jimmy and Johnny, and Faye was able to be a homemaker. She liked that. It made her happy."

Aunt Betty also told me that after Auntie Faye died, she got a call from George Lindley. He knew Jeannie had arranged for her mother's ashes to be sent to Grand Marais to be buried at Maple Hill, along with our other Burge relatives. He had the gall to ask, "When I die, could my ashes be buried next to Faye's?" Aunt Betty told him that neither he nor his ashes were welcome in the Burge family plot.

The truth about how he had continually abused Jeannie and Faye, and how she had taken him back over and over again at the expense of their safety, had finally come out after Auntie Faye's death. If her sisters had failed to protect her in life, they made damn sure to protect her in death. It's a consolation that feels inadequate to me and others in our family, especially my cousin Jeannie, who lived her life thinking no one really cared about her.

My mother told me Faye always held out hope that someday her phone would ring and it would be Jimmy and Johnny. In an imaginary world of happy endings, they would explain to her "how hard it was to find you, but now, finally . . . here you are." They would tell her that "we can't wait for you to meet our families," and, "oh yes, of course we have dogs and cats too." Before hanging up they would say, "Yes, Mama, we are fine and happy, and we hope you're fine and happy too."

But the call never came. The sad truth is that Auntie Faye lived and died adrift in a sea of sadness. She left behind a lot of questions and a lot of people whom she loved with an immensity of intention like her daughter, Jeannie, who blessed her with three grandchildren and, for a time, glimmers of hope that things would get better. For the Burges, there's no balm like bringing a baby home to your mother. Jeannie gave Faye that satisfaction, and I love her for it.

Struggle to Breathe: A Poem for Faye

In a fit of coughing, she struggles to breathe.
If each inhalation takes life in,
there is no time for loose talk or distraction.
When gasping for air—for life,
she is eternally reminded of how bodies disintegrate,
men disappoint,
women disapprove,
and mothers who die on the inside,
are still expected to keep breathing.
If each inhalation takes life in,
then each exhalation is a letting go.
May her struggle to breathe
become oxygen.

Lila

AUNT LILA HAD A DEEP SCAR, shaped like the blade of a scythe, down her left cheek. It began just beneath her eye, curved around her sturdy cheekbone, and ended close to the corner of her mouth. The injury happened when she was a baby. Her mother was bathing her in a washtub of soapy water on top of the wooden kitchen table at the Stelter family farm in Weyauwega, Wisconsin. There was a bottle of rubbing alcohol on the table, along with the baby and the tub of water. It was an oval table made of oak that had metal braces under each leaf; the braces allowed the table to fold into a half-moon shape so that it could sit flush against the wall. Grandma Burge presumably reached for the rubbing alcohol, and at that moment, the table leaf collapsed, sending the baby, the bottle, and the bathwater to the floor. A jagged piece of glass caught the side of Lila's face, narrowly missing her eye. Aunt Faye used to say that the scar accentuated Lila's beautiful blue eyes and dark eyelashes, and called attention to her perfect mouth. This observation tells you something important about each of them—how Faye was able to soothe the wound with a compliment, and just how very beautiful Lila was, in spite of her scar.

In a black-and-white photograph taken around 1946 in the front yard of the Warba farm, Aunt Lila stands at the center of the frame, looking down. A slender beauty with long legs and willowy arms, she has chosen to wear a flouncy skirt and flower print blouse, tucked in neatly at the waist. It's a warm, sunny day, and the afternoon light gives her skin a flawless glow, the perfect contrast between her dark eyes and her nearly black hair, the curls haphazard and wind-blown, as if she had just woken up from a nap. She is laughing at whoever is taking the picture, bending slightly at the waist toward the camera. We see her thin, shapely legs and her lovely eyes, but her hand and fingers deftly cover the left side of her face in a shy and unnatural way. It appears that she is trying to hide the scarred part of herself from the world, but it was her scar that made her one of the most beautiful people in the world. At least to me.

Unlike Faye's, Aunt Lila's room of personal memories is well furnished. After all, I heard her voice before I could talk, and she was likely one of the first people to hold me in her arms other than my parents. She showed my mother how to take care of me as a newborn girl and fielded a lot of questions and calls about babies after I was born in 1967. By then, Lila had already raised five babies of her own; her youngest daughter, Lisa, was just three years old when my mom had me. Lila showed her youngest sister Joyce how to encourage a baby to nurse, how to change a diaper, and how to give a tiny baby a bath in the kitchen sink, a lesson everyone, especially Lila, had learned the hard way. She and my aunt Betty and my mother's friend Lila Monson would visit my mom every day for coffee at the trailer where we lived, a metal-sided Airstream, jacked up on cinder blocks in the Gopher Campground on the eastern edge of Grand Marais. And even though she had already cared for five girls, teaching them all to eat with a spoon, walk in the grass, and play "little piggie went to market" on every tiny toe, she loved my mom and she loved me, and so she helped me learn to do all those things too.

I've often wondered if Aunt Lila's scar was the thing that caused her to make the decisions she made in her life. Was it why she escaped the farm and married at such a young age? Did it dictate how she entered a conversation, or change the way she wore her hair? Was it what made her stronger and more resilient as an elderly woman? Is that indelible mark the reason why she had great compassion for others and why she never had much time for vanity or superficiality, especially in her own daughters? A beautiful lot, the five of them were also blond and blue-eyed at a time when Farrah Fawcett was held up as our beauty ideal, and young girls were taught to hide their smarts because that's not what the world wanted to see. All relatively close in age, these five sisters grew up in a tiny house on a steep hill, with their mom and father, Leroy Garner, whose ethnicity, according to their daughter Lilean, was "a cross between a skunk and a barbed wire fence." The house was next to the First Norwegian Lutheran Church on the corner of First and Third in Grand Marais, Minnesota. The church was built in 1898 and served the very first Swedish and Norwegian settlers on the North Shore of Lake Superior. After a new Lutheran church was built at the top of First Avenue, the old church was used as a temporary school while the new school was under construction, at the top of the hill. After the building had sat empty for a number of years, the Grand Marais Playhouse moved in, converting the church hall into an eighty-seat community theater. In those early days, there was no bathroom for the actors or the audience, and the stage actors and crew would often run through the backyard of the church and into the Garners' back door so that they could use their bathroom during a break in the play. Theatergoers had to park on the street, and during big performances Uncle Leroy would put out a sign out that said PLEASE LEAVE PARKING FOR THE GUY THAT PAYS THE TAXES.

For most of their time growing up, all seven Ls—Linda, Lilean, Loni, Lori, Lisa, Aunt Lila, and Uncle Leroy—shared the same small bathroom, which was painted in a shade of vintage pink, with daisy-shaped flower decals pressed into the bottom of the bathtub. Each person would have to patiently wait their turn to get ready for work or school or church, standing in line to shave or preen in front of the mirrored medicine cabinet that hung above the bathroom sink. As my cousin Lilean says, "We would watch the bathroom door, and when we had a chance, we'd run in really fast! There was always someone pounding on the door, trying to get in." Uncle Leroy's alliterative summary was, "You could shit, shower, and shave all in the same two-foot square."

It wasn't until much later that Uncle Leroy installed a second tiny bathroom at the other end of the hall, since he was probably tired of having to wait to use his own bathroom when there was a play performance happening next door. This was another bathroom so small your knees had to nest underneath the diminutive wall sink when you were sitting on the toilet. I remember both sinks in each bathroom being cluttered with an array of hair implements—curling brushes, hair irons, fat-toothed combs—along with tubes of mascara: cluttered evidence that the bathrooms may have been built by men but they really belonged to females. Lots of females. It was the first time I would experience symptoms of a condition I'm calling "chronic femininity." It's related in some ways to the morbidity of motherhood in that the afflicted person is most likely to be female, but rather than a physical ailment driven by physiology and historical precedent, chronic femininity is more of a mental disorder exacerbated by 1970s sitcoms and Olivia Newton John singalongs. My imaginary dictionary entry would look like this: **chron·ic fem·i·nin·i·ty.** Noun: 1. Persistent and longstanding expectation that women look, dress, and speak consistently with society's feminine ideal. 2. The recurring assumption that when a girl matures into a woman, her primary role is to be pleasing to the masculine eye. Use: "Young girls are often taught the basics of chronic femininity at an early age, learning that attracting male attention is a primary means of praise and self-fulfillment." Also: "Death by chronic femininity is usually preceded by persistent thoughts of confused identity and feeling like a misfit."

The Garner house is where I learned I would never really fit into the Farrah Fawcett mold of chronic femininity, despite every attempt to force me into it as a young girl. For most of my life, I followed the Farrah doctrine until it hurt. When I was nine, I even asked Santa Claus for a Farrah's Glamour Center for Christmas, which Santa delivered with a bow. This brilliantly marketed "toy" was actually a hard plastic dummy of Farrah Fawcett's head and shoulders to which you applied rouge, fake eyelashes, and lipstick. The purpose was to make money off Farrah's poster-girl image while training young girls in the art of feminizing themselves in the Farrah mold—unless of course you were tall for your age, and had brown eyes and black hair like I did. Farrah's disembodied head came with a kit of blue eye shadow, glossy pink lipstick, and the sick feeling that you were a failure if you were unable to achieve the famous Farrah "flip." Watching my own blond, blue-eyed cousin replicate the perfect "flip" every single day in the Garners' tiny pink bathroom compounded my feelings of confusion and utter loneliness. But I don't begrudge my cousin for it. It was awful timing, because I was at a very tender age, missed my family a lot, and wished I could be back in my own bedroom on Eighth Avenue where everything made more sense. There were three bedrooms at Aunt Lila's house, all proportionately small to the rest of the building. The girls mostly shared one room, with Uncle Leroy and Aunt Lila just down the hall. And the house was even smaller in the years when the Garner girls were growing up. At the start of their tenure, the house was almost half the size it was when I lived there. The old kitchen cabinets were still installed on the walls of the first kitchen, years after they expanded the house to include a new living room and the full-size kitchen I knew so well. That was the room that served as the heart of Lila's house. Leroy (or Lee, as he was often called) and Lila slept in a small room at the midpoint of the house. If my recollection is correct, there was a folding screen covering the entrance to their bedroom instead of an actual door that opened and closed. These were all dark little rooms, with even smaller, darker closets. The hallway leading from the living room to the back bedrooms was skinny and dark. I still have dreams about walking down that hallway. Of feeling my way along the walls and being startled by a blast of hot air from the furnace, coming up through the open grates set into the floor.

The cramped spaces of this house would be where I spent some of the saddest and most confusing times of my life. It was the year when my sister, Dawn, and I were split up. She was sent to live across town at Aunt Betty's, and I was sent to live at Aunt Lila's. I was ten going on eleven, and when the time came for us to split up, we were told very simply and plainly that our mom loved us but she needed to be in the hospital very, very far away, and no one was sure when she was coming back. Mom herself had to explain this to us. I don't remember where this family earthquake took place, but I do remember the feeling of it so clearly that my stomach still aches thinking back on it. In a voice so thin it could have been ether, she said, "I want you to know that I love you both so much and that this has nothing to do with you. And it's not because of anything that anyone did. I just need to go away for a while."

I imagine that was probably one of the hardest things Mom ever had to do—feeling depressed and deeply underwater and then having to swim back up to the surface to explain to your two kids bobbing in the waves that you were about to drown. There was no precedent for this in our lives, and as far as we knew, our mom was just . . . Mom.

Dad worked midnight shifts inside the iron works at Taconite Harbor, loading taconite pellets onto ships and eating his lunch from a black plastic lunchbox at 4:00 a.m. He was not able to get us to school every morning and see that we ate regularly. And that's how I ended up in Aunt Lila's care, inside a house that had already raised five girls, going on six, if you include me. The four oldest cousins had moved out, most of them already married with kids of their own. Lisa was the only one left at home and was in junior high school. She and I shared the smallest bedroom during the time I stayed there. She was three years older and slept on the top bunk. That left me the bottom bunk, inside someone else's room, inside someone else's house, with someone else's mother. It wasn't until a friend recently asked, "Why, if there were three bedrooms, did you have to share a room with your cousin?" After all, there was an empty room across the hall, where the older girls used to sleep. It took me forty years to see that Aunt Lila put me in Lisa's room on purpose. She knew I was missing my mom, my sister, and my dad, and she wanted to protect me from feeling alone. It was an illogical way to utilize space in a tiny house, but a very logical way to be an aunt. And that was Aunt Lila to me.

Almost every weekday of that year, Lisa and I went to bed at night, she in the top bunk, me below. Sometimes we would laugh together like sisters, and sometimes we would struggle to know each other like cousins. In truth, Lisa helped me through one of the hardest times in my life by telling me, "I gets better, I promise." Lisa and I were very different. She was a cheerleader and dated a football player and had a lot of friends. I was really shy, unsure of myself, and lived in a fantasy world when it came to boys and the idea of going out on a date.

Aunt Lila would wake us for school each day, no small feat for a preteen and a full-blown teenager. We would eat cornflakes for breakfast in the Garners' kitchen, a room I have reimagined over and over again, both in sleep and in my waking life. By far the largest room in the house, the kitchen was also the room with the most windows, looking out over their backyard. Uncle Leroy's dilapidated garage was in full view of the kitchen sink. A pair of mature apple trees just outside the window would put out big, cottony blossoms every spring. There was a large dining room table in the corner that was always covered with a colorful plastic tablecloth. Aunt Lila's antique English and Canadian teacup collection was perched on a fancy wooden display shelf above the table, on a wall papered in a busy, fleur-de-lis floral design. I'm lucky to have a cup and saucer from her collection, a Christmas gift from her when I was grown-up and living on my own. The set is bone china from England with a delicate spray of hand-painted flowers surrounded by crimson and gold borders. It's perfectly pristine, and perfectly pretty. I don't ever remember anyone drinking tea out of Aunt Lila's fancy cups. That kind of pomp and circumstance would have stuck out like a tiger lily bloom, lost in a bramble of buckthorn.

* * * * * * *

Even though the daily dramas at the Garner house prevented her from hosting fancy tea parties, Aunt Lila still found time for fun and fanciful things. She truly loved the kids in her life, and so every year my sister and I, our cousin Cindy, and most of her daughters (and later her grandchildren) were given free rein as cookie decorators at her kitchen table every Christmas. It was one of our family's holiday traditions, and to this day, the toasted edges of a perfectly golden sugar cookie are forever etched in my mind as the pinnacle of a baker's skill. Aunt Lila would spend days before our decorating day mixing up the dough, rolling it out evenly, cutting it into shapes, and then baking cookies until there was a veritable mountain of Santa Clauses, stars, trees, gingerbread men, and Christmas bells, to use as canvases for our delicious frosted masterpieces. In the cupboard next to the refrigerator, there was a plastic tray of edible sprinkles and dusting sugars in every color. Sometimes with our help, Aunt Lila would mix up an enormous bowl of powdered sugar icing. She would divide the sticky confection into smaller bowls and we would add drops of food coloring to each one, mixing it with a spoon until the slurry was holly green, Santa red, church bell yellow, or sky blue.

Decorating cookies at Aunt Lila's table was perhaps the first time I ever felt allowed to get really messy. She made it OK to have sticky hands, to get frosting on my face, and lose myself creating art that was meant to be displayed, admired, and then eaten in four gulps. This experience would come in handy many years later when I was getting paid to make beautiful cakes and cookies in a bakery that coincidentally looked out over Aunt Lila's row of lilac bushes and into the side yard. The bakery was on the first floor of the old Lutheran church—the same building that once housed the theater. From my bakery window, I could see almost directly into the window of what used to be Aunt Lila's kitchen. So, when I was rolling out pie dough or cutting out my own pretty sugar cookies, I would talk to her inside my head, because she, more than anyone, would understand the dough and know when the cookies were the right thickness, and when they were perfectly done, without being overbaked. I inherited her good instincts with a rolling pin, and in Aunt Lila's room full of stories, kitchen tools and the smell of something delicious baking in the oven are very important aspects of who she was. Lilean, Lila's middle daughter, remembers their house like this: "You would walk into Mom's house and it was coffee on the table and whatever food they had. A lot of times it was fresh fried fish. My favorite were her rhubarb bars with meringue on top. It was always your house, too, no matter what. Even if we were fighting, I'd still go in. She could fry fish so well. She was a great gardener too. She had just a tiny garden. And fresh cookies, always home baked. Mom was always filling Dad's lunch bucket with snacks."

For so many reasons, Aunt Lila's kitchen was a formative place. Both she and Uncle Leroy shared a great sense of humor, and when Aunt Lila laughed, she would laugh with her whole self. I can picture her standing in her kitchen right next to the sink, probably wearing a cap-sleeved nightgown, and something funny would happen and she would just stop what she was doing and scream out a burst of laughter. She was able to fill up that whole kitchen with joyful guffaws whenever she started laughing. Lilean shared that "Dad was funny, but Mom was more on the stern side, and they would laugh so hard. Dad needed Mom's leveling, and Mom needed Dad's lightheartedness, so yes that was really their bond."

One morning during my long stint as a guest in their house, Uncle Leroy woke us up instead of Aunt Lila. He was screaming and yelling from the kitchen. "Get up, everybody! Everybody—get up!" Lisa and I jumped out of our bunks and ran into the kitchen where Uncle Leroy was yelling and pointing out the window. Aunt Lila, still in her nightgown, was peering over his shoulder, attempting to see what all the ruckus was about. "Can't you see it, Lila?" he said.

"No, Leroy. I don't see a damn thing," she replied.

"It's there. A bear eating an apple . . . and smoking a pipe!" Well, Uncle Leroy was so convincing that I actually saw the bear eating an apple while smoking a pipe, even before I looked out the window into the back yard. Sure enough. There was no bear and no apple, and certainly no pipe. There was only a quiet yard covered with the remnants of late winter snow.

"APRIL FOOLS!" he yelled, and then he doubled over with laughter, lines forming around both of his eyes, his gap-toothed smile luring each one of us into his ridiculous joke.

"Leroy!" Aunt Lila said, slapping him on the arm. "You devil!" And then she started laughing, and the two of them were laughing together, and I could tell, by the way they were laughing together, that they truly loved each other. This is a bright, shining memory from a time when most everything seemed dull and uncertain. Looking back on things, it's not clear why some memories are so crystal clear, and why some things remain hidden away, like a scar that's healed, but the memory of the injury stays as acute and sharp as the day it happened.

****

Aunt Lila was seventeen when she married twenty-one-year-old Leroy Garner in Grand Rapids, Minnesota. Uncle Leroy was from that area, and Lila met Leroy soon after he got back from Germany where he served with the U.S. Army in World War II. Like most of the men who served and then came back to the Iron Range, Uncle Leroy worked in the mines and that's how he made a living.

My cousin Lilean explained that her dad had gone into the army as a very young man—the youngest one in his battalion. When he came back home from Europe, it was seventeen-year-old Lila Burge from down the road in Warba who caught his eye. Lila told the story at Christmas one year, above the din of her grandchildren playing together in the kitchen of one of her daughters. She is sitting at the table with Lisa, Lori, and Lilean, who are asking her questions about the past. While she is telling her story, she never fully turns her body toward the video camera. But occasionally, during a pause in the story, she looks over her shoulder and right into the camera lens, as if she is letting her listeners stop and connect with what she is saying. Aunt Lila had an endearing habit of raising her shoulder up and down in little twitches, while bobbing her head just a little bit—a subconscious tic that made her seem flirtatious, or as if she was being a bit of a tease. It was one of the mannerisms that made her uniquely Lila. I'm quite sure this little quirk of hers must have been on full display the first time she met Leroy.

According to Lila, here's what happened that night: "It was in my little hometown. There were maybe thirty people living there. There was a dance that night and this guy asked me to go with him. Leroy had asked someone else to go with him. There was a restaurant with beer next to the dance hall and we were all sitting in a booth. Our friends introduced us and Leroy said, 'Oh, hi, Lila!' The guy I was with sort of dragged me away because he didn't like how Leroy was eyeing me. Pretty soon Leroy took out his jackknife and he carved my initials and his initials in the wooden booth. He pointed at it and said, 'That's the girl I'm going to marry!'"

After the dance I went back to Leroy's cousin's house in Grand Rapids and I had to be home at, like, such and such a time, you know. My dad had given me orders. So, here comes a knock at her door, and Leroy's yelling, "You got any coffee? We need some coffee!" She didn't have any coffee or a fire in the stove. So, Leroy takes that same jackknife and starts carving strips off the beams inside the house, you know, the wooden beams in the ceiling? And he takes these strips and shavings of wood and used them to start a fire in the cook stove so we could have some coffee! I thought, 'What kind of character do we have here?' [chortle] Boy, was he rough! He was so much fun. And my dad was such a straitlaced kind of guy . . . so responsible . . . and Leroy was so much fun. We had a lot of fun . . . he taught me how. I taught him to be responsible and he taught me to have fun. It took a long time to tame him down. [Laughs.] I never really did tame him down . . . I tried, though."

****

Lila was a vision with dark hair and violet-blue eyes, and Leroy was smitten with her. Lilean remembers her dad wistfully telling her that "your mom would wear her hair up in a French roll," and confirmed that he always "loved having beautiful women on his arm." Looking back, she said, "That's probably what it was. I guess she was quite beautiful. The story is, that a circus came to town and they asked her if she would be the woman riding the white horse into town along with the circus parade."

I asked Lilean why Aunt Lila didn't run off with the circus and she said, "She didn't like horses." And then we both laughed, because by all accounts, Lila was a reluctant farm girl, and she didn't really want anything to do with horses or any kind of farm life. Lisa remembers Lila telling her that she would get teased because she had to do farm chores before school and some of the other kids called her "stinky." Lilean said, "Mom told me one time that she would catch the bus in Warba after being in the barn, then they went to school in Grand Rapids. She remembers kids on the bus teasing her about having cow shit on her shoes."

Grandma and Grandpa Burge's reaction to Lila's impending marriage was less than supportive. Back then for young women, it was either finish high school or get married; not both. According to Aunt Betty, Grandma Freda refused to acknowledge it at all, and both she and Grandpa refused to attend the ceremony. If it were not for Leroy's sister Rilean and Lila's sister Faye, there would not have been any family in attendance that day. A memory that is forever paused in my mother's childhood is Uncle Leroy and Aunt Lila driving into the Warba farm on their wedding day. Leroy's car had a horn that played music and the fanfare of their post-wedding debut was one that left quite an impression on my mom, who was eight years old. She said, "Lila was so beautiful. They came out to the farm in Leroy's car after they got married. She may have already been pregnant at the time, and so, Mom said mean things to her on her wedding day."

It turns out that saying mean things to your daughters who were about to be married was a pattern at the Burge farm, certainly for Faye ("You should be thin!") and now Lila ("Dear Lord, Lila—are you pregnant?"). This hardline approach doesn't reconcile with the Grandma Freda I knew, but perhaps by the time she had grandchildren in her life, she had sufficiently seen it all when it came to the lives of her seven children, especially her five daughters.

And so, there was Uncle Leroy, larger than life, taking his lovely new wife out for a drive on a cold November day, all the while blasting "She'll Be Comin' Round the Mountain" on his car horn, to show the

Burges that their cold and unaccepting response to Lila and Leroy's barn-burning love story was not going to make one puny little difference in the grand scheme of things. And really, when I think about Uncle Leroy and Aunt Lila, one of the things I admire most about them is their stubborn and steadfast love for each other come hell or high water. It's what got them through some very ridiculous circumstances, including on their wedding night, which Aunt Lila described like this:

Leroy and all our friends could drink, but I was too young, I couldn't drink. So, our wedding dance was at a bar and everyone would dance and drink, but I could only dance, so I'd dance and dance. And it was November sixteenth and it got so cold . . . ohhhh, it was cold . . . and after the dance we were trying to get into our car and back to our little house . . . we had a little house. And our car didn't start. Here we are on our wedding night and we had no way to get home from the parking lot. We got out on the street and an older couple stopped and we told them it was our wedding night and our car wouldn't start, and we had no way to get back to our little house. So, they said, "We'll take you back to your house," which was about two miles away. And Dad [Leroy] tried to carry me over the threshold—ha!

Before the dance, we had put out some groceries, like jam and maraschino cherries, you know, out on the table, and, ha! He was going to carry me over the threshold on my wedding night, and he couldn't even lift me! [Long laugh, throwing her head back.] Anyway, we got into the cabin and he knocked into the table and everything went crashing! And I was laughing like a dang fool. Anyhow, Bud, Leroy's best buddy, came home with us, and there was only one bed. So, I said, "Bud's sleeping with us?" Well, he hit the bed and passed out cold and so did Bud. And I laid there all night going, "What is going on here?" Ha! The next morning here comes his sister [Rilean]. She stayed across the street at her mother's house, and here we are, Bud, Leroy, and I, in bed together, and there was jam smeared on the floor. Bud had slept on the outside, Leroy in the middle and me, I was on the other side. I didn't get a wink of sleep and so that was my wedding night!

The couple's first home was located in a neighborhood outside of Grand Rapids known as "Skunk Hollow." It was a two-room cabin that had freezing floors in the winter and an outhouse barely hidden in the trees. Almost exactly nine months after they were married, their first daughter Linda was born. Aunt Lila had to haul water to bathe the baby and do the washing. They were so poor at that time that my uncle Pete recalls his sister Lila coming home to the Warba farm and asking her mother Freda if she could go into the root cellar in the basement and get a handful of potatoes. My cousin Lilean described this first house as "a tar paper shack" that was just across the road from Leroy's parents' house. The Garners did not have money and Leroy knew intimately what it felt like to live from hand to mouth. He worked in the mines as a heavy equipment operator, just like Grandpa Burge did. Back then, having a steady job didn't necessarily guarantee a life of financial freedom on the Iron Range. Men who worked in the mines, as opposed to the men who sat behind the desks at the mining company, made a little over $1.00 an hour. Given the history of my own family, it's pretty easy to be skeptical when multinational mining companies come to northern Minnesota and try to leverage our "mining heritage" as justification for excavating and eviscerating our homelands. For me, they are conjuring the old days of boom-and-bust economies and the specter of abject poverty—a reality that was always hanging over the heads of mining families from Grand Rapids to Taconite Harbor. As any mining family knows, once the pockets of ore were spent and shipped out across Lake Superior, the men who sat behind bigger, fancier desks in bigger, fancier cities would make a mint off of the hard labor of men like Uncle Leroy, Grandpa Burge, and my dad, Francis, who worked on the ore boats when he was a young man.

So, during those years in Grand Rapids, and for a few short stints in Minneapolis, Lila and Leroy would scrape by as best as they could, while Lila brought her many daughters into the world, one after the other. Having babies was "easy" for Lila, at least in terms of conceiving children, carrying them to term, and having them arrive in the world healthy, strong, and loved. I'm not insinuating that raising all of these babies was easy for her, because it most certainly was not. And I'm not saying that Lila never suffered a miscarriage or early complications, because it's likely she did, based on family hearsay. And she, like her own mother, and her grandmother before that, would have been forced to endure one or both of those heartaches as a young woman. But unlike her sister Faye, Lila never struggled with the dreadful morbidity of motherhood. Lila was beautiful, after all, and her esteem as a woman and a mother didn't come from a place of longing or sadness. And more importantly, Lila was very much the opposite of Faye when it came to speaking her mind. She was so very quick with words, and never held anything back for very long. This trait, whether inherited or learned, would save Lila from the same sad fate of her older sister.

****

As their young family grew, so did the need for a safe and warm place to live. At some point, Grandma and Grandpa Garner's house across the way in Skunk Hollow burned down, leaving behind a cinder block foundation. Uncle Leroy made it his mission to build his family a new place on the foundation of his parents' old house. From scrap lumber and fixtures he squirreled away money to buy, a new house eventually emerged that had hardwood floors and stud walls to keep the kids in and the cold out. Lilean recalled that Aunt Lila was "really happy" to have a more solid place to raise their family and noted that her dad "always tried really hard to make things better for them." His efforts included setting up a "New and Used" store in one of the sheds at their house. My cousin Linda shared that Uncle Leroy traded a used dresser for their first dog—a black lab puppy named Spike. This would be the first pet in a long line of pets, including an injured crow that Uncle Leroy found on the road one time. He brought it home, built a pen behind the house, and named it Tar Paper. Linda said that her dad taught the crow to say its name, so it would say "Tar Paper" over and over again. Spike would bark at the crow, and pretty soon Tar Paper started barking like a dog! After it got better, Uncle Leroy set the crow free, and Linda remembers that it would come back and visit them, the whole time barking like a dog from high up in the trees.

Not long after they moved into the new house, Uncle Leroy got laid off from the mining company. Desperate for money, he experimented with a steam cleaning business, worked odd jobs, and did what he could to take care of his family. Seeing a niche in the newly developing refrigeration and heating market, Uncle Leroy decided to go in a new direction and enrolled in a technical class on installing and maintaining refrigeration systems. The only difficult part was that the class was held in Minneapolis. Determined to turn their finances around, he left Lila and his young daughters on the Range with the promise that he would be able to start his very own business and make lots of money. I can just hear him say, "I'll make a fortune, Lila! And we'll get a brand-new modern refrigerator too!" At that time, the family was Linda, Loni, and Lilean, with Lori to arrive soon.

When Uncle Leroy was away Aunt Lila took it upon herself to get some first aid training. She always had an affinity for medical-related things. She was not squeamish or faint of heart, and as she would do throughout her life, Lila wanted to help other people. And so, when a man from Grand Rapids visited their house one day and showed her a painful boil on his leg, Lila knew how to properly lance it and treat the infection, using her newly acquired home-nursing skills. Right around this time, a good friend of hers named Marie and a number of other people in Marie's household were suffering from some kind of throat infection that seemed much worse than an everyday cold. Wanting to help, Lila doctored Marie for several nights, but she got sicker and sicker, until it was decided that she needed to go to the hospital. Unfortunately, Marie was infected with diphtheria and died in the Grand Rapids hospital. Diphtheria was treatable at that time, and a vaccine had already been widely used to eradicate the disease by the late 1940s. Sadly, a chiropractor misdiagnosed her illness and neglected to treat the ailment that eventually killed her. Lila developed a somewhat irrational fear of chiropractors because of that incident. In the process, she had also directly exposed herself and her young children to deadly bacteria. Lilean remembers that "the whole family was quarantined for a few weeks. There was Mom, her husband is gone, and all of us little kids running around. Our neighbors would bring food to the door and run! Thankfully, Doctor Brown came to the house and gave us all shots in the butt, and we weren't even able to go outside and play!"

It breaks my heart to tell what happens next. While Leroy was away at refrigeration school, they got behind on house payments and were not able to recover. They lost their new house with the hardwood floors and the stud walls that kept the cold out. There would be no new refrigerator, and no fortune that would come soon enough to save their investment. This was devastating for Aunt Lila. When the bank repossessed their house, Lila and Lee were forced to make a move. It was 1962. Her younger sisters, Betty and Joyce, were both living in Grand Marais at that time and Grandma and Grandpa Burge were still at the Warba farm. The U.S. Forest Service was hiring heavy equipment operators, and Leroy, as a World War II veteran, was able to find a full-time job working in the Superior National Forest outside the town of Grand Marais on the North Shore of Lake Superior.

Their first house was in the Croftville neighborhood, just east of town and right close to the lakeshore, where the whole family packed into a two-room cabin with bunk beds. There was a hand-pumped well in the yard, an outhouse, and a little shed in the back. Lilean remembers that this was the house where the family's black lab named Cookie had twelve puppies. So, that's two adults, four girls, one mama dog, and twelve puppies all rattling around inside two rented rooms; one that was used for cooking and one that was used for sleeping. My mom recalls visiting them just after the puppies were born, which was apparently quite the sight. The Garners always had pets, and Lori, especially, loved to bring home stray animals, including dogs, cats, birds, reptiles, and rodents. There was Frosty the very rotund dog who lived to a ripe old age and Scruffy, a high-spirited bird dog that rode around in the truck with Uncle Leroy, and so many more.

Uncle Leroy continued his full-time work as a heavy equipment operator, running the graders on the old roads that stretch from the bowels of Lake County to the borderlands of the Gunflint Trail. He did some landscaping around the Tofte ranger station as part of his job, and he was also a wildfire fighter. Lilean remembers him bringing the family up the Gunflint Trail to proudly show them the aftermath of a midtrail fire that burned in the area of Hungry Jack Lake. Uncle Leroy was also stationed in Isabella, Minnesota, for a time, which is a very long drive from Grand Marais, especially in the winter. Lilean joked that she and her sisters always wondered who the mysterious other woman "Isabella" was until he took them there to visit the Forest Service office. There are still men and women who remember working with Uncle Leroy. He was well liked and is generally remembered as a very colorful part of the old-school Tofte crew.

With steady money coming in, the Garners were able to secure a little yellow house in Johnsonville, which was at the bottom of Eighth Avenue West just north of Highway 61. Lila's sister Betty and her husband, Lloyd Larsen, had a house two doors up the hill, so Betty and Lila were able to reconnect as sisters and emotionally support each other through some very rocky times, particularly for Lila and Leroy, who by then had four daughters, thirteen dogs, and a widening chasm between the two of them, carved out by a dark and sticky river of Jack Daniels and Coca-Cola.

* * * * * * *

It was a not-so-hidden secret that drinking ruled things in the Garner house for a long time. It hung over Aunt Lila in every place they rented or lived in, between Skunk Hollow and Minneapolis, where they lived when their second daughter Loni was born. Aunt Betty lived with them at that time, and she remembered that while Aunt Lila was at the hospital with a newborn baby in her arms, Aunt Faye was scouring the bars looking for Leroy to tell him the good news about his new, blue-eyed daughter. Lilean confided that when she was a teenager, "The house was claustrophobic. They were poor. Dad would work hard but was a binge drinker. It wasn't a peaceful house. I never felt it was a peaceful house when I was growing up."

Though she was at times a heavy smoker, Lila wasn't much of a drinker and would occasionally have a glass of Lambrusco or Ripple with 7 Up in it. One time, Leroy was out late, drinking at a downtown bar, and Lila decided she was going to go find him and bring him home. There he was with his Jack and Coke. She waltzed into the American Legion and sat next to him at the bar. She ordered a Coke from the bartender, and when he wasn't looking, she would switch drinks with her husband, trying to wean him off the booze so that she could get him home. She said, "Damn it, Leroy, I'm half in the bag . . . drinking your drinks!" Lilean shared that Uncle Leroy had a particularly difficult time making it home on Friday nights. "Not every Friday," she said, "but when it happened it was super upsetting to Mom."

Leroy's own father was an alcoholic farmer who lived in a dirt-poor shack in Grand Rapids that had newspapers stuffed inside the walls to keep the cold out. This is where Uncle Leroy grew up, which makes the Burge farm seem upscale by comparison. Young Leroy was temporarily thrown out of third grade for smoking and then quit going to school completely in the eighth grade. In spite of these rugged circumstances, everyone who knew him recognized that Leroy was charming and always had a twinkle in his bright blue eyes. After quitting school, he rode the trains for a while and then went into the army, which was always a source of pride for him. He served as a truck driver in Germany during World War II, and the story relayed by Lilean is that "toward the end of the war, Leroy had lost his own battalion and while out searching for his compatriots, stumbled upon a battalion of German soldiers, who surrendered themselves to him in the field. Disregarding wartime protocol, Leroy went out drinking with his captives instead of turning them in. Now stumbling drunk and lost in Germany with some new and potentially dangerous drinking buddies, Leroy knew that bringing the Germans in that night would have been incriminating. So, he slipped away from them to avoid tipping off his superiors to the fact that he had temporarily gone AWOL and gotten drunk with, possibly aiding and abetting, the enemy."

When I lived in their house, there was never any alcohol, at least not that I remember. By the time their youngest daughter, Lisa, was a teenager, Uncle Leroy had quit drinking and Aunt Lila was very active in Al-Anon. My mother claims this was when her sister Lila became a "liberated" woman, which in Lila's case, meant that her personal freedom was synonymous with freedom from her husband's addiction. For the first time in her life, Lila would be able to explore her own health and well-being. Because she didn't drink and found solace in helping others, she kept attending and organizing Al-Anon meetings, which helped her sort through codependency and the difficulties of living with a reformed binge drinker. If there was any darkness around Uncle Leroy's drinking, it was not something that ever played out in front of me. It's sort of unimaginable, really, to think of two adults with their own issues, trying to raise their daughters, all of them intelligent, rebellious, and strong-willed, while cohabitating in a ridiculously small space. At times I know things reached the boiling point, and with five girls, you can count on a lot of drama. But somehow, they made it through.

By the time I was ten going on eleven, the house seemed comforting and peaceful. But it was never very quiet. Aunt Lila had a bell on top of the front door that chimed every time a visitor arrived, and a clock that cuckooed and played a song at the top of every hour. At first, I would lie awake at night, listening to the clock tick, unable to sleep through the hourly outbursts. After several weeks, I got used to the noisy sounds of the house and was able to sleep through the night. I remember watching Duluth TV stations in the evening after supper and sitting on the floor between the wall furnace and Uncle Leroy's rocking chair, where he would sit and smoke his pipe and talk about his day or tell us stories about when he was kid. There was a photo of him above his chair in the living room that was taken after a big win in Las Vegas. There he was in the hot desert sun, holding up a fistful of crisp, one-hundred-dollar bills, with his teeth clamped around a fat cigar and grinning from ear to ear beneath his whisper-thin moustache.

After a while I got used to the routine at Aunt Lila's house, and instead of feeling unsettled during the week, I had to ready myself to spend weekends at our own house on Eighth Avenue. My dad and my sister and I would try to create some sense of normalcy, even though nothing was close to being normal. I think the only reason I made it through that year without my mom is because Aunt Lila never made me feel out of place. She loved me and accepted me as I was, perhaps knowing on a deeply lived level, that every family has to learn to live with scars, both physical and emotional, and that we can either choose to try to hide them or we can use them as marks of courage and healing and find a way to live with them. Aunt Lila was an expert at living with battle scars, and she knew very well that it's the scars you can't see that will do the most damage.

* * * * * * *

At some point after Mom had been in the hospital for a few months, my dad gathered Dawn and me up, put us in the car, and told us that we were going to visit mom in Duluth. I remember very little about the ride, or the day, or even what my dad said to us. I don't remember what we ate, if we stopped anywhere, or what happened later. But I do remember very clearly being at Miller Dwan Hospital in downtown Duluth and walking among nurses in white dresses and hose and doctors in coats with stethoscopes, while holding tight to my little sister, who was just seven years old. At the end of a long hallway with polished white floors we paused outside the door of a hospital room and became witness to our mother quietly going crazy. She sat on the end of the bed inside the very clean and orderly enclosure. She was hunched over and nearly undressed—wearing only a pair of purple panties with white plastic rings on each side and a white shirt that seemed too small for her. It was a diminutive and broken version of Mom, and yet I remember her being indescribably beautiful that day, as if I was seeing her for the very first time. The north-facing windows reminded us that it was sunny outside, but the interior of the room was dressed in soft shadows and darkness. Being asked to go inside and expected to engage with the hollowed-out shell that was our mother, is a scenario no kid is ever ready to see or understand. The three of us moved together into the room, like a clump of grapes, and my dad said to her, "Joyce, that isn't the kind of underwear you usually wear."

And her reply was indecipherable. A foreign string of words that may as well have been "I'm sorry." Apologizing to us for seeing her in that state was something she had been conditioned to do from the time she was a little girl, when she was terrified to speak out loud at home or at school. She professes that the symptoms of her obsessive-compulsive disorder didn't show up until she was pregnant with my sister Dawn, but if you count all the times she hid behind her sisters, bit her tongue to keep herself from speaking out, or accepted less because she felt she didn't deserve more, the ravenous and insatiable appetite of her OCD had been fed enough red meat throughout her life to grow inside her like a hungry lamprey. And so, it was at Miller Dwan that the doctors decided to erase Mom. A few weeks before our visit, they had ordered up a series of electroshock treatments combined with lithium and other antipsychotic drugs, with the goal of killing the parasite that would likely have killed her.

Even though they did their awful best to wipe her slate clean, my mother's formative childhood memories stayed intact, and can still be written out like white chalk on an ebony blackboard. I'm very thankful that some of her memories made it through the electroshock sessions, similar to how Grandpa Burge survived his lightning strike. Because without her help, we would be all alone, trying to make sense of the Burge family secrets all on our own. The very wise U.S. poet laureate Joy Harjo has described a family as a "connection and a collection of hearts, minds and stories." It's also a place where layers of old trauma and darkly hidden secrets live. Harjo's view on family, as well as the views of some of my own relatives, have instilled in me the idea that family stories and memories are ancient living things and that "our ancestors come to us through our collective memories."[1] When you think of your relatives in this way, you have an opportunity to nourish the roots of your own family tree. What are we if not new needles formed from the fibers of a gnarled and wizened old-growth conifer? Those who wish to heal from the bad things that happened in the past and move beyond them into a new phase of our collective family story may still find that the residue of these damaging things always stays barely visible, like a hatchet scar on the trunk of a great red pine, or the traces of writing left behind on a chalkboard, after trying to wipe it clean with a dusty, gypsum-coated eraser.

Growing up on the Warba farm was complicated. My mother once explained that her mother, Freda, would play favorites with the kids and chose to "pick at" Betty and Lila. So, Grandpa, trying to defend the two, would take their side against his wife, which would result in a big fight. My mother said, "I don't like fighting. There were terrible fights. One time we all ran into the woods. Dad threatened to leave, but he never did." And here's where my mother's voice becomes her mother's voice, melting together like butter in pot. She said, "Mom [I] felt like she [I] had to be perfect."

And so, little Joyce resolved, "I'm not going to be bad. I'm going to be perfect." Ironically, my mom's nickname when she was very little was "Fire Engine" because she screamed and yelled so much. But then as she got a bit older, she stopped screaming and got quiet. And Joyce stayed quiet all throughout school, past her days as a new bride, through the birth of her first child (me), and she persevered until her second child (Dawn) was born. It's this painfully shy version of mom that is hard for me to envision now, so many years later. Deciding to be quiet as her way of being perfect made her the prettily perfect host for obsessive-compulsive disorder. OCD is passed along through generations of family and manifests itself in different ways, depending on the person afflicted with it. It is a mental disorder caused by a chemical imbalance in the brain and can't be cured without a combination of therapies. In Mom's case, the OCD was like a never-ending loop of terrible thoughts she was unable to stop or control. So, imagine the worst thing you can think of (the death of a child, a car accident, airplane crash, violent assault, dog killed by wolves) and play that scenario over and over in your mind without end. That's what having OCD was like for Mom. Her dreadful thoughts would compound on themselves and by the time she was hospitalized, she was in a deep, life-ending depression. The day we visited her at Miller Dwan, her fight against the disease had only just begun, and it would be a full two years before Mom would be able to function as a day-to-day mother and wife back at our house on Eighth Avenue. Mom's scars are the ones she carries inside her head. You can't see them, like you can Aunt Lila's scythe-shaped scar, but we all know that they are there just the same. I asked my cousin Lilean if she thought Aunt Lila's scar affected her as a person, and she said, "I don't remember her being overly sensitive about it. She wore her scars proudly. She never tried to hide it. The only time she ever brought it up, was when Lori [Lilean's next youngest sister] had a car accident and she cut her nose badly. She remembers Lila lamenting, 'Oh no, she'll have a scar like I do.'"

For the Burge women, the scars you can't see are carved inside our guts, hearts, and throats. These scars were inflicted by other people and include getting cornered by your mom's best friend's husband down in the root cellar at the farm. Being molested by that same neighbor man while riding a horse. Being propositioned outside the principal's office when you are eight years old, by the principal himself. "Don't tell anyone I asked you that," he would whisper. There are the scars imprinted because you are having an affair with a much older man whose children you babysit for or denying the fact that your boyfriend is an abusive child molester. And in my mom's experience, suffering something unspeakable as a child—something so awful it remains blocked out of your mind until you are seventy years old, when it pops back into your consciousness, like a dead and bloated moose carcass on the surface of a lake. All of these traumas are just the emotional wounds and scars that I'm aware of. One of these scars belongs specifically to me and yet, within the continuum of family, they all belong to me, just as my scars belong to all the women in my family.

The women in the Burge family were taught to be invisible and find self-worth only in their ability to attract a husband and have lots of children. Mix the morbidity of motherhood with chronic femininity and you get big heartache with a fatal dose of low self-esteem. Each one of the Burge sisters were mishandled by men, and though they discussed these things among themselves, they were not taught the tools of self-care that were necessary to relieve them of their burdens. And in all cases, no one made an effort to hold these men accountable. When I asked my mom about their neighbor at the farm, the one who grabbed her when she was on a horse and the same one who cornered Aunt Lila in the root cellar, she said simply, "No one ever told on him." Like an untreatable, malignant tumor, this man's abuse of children just continued to spread, year after year, until all the Burge daughters had grown up and moved away.

* * * * * * *

If Aunt Lila's instinct as a young woman was to cover her scar, that same compulsion caused her to try to conceal her beautiful inner self. From the time she was a young girl she was told that a woman's worth was based on raising children and keeping a man happy, and yet, when she proved she was very good at both of those things, she was shamed for doing it wrong and doing it too soon. Her parents chastised her for being too young and made her feel as if she was reckless and disgraceful. Lila was expected to carry the responsibility of being a mother, but only when the time was perfectly ripe. The reality is that from the time she was seventeen, Lila mothered and grand-mothered and surrogate-mothered most everyone in her life. She was forced to accept all the burdens of being a mother and a wife, and she carried those heavy pails of responsibility with a steady hand, like carrying pails of water from the well to bathe your newborn daughter.

A natural helper, and a very resourceful and curious person, Lila was able to function with very little help from others, but at times the burden was too much, even for her. When Lilean was growing up she recognized that life at the Garner house could be overwhelming for her mother. She said, "I felt like Mom was screaming all the time . . . Mom was frustrated. She was married to a binge drinker . . . In the teenage years, we didn't get along. I avoided the home setting. I spent my high school years showering at the school, and I came home in time for dinner." She went on to tell this story: "I remember one time in my rebellious teen years, Mom and I were fighting and I asked Dad, 'What did you ever marry her for?' He got so mad at me and said, 'You don't even know what your mom was like. She was like a little deer jumping from rock to rock.'"

Is there anything more vulnerable than a little deer traversing dangerous, rocky terrain? This may have been Leroy's way of claiming that he saved Lila from a precarious situation, which is probably very true. Lila was just seventeen when they were married, and given what we know about life on the Warba farm, there were not a lot of exit ramps, short of running away with the circus. In that little deer, I see a vulnerable, singular being, but I also see a beautiful wild creature that's completely free. Lila's freedom was hard fought, and it took many, many years for her to rediscover that same sense of freedom and liberation, because she had a lot of girls to raise first.

When Linda, the oldest L, started her last year of high school, Lila learned that she was pregnant yet again. As Lilean said, "Lisa was a surprise. I remember Mom in her maternity clothes and Aunt Faye asking me, 'What would you think about having a baby sister?' I thought, 'It's just one more kid.' So, Lisa was kind of my sidekick when she was little."

Lisa, the fifth Garner daughter, was born the same year her oldest sister, Linda, graduated from high school. And by the time Lisa was in kindergarten, three of the older Garner daughters had already made Lila and Leroy grandparents. And so, Aunt Lila raised her own kids over a span of thirty-four years, had a big hand in raising her grandkids, and also helped raise me. Thank goodness.

Mom was away from us for a year. After she was released from the hospital, she went to a full-time care facility in Prescott, Wisconsin, for intensive therapy, including individual counseling and group support. While she was there, she made us little gifts in the craft room, like a clumsily shaped clay vase and some cards. We visited her there one time, and she seemed like a stranger to me. I think she probably felt like one too. I don't really want to imagine how things would have been different for me had Aunt Lila not taken me in. And other aunties helped, too, like Aunt Doreen, my dad's oldest sister, Aunt Betty, who took care of Dawn like Aunt Lila took care of me, and our cousin Sue Ellen, Aunt Doreen's daughter, who stayed with us a lot on the weekends while Mom was gone. Dad, of course, had to continue to go to work to keep the bills paid and the lights on. Being a product of his own family's brand of dysfunction, Dad was also living with a whole different kind of expectation. He was a man trying to measure up to 1950s masculine ideals, according to which the woman kept house and took care of the kids, and the husband worked hard each day to take care of the family and then pretty much did whatever else he wanted to do, because that was a man's prerogative. And in Dad's case, the wretched history of the way his own father treated his mother would complicate things for him and, by extension, our family for the rest of his life. For this reason, when Mom's depression reached the clinical stage, he struggled to understand what was happening, why it was happening to us, and why he couldn't fix it and make it better. As part of her recovery, Mom had to reclaim her true, authentic voice, and part of that was explaining to our dad that she needed him to change too—and in fact, that her life depended on it. Because of his love for her, he worked very hard to evolve the way he thought about women—in particular, the role of wives and husbands in the age of chronic femininity, which empowered men and diminished women, anointed the male gaze as the sanctioned, primary lens through which the world saw beauty, and, as a result, caused many generations of women and girls to fail miserably, especially if they didn't look like Farrah.

After Mom got out of the hospital, Dawn and I returned home to Eighth Avenue and our weekly routine went back to seminormal. Mom continued her treatments and for the past forty-two years, has taken just one-half of a pill every day, which, she proclaims, saves her life. That little bit of medicine stops the bad thoughts from circling around and lets her mind rest. Life for our little family and our extended family slowly got stitched back together, and I believe we all grew much closer because of that long stretch of time away from each other. Mom is the only person who knows to what extent those old, deep scars have healed inside her mind, but like Aunt Lila's half-moon-shaped mark, it's her scars that make my mom even more beautiful to me, because they are evidence of strength and resilience. She is a living survivor of perfect imperfection.

****

Aunt Lila's house would continue to be a place of warmth and good times for us. She would annually host cookie decorating on Christmas, and her kitchen would often be the hub of Thanksgiving celebrations for a big part of the family. Aunt Lila, Aunt Betty, my mom, and all of the Grand Marais Burge cousins would go over to the Garners' on Thanksgiving Day for dinner. There would be turkey and ham, a moose roast if my dad had a good hunt that fall, scalloped potatoes and mashed potatoes with turkey gravy. Bread stuffing, homemade rolls, sweet potatoes, buttered rutabagas, green bean casserole with "French" onions on top, lime Jell-O with some bizarre ingredients mixed in, wild rice casserole, jellied cranberries that retained the shape of their tin can, and homemade pies of all kinds. The Burge family always had real whipped cream and Cool Whip for pie, and while Uncle Lloyd and my dad would have beer with dinner, Uncle Leroy would drink coffee. After dinner the kids and the women would go into Aunt Lila and Uncle Leroy's bedroom and relax on the bed to digest the feast. We would giggle, laugh, share stories, and wait for our full stomachs to empty out a bit so that we could eat another plate of food, or even nibble on a few little sandwiches made of turkey on home-baked dinner rolls with salt, pepper, and mayonnaise. Food was, is, and might always be the way the Burge family shows affection—a mixed-up way of loving life and loving each other. If food was love, we would all be positively stuffed to our stocking caps with it. This family value would prove problematic for a lot of us, but back then, Thanksgiving was frenzied and wonderful—something I've not yet reconciled or managed to break away from completely.

So, while the women and kids lounged around on the bed and

later cleaned up the kitchen, the men would "visit" with each other while watching football on TV. "Visiting" was my dad's code word for taking side-by-side naps in the living room chairs. The men would sleep and snore and sputter. And once in a while Uncle Lloyd would wake up with a start and grumble something unintelligible before falling back to sleep. As we were packing up to go, my dad would always say, "Nice visiting with you, Lloyd." Then everyone would laugh heartily, and it became part of the tradition every year—the women doing the cooking, putting the food away, washing the dishes, and interacting with the children, all while the men napped on the couch.

In a letter Lilean wrote on August 17, 1980, to Grandma and Grandpa Burge, who were living in Tucson at the time, she acknowledges a new phase in Lila's life: "Mom is working at the Tourist Information Booth and really seems to like it. I think it is good for her to get out now that Lisa is getting more and more independent. Lisa is very involved with her work at the Dairy Queen and friends, and really isn't home a lot. I'm sure Mom has got to feel a little like an empty nest after having so many kids dependent upon her for so long, so this job is really good for her. She looks good and gets all dressed up and seems much happier."

Aunt Lila went through a kind of renaissance period after all her daughters were grown. Many of them already had kids of their own, and so Lila was never really lonesome for the company of a little one. She took all of us in and took good care of everyone, because that's who she was. Her first batch of grandchildren, Kari Lee, Melissa, Aimee, Kris, Eric, and Gina, all spent a lot of time with Aunt Lila and Uncle Leroy, eating from TV trays in the living room, listening to records on the stereo, and playing games at the kitchen table. They all know that house just as intimately as I do, and each of them has their own set of memories and stories to go along with it. Gina, like the others, was very close to her grandma Lila when she was a kid, and her mom, Lilean, laughs about it, saying that "Gina would have her lunch at Grandma's when she was in high school. They would sit and watch *Days of Our Lives* together."

Kris, my cousin Lori's son, was having a hard time, and according to my cousin Lilean, "had to learn to control his temper when he was a little boy." His grandma Lila knew exactly what he needed and had him outside harvesting night crawlers from their backyard in the dark, and they looked up at the stars together, a little boy and his grandma. His reward for slowing down and being patient was that he got to use his night crawlers to go fishing with his grandma and grandpa. And fishing is the ultimate test of patience, as anyone who has tried to catch a walleye dinner on Elbow Lake knows firsthand. Kris grew up to earn a black belt in karate and now works for the State Department in Africa. I'm guessing he still likes to fish too.

Kari Lee, Lila's granddaughter, once said it perfectly: "I was her favorite grandchild. So were all of her grandchildren; she made all of us feel like we were her favorite." Indeed, during the year I lived in Aunt Lila's care, she made me feel like I was her favorite. She never made me feel like I was a burden. She was happy to have me and she always made me feel that way. She was as generous with her love as she was with her sugar cookies. I was just another lucky kid who was able to live at Aunt Lila's house for a while and know what it felt like to be accepted and loved by her.

With far fewer people in the house, Lila got involved in many community things. It was in her nature to try to help people and she continued to do just that. As Lilean said, "I'm more and more aware of how many people she impacted." She became even more active in Alcoholics Anonymous and she reached out to many people in the Cook County community through that organization. She would hold and organize Al-Anon meetings in Grand Marais and mentored a number of people, all the while keeping their anonymity, which is not easy in such a small town. She would invite troubled people into her kitchen and talk with them. She was always really easy to talk to, and I'm guessing that everyone who sat down with her was made to feel special. Plus, there was always coffee and snacks, and her kitchen table served as a place of comfort for a whole lot of people who really needed a friend and a sympathetic ear. If her circumstances had been changed, I can easily envision Aunt Lila working as a human services director, a counselor, or some other form of humanitarian advocate. Lilean describes her mother's life like this: "Mom was very intelligent. She was always a frustrated professional person. She had five kids and not much to go on for her. She always wanted a challenge. She always felt there was more. She was capable of so much. She got her insurance license. She took advanced first aid classes. She was always grasping for more knowledge. She had a very active mind!" Lilean went on to admit that in retrospect, "It's hard to be objective about our mothers—they have a separate world that we don't really know."

It's also hard for mothers to be objective about their kids. As my mother has shared, Grandma Burge was always hard on Lila. She picked on her when she was a little girl, fussed about Lila's outspoken personality, and shamed her for quitting school and getting married at seventeen. And yet, when Grandma Freda and Grandpa Bill bought a house in Grand Marais after selling the Warba farm, they chose a house just a few doors up the hill from Lila and Lee's. Whatever old business was left over between Grandma Freda and Aunt Lila didn't seem to matter much as the years went on. In Grandma's old box of letters and Burge ephemera, there was a carefully saved newspaper clipping of Aunt Lila's Royal Neighbors of America Insurance advertisement. Lila's picture, address, and phone number are on the ad: *Mrs. Lila Garner, PO Box 652, Grand Marais, MN, 387–1664.* Grandma was proud of Lila, who had always been in the world, but had finally arrived in Grandma's world of expectations. She sold insurance to people who needed protection from the unexpected tragedies and losses in life, and she was perfectly suited for that because she had lived it herself. She had lived all of it, and then some.

With their brood now mostly self-reliant, Lila and Leroy continued on with their love story. The two of them had always liked to go on excursions in the woods together, first in Grand Rapids and later on the North Shore. He knew the forest map well because of his job, and she would regularly accompany him ricing or fishing in his old boat. The front of a postcard Grandma Burge wrote to Leroy on June 21, 1985, shows a cartoon of a man in a fishing boat overflowing with his daily catch. The caption is, "Hain't never seen a man who could fish and worry at the same time."

On the back of the card Grandma wrote, "Hope you are getting your limit, don't let Lila beat you. We are eating trout and silver salmon. Are the mosquitoes biting? Be good, Mom." This is in reference to a story Lilean loves to tell about when Uncle Leroy threw Lila's big fish back in the water one day. She prefaced the story by saying that "Mom was spunky, too!" and then she went on to tell the tale:

"Dad was a walleye fisherman but we [she and her husband, Chris] took them trout fishing one time. Lila caught the first trout before he did and Leroy threw her fish back in the water, saying it was too small. And Mom got so upset! There she was, beating him over the head with her fishing pole in the boat. What a stinker! Dad was mad that he didn't catch the biggest fish!"

Uncle Leroy commemorated this incident by painting a poem for Lila on his old minnow bucket in bright red letters: *Don't beat me or bang me, or say you could hang me, for turning your little fish free.* I'm honored to have that old minnow bucket—a treasure given to me by Linda and Lilean, along with two pairs of hand-fashioned wild rice knocking sticks from the days when Uncle Leroy would rice in Grand Rapids. He would pole the canoe through the rice bog, and Lila would knock the ripened rice grains into the boat. I was able to use a pair of those sticks this past fall, on a ricing lake not far from where I live. The sticks were worn down at the places where Aunt Lila used to hold them, but they were still very sturdy and capable. As we moved through the tall plants, the rhythm of the knocking sticks, as we bent and beat through sections of hay-colored rice stalks, was mesmerizing. Those simple tools made it possible to bring food into the boat, while reconnecting with Uncle Leroy and Aunt Lila so many years after they themselves had been out on a lake. Ricing is difficult work, especially when the air is cold, the wind is tricky, and the rice bog is full of spiders and other creepers. Good work done with strong hands can help us heal from the hurts of the past. With every knock of those sticks, I felt a sense of satisfaction and gratitude, knowing that the pain can be reckoned with and moved through, even if sometimes it's measured by one canoe length or one grain of rice at a time.

In March 1998, Uncle Leroy suffered an aneurysm and massive stroke. My cousin Lori described what that day was like for her: "When Dad had his aneurysm, I lived in Duluth. I got to the Duluth hospital first, and Mom and Lilean got there shortly after. In the beginning, Mom took Dad's hand and told him, 'Hold on Leroy.' After the CAT scan and all hope was lost, Mom, Lilean, and I (and our husbands at the time) were around his bedside. The other sisters were desperately trying to get there. We were standing around Dad's bed as they stopped the air bag that was breathing for him. I can still clearly see her hold his hand and her calmly telling Dad that 'it's okay to go now.' She set the tone for all of us there, for Dad leaving us. And we were able to let him leave this world respectfully and with peace and love, though our hearts were broken. There was no wailing, no outburst. It was peaceful and no drama—something poor Dad saw little of, raising five girls."

When Uncle Leroy died, I was living in Minneapolis and had my first real job. When I got the news, I used my first credit card to rent a car and made the trip home for his funeral. It was at the Congregational church and everyone was so sad. Leroy's loss greatly affected his five girls, and his absence would mean that Lila, his wife of forty-two years, would have to learn to live alone for the first time in her life. But rather than fold up into herself, Aunt Lila opened her arms to the heavens and braved what she feared the most. Said Lilean, "Mom said she felt the sky open up at his funeral and felt at peace. Mom amazed me with her grace at that time."

Even though life with Leroy was not perfect, Aunt Lila's life with him was thrilling, right from the very start. They were a couple who proved the cliché that opposites do indeed attract. Aunt Lila told the story of when their courtship first began. It was not long after the night he carved their initials into the dance hall booth, but just before Lila set Leroy straight on what kind of woman she was. She said, "[Leroy's] cousin John was seeing my friend and they came to the Warba farm so they could take us out to Little Falls. And Leroy had the money because he was just out of the army, so he bought the booze and the gas . . . and he made it clear right away that he was picking me up so he could have sex along with his booze. So, my friend and I ended up hiding in the attic of this lady's house in Little Falls, hiding from him and John. That was his first impression of me, and well . . . he was wrong about that [laughs]!" In her reminiscences about the early days of her marriage Lila admits, "That's the way my life was . . . so exciting! And now it's so boring."

****

For more than thirty years, Lila's day-to-day routine was very much rooted in making a home for her family and taking care of the Garner household. She never had time to be bored because there was always something to attend to. For those many years, life in the Garner house was just focused on preparing one girl to leave the nest, and then moving onto the next. Linda, the oldest daughter, left home right after high school graduation. When all five girls were living together in the house, the oldest four shared the tiny front bedroom with two bunk beds. There was one closet that was always crammed full of clothes and toys. Back then, Lila washed the whole family's laundry in a wringer washer and hung everything out to dry. The house had an extensive back porch that ran almost the entire length of the original house, and when Linda was older, she slept on a cot on the porch and her four younger sisters moved into bunks. Lilean said that she was in eighth grade when they added on the living room, Lila's full kitchen, and the second half bath, the one that actors from the Playhouse would use during intermission next door. When they cut into the old house for construction, there were old, hand-hewn timbers inside the structure, which makes it likely that the house was built around the time the neighboring First Norwegian Lutheran Church was built in 1898.

When the house was at full capacity the family regularly spilled out into the yard, especially when it was relatively warm outside. And while the front yard was rather small, the backyard was relatively large—enough space for two apple trees, a few different gardens, and of course, the garage. Lilean used to say that "Dad lives in the garage," and it's easy to see why Uncle Leroy would have spent so much time out there. His garage was packed full of refrigerators, fishing gear, random tools, and things made out of metal. It was his palace, while Lila tended to the inside of the house and the yard. When thinking back on their childhood days on First Avenue, Lilean said, "God sprinkled a handful of black dirt in that rocky country, and it was located in Mom's backyard. She loved gardening. When I built my log real estate building in downtown Grand Marais, Mom took it upon herself to landscape around the sign, putting in a base of big rocks and planting flowers. She turned it into a beautiful rock garden of flowers. She worked so hard. Family was everything to her."

Aunt Lila never moved from that house, even after Uncle Leroy died. Those who knew Lila, knew that having the stability of a house to live in was primary to who she was as a person. Lisa remembers her mom telling her a sad story about when she was a little girl. The Burge family was facing one of their many moves due to a change in Grandpa Burge's job. In the middle of the night Grandpa woke all the kids up and told them they had to get ready to leave, ordering them to pack up their belongings. When they were gathering their things, Lila put her clothes in a pile and held on tightly to her favorite baby doll. The bags were all full to bursting and so Grandpa Burge took Lila's precious dolly out of her arms, told her that the family didn't have room for it, and threw into the fireplace. She just stood there crying and watching it burn. This would have been Lila's first lesson in what it means to lose control at the hands of someone else. After that experience, it seems that Lila spent a lot of her life trying to hold on to the things she loved, in an attempt to stay on solid ground. And when her life felt the most precarious, like when the bank repossessed their house in Grand Rapids, or when she had to watch her little doll melt into the fire, Lila learned that the safety and stability of having her own home were more important than almost anything else in the world.

After Uncle Leroy died, Aunt Lila spent many years at the Garner house all alone, tending to her rows of tiger lilies and irises along the south side of the house, picking rhubarb every June, and doing her best to nurture anyone who needed her, including her own grandchildren and other people in the community who required a helping hand. The whole time, she missed Leroy and the immediacy of sharing her life with a man who sometimes made her crazy but was always delightfully unpredictable.

One day about ten years after she lost Uncle Leroy, Aunt Lila was away from her home, visiting her daughters in Chicago over the holidays. She began to have symptoms of heart trouble and her daughters took her to the hospital. She had blockages around her heart and ended up having to have emergency quadruple bypass surgery. And while it initially seemed as if she would survive that very traumatic procedure, a misstep by someone who should have known better would force Aunt Lila to face what would be the biggest challenge of her life.

After her open-heart surgery, Aunt Lila spent a long recovery in the hospital and before she was sent home, she was put on a blood thinner, which is a routine treatment for post–heart attack patients. At some point, her doctor at home decided to take her off that medicine, and the clot that formed soon after, bypassed her heart and lungs and went into her brain, causing her to have a stroke. She was out having lunch with a friend and the stroke symptoms started in her friend's car on the twelve-mile drive back to Grand Marais. My mother and her daughter Lilean were with her in the emergency room, and my mother remembers helplessly watching as her beloved sister had little strokes, one after the other. She spent some time in the hospital in Duluth at first. The stroke had wiped out many of her basic functions, and she remained in a precarious state of health for a number of weeks. We were all so afraid that our dear Lila would never recover from it. My mother visited her in the hospital, and her loving sister, the one who always tried to take care of things, didn't even know her own name. My mother would touch her on the arm and say, "Lila . . . you're Lila." And Auntie would shake her head and cry, unable to say the words. For someone who was blessed with the gift of communication and was known to never mince words, losing her ability to speak was the worst kind of torture for her. It was because of her own perseverance and strength that she got through that terrible time. For several weeks, Aunt Lila continued to have small strokes that would set her recovery back. She would make progress, and then suddenly she would be forced back to square one. This would be a solitary effort, and no one was going to be able to do the necessary pile of work that had to be done except for Lila.

When she finally started to come out of it, her daughters would visit and talk to her, saying her name, saying their names, talking about her grandchildren and making small talk about what the weather was like outside. Here's what Lilean remembers about her mother's slow recovery: "We'd be talking and I'd spell out her name in letters on the page—L . . . i . . . l . . . a. Then I'd give her the pen and paper and she'd write her name. It was like, all of a sudden, it was, 'Bing! . . . I'm Lila! I'm Lila!'"

When it was time for Aunt Lila to come home to Grand Marais, she was in a wheelchair and required daily physical therapy and speech therapy. The stroke had severely disabled her, but clearly, she still had work to do. One of the hardest changes for everyone was that she would never be able to go back and live in her beloved house on First Avenue, which had steep front stairs and those cramped little hallways that could not accommodate a wheelchair. The decision was made to sort through a whole lifetime of things and secure a room for her at the Northshore Hospital and Care Center in Grand Marais. It was here that she would live out the rest of her life. Lila and her granddaughter Gina were always very close. After she graduated from high school, Gina had served in the U.S. armed forces, just like her Grandpa Leroy had. Gina was married and had a family of her own, and her bond with her grandma grew stronger than ever. When she had her second baby, she brought her up to the Care Center, laid the baby on her grandma's chest, and said, "Lila, meet Lila." Gina's mom, Lilean, was there and said that "the baby and great-grandmother looked deeply into each other's eyes" in recognition of their shared lyrical name, which had become a sort of battle cry, after Aunt Lila had to fight so hard to bring that name back into the world.

I would pop in to visit her whenever I came home for the weekend. It was remarkable the amount of progress Aunt Lila had made, from being near death at the hospital in Duluth, being bedridden and relearning her own name, to sitting up in a wheelchair and learning the names of everything and everyone else. It was like she had gone backward to the age of two or three and then catapulted all the way back to being a grandmother, mother, and auntie within the span of a year. Occasionally I would read to her from *Gone with the Wind*, one of her favorite stories, and sometimes our visit would be cut short because it was time for her to go to speech therapy or spend time in the crafts room. A year into her residency at the Care Center, I came home for Christmas and under the family tree there was an envelope with my name on it, the letters written out in what looked like the hand of a four-year-old child. Inside the envelope was a Christmas tree ornament made from a dried apple slice, some little white straw flowers, and tiny artificial holly berries. The card inside said, "To Staci, Love Aunt Lila," written in those same, little-kid letters. I still treasure that ornament as a symbol of Aunt Lila's love, perseverance, and courage.

It reminds me that there can be perfection within imperfection, and that if life forces you to lose ground or shift gears unexpectedly, it is your own strength of mind and strong sense of purpose that will help get you back on track.

Not surprisingly, after she regained her identity and her ability to read and write (with her left hand), Aunt Lila became an advocate for others who could not manage things on their own. While at the Care Center, she arranged Al-Anon meetings, and people from all over came to those group sessions. She kept an eye out for the unfair treatment of people who were more vulnerable than she was, and on more than one occasion, she bravely took an issue or a complaint to the managers about something that was adversely affecting the quality of life for residents there. One of the causes she took on wholeheartedly was the lack of privacy for families who were going through end-of-life care. She felt bad for the people who were dying and had to share a room with another resident. She experienced firsthand that it was a terrible situation for both the grieving family and the resident, who had no place else to go. She took it on, organized a plan, and then attended a hospital board meeting in her wheelchair to advocate for the construction of a hospice room where families could spend the last days with their elderly relative in private. Lilean described her mother as "the driving force" in that effort, and Lila followed the process through until the hospice room was finished. Lilean also helped and volunteered to hang wallpaper in the new room. She said that Aunt Lila sat inside the new room in her wheelchair and "was with me overseeing my wallpapering job!"

Aunt Lila was also involved with the paving of the Sweetheart's Bluff hiking trail in the Grand Marais Rec Park. The well-loved and well-used historic trail was not wheelchair accessible, and in fact, very few paths or sidewalks in Grand Marais at that time were suitable for nature lovers with disabilities. And so, Lila, along with a group of likeminded citizens, petitioned the city to pave the trail so that wheelchair-bound people would be able to explore the woods and the lakeshore from that very beautiful vantage point, just like anyone else could. It was around this time that Aunt Lila was named "Senior Citizen of the Year" during Fisherman's Picnic, an annual summer festival. She was now local royalty, and her daughters came home for the celebration and parade. Aunt Lila was so happy and looked so beautiful that day. She wore a dark blue sweater that set off her violet-blue eyes and complemented her silver-white hair perfectly—so radiant, so fierce, and deeply loved by many. And still, Lila had more work to do.

* * * * * * *

In September 2001 I was living in Duluth but was fidgety about where my life was headed. I had gone through a bad breakup with a man who had abused my trust, and more than anything, I just wanted to go home and recoup my losses. A halfway step between the Twin Cities and Grand Marais, Duluth provided a good transition for me, and my job was steady and stimulating, until things started to go wrong at work. I was dragging my feet the morning of September 11, when my sister called and told me to turn the TV on. I collapsed on the couch and watched the Twin Towers fall while the world as we knew it changed forever. I called work to say I wasn't coming in, got in my silver Subaru wagon, and drove the 110 miles home. For me, when the world comes crashing down, there is nowhere to go but north. I visited Aunt Lila while I was there and also my auntie Gloria, my dad's sister, who was helping me put together some family history for my graduate thesis—the story of Chippewa City, an abandoned village that was once east of Grand Marais, where the Drouillard side of my family was from. I know that 9/11 changed a lot of things for a lot of people, and the change that it created in me was knowing that I needed to return home. The work I was doing for my history project was intimately connected to home, and there were some other romantic thoughts that needed to be followed up on. I sent one email to my friend, the artist and author Betsy Bowen, that said, "Dear Betsy, I'm thinking of moving home. Do you know of any jobs in Grand Marais?" And Betsy emailed me right back and said, "Betsy Bowen Studio needs a manager to tell us if we can afford a manager." I took her up on the offer, gave my two-week notice at work, and made plans to move. Everything fell into place, much as it has in the past, when you know you are on the right path. With my dad's help, my two cats and I piled our things into a trailer and settled into a rented apartment downtown. After a year, I moved into what I'll call Cabin 2, a vintage vacation cabin just down the street from the Care Center where Aunt Lila was living. I was able to walk to work, walk to visit Aunt Lila, and hike the old trails of my youth without ever having to start my car. Small town life isn't for everyone, but the simplicity of it was liberating for me. And just like I had learned from Aunt Lila, when you have plenty to do, chances are good that you will flourish.

That first summer in Cabin 2, I set up a luncheon on my little deck. I invited my mother over and called Aunt Lila to ask if she would like to come to my cabin for lunch the next day. She was thrilled by the invitation, and so that late morning I walked one block up the hill, wheeled Aunt Lila out of her room, down the hall, into the parking lot, and down the street to my little cabin. A carpenter friend had helped me with a makeshift ramp so that Aunt Lila could be wheeled right up onto the deck. She and I laughed so hard on the walk down the hill. It could have easily gone wrong, with me hitting a big rock and spilling her into the street, but she didn't seem to care. She was just along for the ride and trusted that I would get her back to her room eventually. There was something about the stroke that affected Lila's lifelong compulsion to remain in control of things that were not easily tamed. It was what added spark to her relationship with Uncle Leroy, even though her efforts weren't always successful.

Lilean recognized that her mother's health crisis somehow eased Lila's grasp on some of her rigid ideas from the past and enabled her to live in the moment—something Uncle Leroy had always helped her experience but that didn't come naturally to her. Lilean said, "Once I drove her to Chicago in the wheelchair van. Someone cut right in front of me on the expressway going into the city. I slammed on the brakes, and it was really scary. We came really close to being in a bad car accident. I looked over at Mom to see if she was OK, and she was smiling! And she said, 'Well, if I was going to die it would be doing something that was making me happy.' That's living in the moment."

So, being properly in the moment that day, the three of us had a long, leisurely lunch in the sun. I showed her my garden, we made small talk, and it felt really lovely to be able to do that for her. To spring her out of the antiseptic hospital, feed her homemade food, and share some iced tea with her while sitting in the warm sun. She was beautifully present, and it's a memory that always makes me smile.

Being home ended up being a good move in more ways than one. In the process of exploring my romantic ideas about home, I met someone who was the most interesting, solid, and accessible person I had ever met. This person was unlike any other boyfriend I had ever had in my life because, well, she was a woman. And here's where chronic femininity made its last stand in the battlefield of my life. Because if your psyche is tailored to believe that attracting a man is primary, and having children is what you are supposed to do as a young woman, then falling in love with another woman smashes through those kinds of expectations with the force of a thousand waves hitting the break wall of one's heart. And it's a terrible thing, to feel the force of those waves and also be made to feel as if you are obligated to keep it all inside you. I managed to contain the floodwaters for about two years. As Cathy and I navigated the exciting and thrilling days of a brand-new love, we also had to sidestep the people who were the closest to us, because we just didn't know how to tell everyone the truth. You see, the overused closet metaphor doesn't fully express what it's like when you are the one locked inside that closet. As the writer Hannah Gadsby has said, being "in the closet isn't a safe place," because it's dark in there, and it's filled to the rafters with fear and trauma. For me the feeling was more like floodwaters deluging a levee. And those floodwaters just continue to rise, until they eventually have nowhere else to go, and then one day the levee is breached. My biggest fear was having to tell my mother that, in reality, the time I was spending with Cathy was anything but a platonic friendship. Mom was, after all, the person who was supposed to pass the candle of motherhood and marriage over to me, her eldest daughter. And after generations plagued with the morbidity of motherhood, and chained to the expectations of chronic femininity, I knew that Mom was not really ready to let go of her ideas about me—her first daughter, the one with the Farrah Fawcett fixation and love of high-fashion magazines. But what I've discovered is that sexuality and love are not about whatever *ideas* you have about people; they're simply about people being people. Ideas are supported by preconceived notions, the assumptions and expectations of others, and our own prejudices. This is not reality. People fall in love with other people, and that's the simple truth. People will. And they do.

****

It was right around this time in my life that Aunt Lila's health started to decline. I was in a mess, because my well-meaning sister unburdened me of my secret love affair and broke the news to our parents before I found the courage to do it myself. I was simultaneously relieved and also terrified. The lever on the dam had been tripped, and the whole family was flooded out for a while as a result of it. As our nuclear family tried to divorce their ideas about Staci's love life from the reality of it, Aunt Lila suffered some terrible digestive symptoms and she got very, very ill. I went to see her, and it was awful to see her so clearly in pain. I think she knew she was dying, but in spite of that, she took some time with me that day. First, she tried to give me one of the plants from the windowsill in her room, which I was not prepared to do in any way. If Aunt Lila was trying to give things away, that meant she was preparing to leave us. I politely weaseled out of it, telling her I would come back sometime soon and we could talk about it then, a ploy I'm sure she saw right through. As I was getting ready to go, I told her I loved her and she said to me, "I love you, no matter what." And then I knew that she knew. The floodwaters had engulfed me, and then Dawn, then Mom, and finally Aunt Lila, who was always my mother's closest confidante. And here was Aunt Lila reaching out her hand to a drowning woman, wanting me to know that it was going to be OK, "no matter what." As she was leaving this world, my dear auntie was still loving me and trying to take care of me. Just like she had back when I was ten and she had me sleep in my cousin's room instead of letting me be all alone. It was a very illogical way to say goodbye, but a very logical way to be an aunt.

This kind of selflessness is also how Lila handled her final exit with her own daughters, which according to Lilean was a long process of Aunt Lila letting go: "Our family used the hospice room she had advocated for to be with mom at different times, as she was at death's edge many times. Of course, she rallied so many times when her family was called! She just wouldn't leave us! We all had to leave her alone for her to finally let herself go. She died many times . . . and didn't die. Dr. Stover called and would say, 'I think it's time.' And then she would bounce back. My sisters would say, 'You have to tell us when it's time.' And I would call them, and they would make the trip home and we all gathered around her, and she would open her eyes. And then she would be around for a while longer. 'We had to leave her alone so she could die in peace.' Mom was afraid of the process of dying, but she wasn't afraid of dying."

Aunt Lila would wait until all her girls were together, far away from Grand Marais on Thanksgiving. They had plans to meet at Lisa's, in a northern suburb of Chicago. Lila knew what their plan was and confirmed it over the phone with all her daughters. As Lilean related, "We were all going to meet at Lisa's for Thanksgiving. All the sisters, except maybe Lori. I talked to Mom the day she died—she had called me. And she said, 'Now you're going to be at Lisa's for Thanksgiving . . . I want you to be all together at Thanksgiving.' I was so worried that she would feel left out, being all by herself. It was really important to her for us to all be together. I said, 'Are you OK?' And she said, 'Yes, yes, that's what I want.' She was mama hen looking out for her crew. And that was the last time I talked to her."

Linda shared that on her last evening on earth, Aunt Lila was laughing at dinner with her Care Center friends. She went to bed and the nurse looked in on her at midnight and asked if she needed anything. She said, "No, I'm fine," and an hour later, she was gone.

Aunt Lila made it eighteen years without Leroy. Considering how many times she reinvented herself and how many people's lives were made better during those eighteen years, her days as a widow were exceptionally well lived. Was she ever perfect? No. She lived with heartbreak, poverty, the frustrations of raising five children, and plenty of scars, both hidden and in plain sight. But because of this, Aunt Lila taught me that beauty has nothing to do with what you look like. She showed me that perfection can live inside imperfection, something I'm reminded of every Christmas when I carefully unwrap the handmade tree ornament that she made while she was relearning everything—teaching her hands how to be hands, while her mind struggled to find the correct words. That crispy little piece of dried apple is just as beautifully perfect as the fancy

English teacup that came from Aunt Lila's collection of precious things. They are both delicately fragile, easily broken. The treacherous beauty of life is something Aunt Lila was forced to reckon with, beginning the day that she, along with the bathwater, went crashing down to the floor.

Scars on the Inside: A Poem for Lila

I'm Lila, she crashed.
Being hurt is survivable.
I'm Lila, she pointed.
Like a little deer
jumping from rock to rock,
bravery is not outside us.
I'm Lila, she said.
Our scars on the inside
are what make us stronger.
I'm Lila, she yelled.
Perfectly imperfect
a life in beauty.
I'm Lila, she laughed.
We will never let you go.

Doreen

MY SISTER SAID the first time she saw our dad cry was the day we buried Aunt Doreen. Dad never crumbled or cried all through Mom's absence and hospitalization. I'm not sure what would have happened if he had cried, but it certainly would have been memorable. And on the surface, he faced the deaths of his own father and mother with a sense of duty and stoic resolve. I remember a lot of people crying when Grandma Lola died, but Dad wasn't one of them—at least not in front of his family. It took the loss of his older sister for Dad to break with his role as family caretaker and show the world what his version of heartbreak looked like. Because of my age and tendency to swallow up sad things, like a big fish swallows up minnows, it was the first death with very real consequences for me. Aunt Doreen was everyone's best champion, and she wielded words of encouragement as freely as she would a threat to "strike" someone who was behaving badly. This was usually a hollow threat, or something she said to make us laugh, but you got the feeling Aunt Doreen actually would smack someone if they really had it coming.

When my dad was a kid, times were really tough, especially if you were part "Indian," or just "Indian" as the case was back then. He said not a day went by when there wasn't some kid calling him names or starting fisticuffs in the street because someone called him a "redskin" or "Tonto" or something. One time he got trapped by two mean kids on his way home from school. He was outnumbered and scared that if he got beat up in town, his own dad would take it out on him again when he got home. Two beatings for the price of one. He thought he was a goner, but just when things were getting really rowdy, his older sister Doreen showed up and started beating the hell out of the kids who had him cornered. She was just three years older, but that was big enough to have the upper hand and strong enough to send the mean kids packing and licking their wounds.

Her given name was Lola Doreen Drouillard, but everyone knew her as Doreen. Named after Grandma Lola, she came in a similar diminutive package, but she was anything but small. Aunt Doreen was the person who instructed us to be proud of who we are. And when your aunt tells you this, it really stays with you. After years of my knowing very little about the Drouillard family history, Aunt Doreen's words were the catalyst for an extensive personal look backward at the past. If it were not for Aunt Doreen, I may not have ever learned how Great-great-grandfather Nelson Drouillard had served as the very first blacksmith for the Grand Portage Reservation. Or how Great-great-grandmother Archange accompanied Josephine Godfrey to the top of the mountain in Grand Portage that would be named "Mount Josephine," at least by the non-Native people who came to live at the fur trading post on the North Shore of Lake Superior. Aunt Doreen was the carrier of our family Ojibwe history, and it was something she proudly and fiercely protected her whole life, just like she protected her little brother that day in the street.

The first daughter of Fred Drouillard and Lola (Linnell) Drouillard, Doreen was always a scrawny kid. With slim shoulders and hips, flat-chested and with tiny feet, she mostly wore loose jeans rolled up at the ankles, white Keds tennis shoes, and thin cotton anklets, which she liked to call "an-kell-ettes." She had a fondness for boy-style comfy sweatshirts, and even in her forties or fifties Aunt Doreen almost always went around the house in a soft gray sweatshirt wearing a pair of elastic waist slacks of some kind. What she lacked in stature she made up for in attitude. In one of my favorite pictures of her, she is about eighteen years old and is standing in the piney woods with one arm leaning on a wooden picnic table and the other relaxed in front of her. Her right leg is crossed casually over the other and her chin is up slightly, giving her an air of defiance. The soft lines of her mouth, that distinctive Drouillard nose, and the shape of her face are so familiar to me, it's like finding an old picture of a long-lost relative and seeing an amalgamation of people from your family joined together in black, white, and gray. I search the photograph for signs of me, and signs of my sister, and all of those little things about her that make me a part of who she was. Just looking at Doreen's face brings a feeling of validation and a sense of belonging. From her Keds sneakers to the dark, rakish curls that ornamented her face, Aunt Doreen was a force to be reckoned with. Because if she loved you, she would dash out into the breakers to save you, or at least that's how I felt about her.

And so, after she died, our family lost our collective spirit for a time. I was eighteen years old. It was June 23 and I was preparing to go off to art school in Minneapolis, leaving Lake Superior and my family behind. Doreen was fifty-four years old when she died, which is just one year older than I am as I write this chapter that is named for her. She was sick before that, but none of us knew how sick she really was. By the time she went into the hospital in Duluth, she only had a few days left on earth. *Anishinaabewaki*—the earth she held in her fists as a young woman, like an Ojibwe version of my childhood heroine *Ramona the Brave*, with bare hands full of beach gravel telling a story about running wild where Lake Superior meets the forest on the North Shore, her birthplace.[1] That may sound dramatic, but in my imagination she really was that fierce. Losing her at such a young age meant that there would never be any more stories about growing up in the woods, or about the mystical things that used to happen when the world was spinning at a much slower speed. It also demanded that I confront one of the harshest realities of death—that bones, teeth, and blood amount to nothing once the feisty spirit of a person is gone. Losing her was when I connected with death in a final and visceral way. As a sullen teenager obsessed with the dark side of music, art, and the even darker side of humanity, I pretended that dying was no big deal, and wore my fascination with the macabre around my neck like a spiked dog collar. Eighteen-year-old kids cheat death all the time, whether it's in the form of destructive behaviors, messing around with drugs or sex, or driving your dad's car way too fast around Dead Man's Curve, where more than one drunk teenager found themselves hurtling over the side of the guard-rails and into the Devil Track River. I relished death stories and near misses, and on more than one occasion, I just wished I could evaporate into the dark, never to be seen again.

* * * * * * *

Aunt Doreen's funeral is still a blur. There were a lot of people crying and many of the people at the church were in deep mourning to see her go, including all her children, who were losing their mother too soon. She would never meet most of her grandchildren and she was cheated out of her birthright to be the Drouillard family *mindimooyenh*—a wise old woman whose job it was to tell the stories, hold the babies, and keep the family together. To an outsider, a Catholic funeral is a strange experience, with its many instances of standing up, then kneeling, then sitting, then standing. Those of us raised as intermittent Lutherans can never keep all that Catholic pomp and circumstance straight. The incense tradition was particularly odd to me, though of course now I completely understand the ritualistic way to clear a room with burning sage, but at eighteen it was disjointed from the world, and certainly irrelevant to Aunt Doreen, who to me, always smelled like freshly baked bread. At the grave site in the Catholic cemetery along the highway in Grand Marais, there was a casket-size hole dug into the ground and a pile of sod standing by to cover up the beach gravel and clay wound left by the digging. We stood there, watching Uncle Al and some of Doreen's brothers, including my dad (who was sobbing so hard he couldn't see), help lower the casket into the ground. Aunt Doreen was so petite, and after her physical self was decimated by cervical cancer, I'm sure the casket weighed more than she did. The crypt swallowed her up, and it was then that I knew she was dead and that death meant darkness and dirt and tears and heartache. When I see her face in pictures now, she beams out of the photographs like a sort of angel. Not like an angel that has accidentally fallen to earth from the sky, but an angel of earthly grit, laughter, and milky hot chocolate with whipped cream on top.

I was recently going through a bin of old letters and found my graduation card from Aunt Doreen. "Dear Staci," she wrote. "I'm so sorry we can't be there with you to celebrate your special day. We love you, Aunt Doreen and Uncle Al." High school graduation took place in early June, just a few weeks before Aunt Doreen died. She must have been so very, very sick when she sent it. To think that she took the time to write me a card, put a little money in it, and mail it from her house in Eveleth is almost too much to bear. Aunt Doreen was always clear about how very much she loved you, and she was never afraid to say it or to show it, at least to me. Showing love and acting love are sometimes two different things, and motherly love often is complicated by expectations or a series of disappointments. As her niece, I always felt a lot of love and affection from Aunt Doreen, and it seemed very uncomplicated, at least within my experience of knowing her. Though she was fearless on the outside, there was something tender about her—an element of vulnerability, like skim ice on the surface of a lake—which was apparent in her soft brown eyes. My first memories of Doreen are of her laughing and dancing in a freewheeling way, while whirling her index finger up in the air like a tiny waterspout. She loved any song that had a beat. She loved to dance, and she loved to have a good time, something that would end up being her Achilles' heel at certain times throughout her life.

Aunt Doreen would come and stay with us from the time that we were little. She was the one who gave my sister her nickname, "Gullygoo," which mimics the noises she used to make when she was a tiny baby and was sucking on a pacifier, a gadget Aunt Doreen called a "plug." She also stepped in as our surrogate mother-auntie for a time when Mom was in the hospital and my sister, Dawn, and I were separated between Aunt Lila's and Aunt Betty's houses. There were times when we had to go back to our own house and we needed someone at home to get us up for school and make sure we had breakfast in our bellies, some food in our metal lunch boxes, and a hot meal at night. I remember her standing in the Eighth Avenue kitchen, about to serve up a thick pot of beef stew or chicken and dumplings. A wickedly good cook, Aunt Doreen made breakfasts, lunches, and dinners for a lot of people throughout her life. As the oldest sister, a mother of six and a woman who once owned her own restaurant, she baked bread, made multicourse meals, and fried fish fillets for thousands of happy eaters.

Aunt Doreen loved to feed people. I remember visiting her at her house in Eveleth after her restaurant days were over. It was a huge, old, multistory house with expansive rooms, including the kitchen at the back of the house. We got up in the morning, wandered down the wooden stairs, and Aunt Doreen was already up, making buttered toast out of homemade bread and hot chocolate with whipped cream on top. She called it "chocolate mustache," and it was the breakfast of choice in Aunt Doreen's kitchen. Putting butter on bread for others was something she had learned to do as a girl. My dad remembers their family sitting down for a meal, and his sister Doreen would take a chunk from a crusty loaf of bread and grace it with a piece of cold, hard butter right in the middle of the slice. She'd hand it out to her siblings one at a time, and they would all complain to her about her lack of ceremony and moan about being served an offensive lump of hard butter.

"C'mon, Doreen, spread it around," a young Pooty or Bruce or Gale would say.

"JUST eat it!" was her curt reply, with strong emphasis on the "JU—."

So, Aunt Doreen was used to buttering a lot of other people's bread, so to speak, and by the time she would make us toast in the morning, it was a crispy thing of beauty, buttered from corner to corner. We dipped that toast into our cups of homemade hot chocolate, and my mouth waters now, just thinking about it. Only people who love you a lot will take the time to make you such a grand and comforting breakfast. Everything about Doreen's life had conditioned her to feed other people, and so she learned to find joy and satisfaction in watching other people eat what she had made. My imaginary dictionary entry for this nondiscriminatory feminine/masculine personality trait would be e·ma·ci·feed·ing. *Noun*: 1. Compulsion to care for and nurture others through food to one's own detriment. 2. The filling up of others while starving yourself of sustenance. *Use*: "Driven by her need to care for others, Doreen, a motherly emacifeeder, cooked all day but went to bed with an empty stomach." *Also*: "The skinny chef's emacifeeding compulsions caused him to feel fully satiated while watching his clients devour the evening special."

Aunt Doreen was very much like that. She would work for hours on end, making sure everything was perfect, and at the end of the meal, when everyone else was full, she would sit at the end of the table pushing untouched portions of food around on her plate, all with a contented smile on her face. Feeding people gave her purpose, and it was something she was very, very good at. My cousin Sue, the middle child of Aunt Doreen's pack, told me that when they were kids, her mom would cook a big dinner every night, especially on Sundays: "She'd always put all the food in separate dishes. She wanted it to be formal. No matter what, you'd better be home for Sunday dinner. She never ate very much. She sat at the table but she didn't eat. She loved soft-boiled eggs on toast. That's what she'd make herself later, or late at night after everyone went to bed." And then Sue added this observation about her mother: "She would take care of all of us but she wouldn't take care of herself. When I was older, we would go round and round about it. She would call me a 'know-it-all little brat' and then tell me, 'I can take care of myself.'"[2]

Unless you knew her well, hearing that Aunt Doreen called her own daughter a "brat," might make you distrust her or question her mothering abilities. But the way she would say these things was meant to be funny, like a word she reclaimed from the days of hearing her own father say similar things to her. Except in his case, mean words would usually go along with a hard slap in the face, or a bona fide beating, which would then erupt into a big family brawl. Grandma Lola would try to intervene, causing Grandpa to turn his attention from whatever kid he was raging at, and take it out on little Grandma Lola instead. Experiencing that kind of terror as a kid had taught Doreen what it was like to live in a fearful, unstable home. She resolved to break the cycle of abuse with her own kids. And so, when Doreen delivered a threat, she would stop with words as your warning, or deliver her infamous "look" in your direction, which meant "stop what you are doing, or else!" Her youngest daughter, Tina, said, "When we acted up, we got 'the look,' which usually worked. She would say, 'I'm gonna strike you!' Or, 'I'm gonna cuff you,'" and she would gesture succinctly, cupping her hand in the air and gritting her teeth real hard, while delivering this hollow threat. Chances are good that Aunt Doreen would never strike you. Tina said that her brother Ralph told her how he got into some trouble at their house in Duluth one time, and "Mom said, 'Get yer butt up across that bed and I'm gonna give you a spanking.' And then she went about her day, cooking dinner and puttering around the house. After a long time, Ralph yelled, 'Mom, are you going to come and spank me?' And she said, 'You just wait . . .'"

****

As the oldest daughter of Fred and Lola Drouillard, a very softhearted Doreen grew up seeing and experiencing some things that she never should have. I asked some of her kids if she told them any stories from her childhood, or if they knew anything about the circumstances of her birth, but none of them really knew much about her life before she had children of her own. She was born in February 1931, following her older brother Fred Jr. (Monty) into a family of two different cultures. Gloria, Doreen's younger sister, said that Doreen was born in a tiny log cabin, less than a block above Grand Marais Harbor. There were two cabins that looked alike, and both were painted dark brown. There would likely have been ice on the harbor the day she was born, as well as deep snow that covered everything, like a layer of whipped cream on top of a slice of chocolate cake.

Her mother, Lola Marie, was English and Dutch with a touch of Irish mixed in. She was born in Black River Falls, Wisconsin, in 1908. Her parents were Sam Linnell and Lois May (Berry) Linnell. Their very large family later moved to a tiny, remote place called Mineral Center, which has now completely disappeared, except for a graveyard, but at one time had its own church and school building. Mineral Center was inland from Grand Portage, on the old dirt road that used to cross the Pigeon River into Canada via the "Outlaw Bridge." Grandma Lola's family of sisters and brothers would rival the Burge clan in terms of numbers, with Great-grandma and Great-grandpa Linnell raising ten children in all, eight girls and two boys.

As a young woman, Lola met her husband, Fred Drouillard, at the Grand Portage border crossing, where she was working as a waitress at a café. Fred, or "Freddy," as she called him, pursued the diminutive Lola aggressively. A handsome and charming man with dark skin, dark hair, and brilliant blue eyes, Fred Drouillard was well liked and respected by a lot of his fellow townsmen. He was a skilled woodsman and fisherman, who also served as a moose-hunting guide all throughout the ceded 1854 Territory that encompasses far northeastern Minnesota. He and Lola had a quick courtship, and in 1928, not long after they met, they got married in Virginia, Minnesota, where Fred was working as a pulp logger. The two of them moved back to the North Shore that same year, living in that little log house where Doreen was born. By 1932, when their third child, Gloria, was born, Fred and Lola had bought a house situated in the thick woods, about halfway between downtown Grand Marais and Chippewa City, where Fred's mother and a number of his Anakwad (Cloud) relatives lived.

Coming from an off-reservation, mixed-blood family, Fred Drouillard was 50 percent Anishinaabe and 50 percent French. Born in 1907 as the youngest of twelve children, Fred was raised with both French and Ojibwemowin as his first two languages. His father, John Drouillard, was also fluent in French and Ojibwemowin—languages he learned as one of the first white children to attend school on the Grand Portage Reservation in 1856. The English language came into play sometime later for Grandpa Fred, although Great-grandma Elizabeth Anakwad Drouillard (also called Chi'zubet, or Big Elizabeth) never spoke much English at all. The Drouillards were skilled at life in the backwoods, and all of Fred and Lola's children would grow up feeling very much at home in the wilderness. Both the boys and the girls learned firsthand how to clean and dress rabbits, pluck and gut partridges, field dress deer or moose, and all of them grew up fishing. These foods were staples on the Drouillard dinner table, until later when Grandma Lola would bring home leftover food from the restaurants where she worked downtown. The house was very small and so the kids, including Doreen, spent most of their time outside in the woods that surrounded the house.

Back in the late thirties, roads were scarce, and most of the people who lived outside Grand Marais would walk on trails through the woods that would take them from place to place. The Drouillard kids would walk a trail to school, take the path over to their neighbor Lucy Caribou's house, or make their way through thick spruce and birch stands to get downtown where the stores and restaurants were. If you are familiar with the density of the untouched forests along the North Shore, you will be able to imagine how both days and nights at the Drouillard cabin would have been very isolated, and probably

quite dark, even at high noon. With trees and underbrush as thick as
it was back then, the sun would have had a difficult time penetrating
through the branches, even in the summer.

It was a hardscrabble life by any measure, and as in most other
families at that time, Grandma Lola, within the prevailing morbidity
of motherhood doctrine, was expected to start having babies as soon
as she was married, and continue on having them, one after another.
And that's exactly what she did from 1929, when Uncle Fred (Monty)
was born, until 1939 when their youngest child, Diane, was born.
Within those ten years, Fred and Lola would bring seven children into
the world, all of them born at home, and most with the assistance
of a midwife, usually someone from the family or a close friend like
Catherine Scott, who delivered a lot of babies in Grand Marais and
Chippewa City. My dad told me that when he was a kid, there was not
a local "doctor's office" in town and that in fact, most of the white
doctors who served Grand Marais in the 1920s and '30s would not
make house calls to help the "Indians," even if a mother or baby's life
was in danger. This is where the differences between my Burge family
relatives and my Drouillard family relatives will diverge greatly, with
one side having the benefit of German and English ancestry, and the
other side suffering the repercussions of racial prejudice while living
in a state of perpetual poverty. At that time, anyone who carried any
amount of "Indian" blood in their veins was subject to the historical
realities of the time, which included varying degrees of locally bred
racism, as well as the far-reaching effects of federal Indian policy. The
Burge family may have been poor farmers and suffered through other
societal troubles, but my mother and her kin would never experience
the difficulties my dad and his family went through as Anishinaabe
people born and raised in far northern Minnesota.

* * * * * * *

Grandpa Fred lived life on the precipice between these two worlds. In
some ways, he could be construed as a romantic sort of character, in
a world that likes to put Indigenous people in a box, neatly labeling
them as mystical, stoic, at one with nature, or as a tragic by-product
of this country's colorful history. And Grandpa certainly was a quiet
and intelligent man, who was very capable and yes, knew how to be at

one with nature—but not in a romantic way. Because to truly connect with the natural world, you have to be ready to turn over your blood, guts, hands, feet, eyes, and sometimes your life to the forest in order to become "one" with the wilderness. Your survival and your family's survival depended on what was actually a great, personal gamble. And by all accounts, Grandpa did just that, and did it most of his life. But even if he was known as the "best" fishing guide on all of Saganaga Lake, Grandpa Fred would always have a more difficult path to self-sufficiency. This is because he was starting from the clay soil on his boots, while transplanted white settlers on the North Shore by and large had the benefit of accumulated wealth and the ability to jump into the economic support systems easily, because they came here and created those systems themselves. Grandpa Fred was raised with a very different view toward land "use" and resources. Based on some of the stories I've heard about Grandpa Fred, his own self-worth was measured by his ability to fish, hunt, and provide for his family, and at the end of the day, he would have a week's pay in his pocket, but he would never earn enough money to own his own guide service or grow his own establishment, even though that was something he dreamed about. And, truth be told, the family would never have made it on his paychecks alone. Grandma Lola always worked, and she worked damn hard all her life. Grandpa Fred was often able to maintain the facade of the "wise and stoic" outdoorsman, but on quite a few work nights he would get into a bottle of whiskey with his fellow woodsmen. The word for whiskey in Ojibwemowin is *ishkodaywaboo* or, quite literally, "firewater." And when he drank that powerful medicine, his personality transformed him into his own family's hellish nightmare, as destructive and unpredictable as a wildfire burning out of control.

The story of the Drouillards and alcohol goes all the way back to the first time a white shopkeeper stole a piece of tribal land by plying the rightful landowner with bottles of booze. It happened right here in Grand Marais and Grand Portage, just like it happened all over the United States. The historical relationship between Indigenous people and alcohol is complicated by many things, including "environmental elements, historical factors, and issues of poverty."[3] And while I can't make excuses for Grandpa Fred, I can point out the complexity of his life, and how he was the first generation of my Anishinaabe relatives to have his culture beaten out of him, literally and figuratively. Unfortunately, cultural regeneration and a return to "the old ways" was not an option for him, and he suffered for it. He had seven mouths to feed, and he lived his life on a saw blade's edge between the traditional world of his Anishinaabe mother and his well-known, French father, a land prospector, "Indian" agent, and politician who served on the first Hovland Town Board. And because of the racial prejudice that existed between the European settlers and visitors to the North Shore in the 1930s, Fred taught himself, and then taught his children, that speaking his first language and looking and acting like "Indians" would make life a lot harder for them.

My aunt Gloria told me Grandpa Fred made it to fourth grade before he quit school and that he was working as a moose-hunting guide in Canada by the time he was ten. "He always thought of himself as self-taught," she said. And so, from the time he was a young boy, Grandpa Fred worked a grueling seasonal life as a guide, hunter, and trapper. This is how he made a living for most of his life. In 1938–39, Fred secured work as a fishing guide at Chik-Wauk Lodge on Saganaga Lake at the end of the Gunflint Trail, and he brought Lola to Saganaga with him that summer. She worked as a cook in the lodge's kitchen, making three meals a day for guests staying at the resort. Her job included frying the visitor's daily catch of trout or walleye, taking extra care that each fisherman got their own fillets from what they caught that day. The fish was lightly breaded and presented on a dinner plate, along with some mashed potatoes, corn relish, and freshly baked rolls. A number of my aunts and uncles worked at Chik-Wauk alongside Fred and Grandma Lola. And Grandpa taught my dad a lot about fishing, boating, and guiding on the Gunflint Trail. At the age of sixteen, my dad was already guiding trips on Saganaga Lake and points north.

The 1920s and '30s were an era of change for people who were born and raised in the now-familiar tourist destinations on the North Shore—towns and villages that were once seasonal, Anishinaabe fishing encampments. As more and more Europeans opened businesses and shops, the people in these towns and villages gradually began to make money by offering an "authentic" fishing experience to visitors. This experience often came with a knowledgeable and handsome Chippewa guide who ran the boat, baited your hook, took your fish off the line, and then would cook it over a fire with bacon and beans for "shore lunch." And while you enjoyed the beautiful scenery or took a dip in the cool and clear water of Saganaga, your Chippewa guide would clean up the dishes, repack the boat, and make sure everyone returned safely to the landing. He might even throw a line in at the narrows on the way back, just in case his clients wanted walleye for supper that night.

When I was first born, Grandpa Fred came to my parents' trailer to see his new baby granddaughter. My mother said that she was beside herself with fret and worry, convinced that something terrible was going to happen to me. She read and reread Dr. Spock's *Baby and Child Care*, and anytime I would cry she would pick up the book to make sure there was nothing abnormal about my behavior. While Grandpa was there, I started to fuss and she instinctively reached for the book. She remembers Grandpa Fred sitting quietly in a chair, grinning at me while I fussed but never offering up his advice, even though he had seven kids of his own.

Based on what my dad and others have said, Grandpa was stubbornly independent. He worked very hard and saw an awful lot of change throughout the course of his life. As a young man he experienced a colossal shift in which Anishinaabe people struggled to maintain cultural ties and secure a place for themselves in a changing local economy that for him bordered on exploitation. And so, he sometimes drank whiskey and every time, the whiskey got the best of him—or the worst, as the case may be. His addictive relationship to alcohol is something that affected all his children. Their father's poison would end up being the poison of choice for some of my Drouillard relatives, while others were able to quit drinking for good, which is what Aunt Gloria and Uncle Monty eventually did.

My dad learned about drinking from his dad, and so did his brothers and sisters. There was always drinking at our house, and he was known to spend a lot of time in the bars downtown, especially in the early days of his marriage to Mom. And certainly, whenever our Drouillard relatives would visit, there would always be rounds of drinks on the table. Always. Aunt Doreen drank whiskey, something she had in common with a number of others in the family. So, every

time Aunt Doreen was at our house, there was the excitement of delicious homemade food, but also plenty of caramel-colored cocktails—
ice cold and ever-present. It's so easy to see her in the little kitchen
of our house on Eighth Avenue. She's wearing a clean, gray, cotton
sweatshirt and tidy black pants—her feet covered in thin, white cotton "an-kell-ettes." She has a delicate silver heart pendant around her
neck, and her hair is cut very short. Aunt Doreen was not ever someone who fussed about girlish beauty or clothing, and she never tried to
put on airs that she was anyone other than who she was. The trickster
known as chronic femininity was not something that Aunt Doreen
ever fell for or subscribed to, because that was too complicated for
her. Growing up in the woods helped her be solidly planted inside her
own skin, and it never mattered much to her what someone looked
like on the outside. This realization about Aunt Doreen feels purely
inspirational to me now that I'm able to see it more clearly. She was
the antidote to the mean words and bullies of the world, and she was
always unabashedly clear about what side she was on.

So, back on Eighth Avenue, it's a festive occasion, most likely
New Year's Eve, and Aunt Doreen is serving as our babysitter while
our parents are out for the night. Our cousin Tina, Doreen's youngest
daughter, is also there and the four of us are having "girls' night" together. We are standing at the counter, and Doreen is showing us how
to mix a proper drink. It's a lowball, about 50 percent whiskey and
50 percent water from the tap. She throws in three or four ice cubes
and, turning her head in our direction, takes her tiny waterspout of an
index finger, twists it around in the cocktail to give the whole thing
a vigorous stir, sticks that finger in her mouth, to not waste any, and
says, "That's what you'd call an old Indian trick!" And then she would
take a sip and laugh, her dark eyes twinkling, completely satisfied at
having passed along this clever nugget of family tradition to the next
generation of girls.

My aunt Gloria remembers that when they were kids, their house
in the woods was often a stopping place for friends and family making the walk to town and back from Chippewa City. Uncle Charlie
Drouillard would drop in unexpectedly and ask to talk to Grandpa
Fred and so would other neighbors, like Basagee, which was what everyone called Jim Morrison, a friend who would drop by for a rest, or

a cup of coffee, before making the last half mile back to Chippewa City. My aunt Gloria said that my dad's dog, Duke, hated Basagee for some reason, so he would stand outside their house at the edge of the woods, with the dog barking furiously, along with Fred screaming to "shut that damn dog up!" Grandma Lola or one of the kids would call the dog off so that Jim could come sit on the porch. Grandma Lola would likely have made him a mug of tea or put on a pot of coffee, and if she wasn't there because she was downtown working as a cook at LeSage's Restaurant or Mabel's Café, Freddy might make some tea for their guest, pouring it into a bowl and not a mug—something that was common back then. I can picture Aunt Doreen as a young girl, watching him pour the tea into a wooden bowl and he would say, "Old Indian trick, ayy DRAIN," laughing at the ruggedness of it.

According to my cousin Tina, Grandpa Fred sometimes called his daughter "Drain," or "Dor," because he had trouble saying "Doreen." He also called her "Sister," which tells you more about her role in the family. The original "old Indian trick" came from Grandpa, and then Aunt Doreen passed it along to us kids. She would use this turn of phrase for other things, not just for pouring tea or stirring up a whiskey cocktail. As Tina clarified, she would use it "anytime she felt an explanation for something would fall flat." We always thought it was funny. But it's also sad when you think of the damage one tiny waterspout could leave behind, once one old Indian trick becomes many.

* * * * * * *

Liquor and binge drinking were introduced to the Indigenous population of the North Shore by European traders. In her book *Holding Our World Together*, Brenda Child tells the story of an Ojibwe woman named Netnokwa and the early "'seasons of drunkenness' in fur trade society." In one case, Netnokwa, the adopted mother of John Tanner, a Euro-American orphan, "intended to take a considerable supply of beaver and otter skins to Mackinac. When they were detained at Grand Portage, Minnesota, she asked a female relative to take the furs on to the island. A French trader of the North West Company issued a 'due bill' [invoice] for the furs, but it was destroyed when fire engulfed their lodge. Netnokwa never received compensation for losing what amounted to months of labor, and Tanner observed that she 'began to drink' after 'the disappointment of her hopes of returning to Lake Huron, and other misfortunes.'"⁴

The "disappointment of hopes," lost and wasted, like a rogue barrel of salt herring dashed into bits against the sharp basalt at the edge of Lake Superior. This is just one example of how the relationship between alcohol and Indigenous people is complicated by a clash of cultures and the dark circumstances of history. It's important to remember that Indigenous people do not drink any more than Europeans do, and in fact, Native traditionalists strictly forbid the use of alcohol in ceremonies, at powwows, or at the family dinner table. If you'll recall, Great-grandpa Stelter, a full-blooded German, died at a young age of cirrhosis of the liver. For the Germans, drinking culture is embedded in our American cultural tradition, especially around Milwaukee, where my Stelter relatives came from. So, while Great-grandpa Stelter was brewing beer in Milwaukee, the government was trying to force Great-grandma Anakwad to move to her land allotment on the Grand Portage reservation. And during my grandpa Fred's time, there were still signs outside the bars in downtown Grand Marais that said "No Indians Allowed." This was not to protect the Indigenous people from harming themselves with alcohol; it was to keep them separated from the whites.

It's a widespread misconception that Indigenous men and women are more susceptible to alcoholism, or drink at higher rates than other ethnicities. Both of these associations are untruths nurtured by the prevailing mainstream voices in history that try to justify white society's continued discrimination against Native people and rationalize the unjust treatment of Native men and women by police and other authority figures. The unvarnished truth is that liquor was introduced to Indigenous people here on the North Shore at a time of great change and intergenerational, collective trauma, when the people were suffering a paucity of hope.

Their reasons for hopelessness were many. The people's connection to the land was systematically being cut off through multiple treaties with the U.S. government; the seasonal and traditional way of life was changing rapidly along with the local economy; people were sick and dying from a spate of European diseases, such as influenza and tuberculosis; families were experiencing the forced assimilation of Indigenous children inside white boarding "schools"; and land allotment and coerced religious conversion were devastating traditional tribal societies and family structure. These layers of environmental and cultural trauma have, over time, worked their ways into the bloodstreams and bones of our relatives, and if you are sensitive and marshmallow-soft, like Aunt Doreen, trying to drink away sorrow was her way of insulating herself from the truly awful things in life and as respite from the burdens she carried.

Tina remembers her mother talking about how she took care of everybody when she was a kid—freely admitting that life for them was rough, but that she also felt a sense of pride about being able to help: "She talked about the old days with such a sense of reverence about it. They didn't know any different. She took care of her siblings, and she always felt she was the caretaker of the family. She helped take care of everybody—and so she was always a mom, even before she had her own kids. When Grandpa wasn't behaving himself, she helped with the younger kids. And she would cook meals and help Grandma Lola at their house and up at Chik-Wauk in the kitchen. She had to bring in firewood, do the cooking, and make sure all of her younger siblings did what they were supposed to."

Tina and I discussed how the family had a disjointed way of growing up, often with their parents away at Saganaga every summer. She observed that "they had to look out for each other. The family had to do what they had to do. Mom never made it sound like her childhood was unhappy. I think they all just looked out for each other because life was so hard."

The Drouillard kids' lives were made more difficult by the unpredictable behavior of Grandpa Fred, who one minute would be as sweet as maple candy and the next as violent as a bull moose in rutting season. Doreen shared this story with her daughter Sue, about growing up in the woods: "It was really wintery out. Grandpa had come home late and the kids were sleeping. There wasn't enough firewood in the house, at least not enough to suit him. So, he got teed off and woke everyone up and made all the kids go out and fill up the wood bin in the middle of a big storm."

This might explain why Doreen tried so hard to make sure all her younger siblings did what they were supposed to do and that all the household chores were done. From an early age, she learned various ways to protect her younger brothers and sisters, or at least do her best to keep them from harm. It's the diabolical pattern of an alcoholic family, where some people take on the role of caregivers as a way of asserting their control over unstable circumstances. While it may have helped soften her own pain, the pain of watching someone you love hurt themselves because of their addiction is often too much to bear, something all her kids experienced firsthand. Sue was really honest about how Aunt Doreen's drinking affected her when she was growing up: "The combination of being a middle child, and then when there was drinking and stuff, I didn't like it. I distanced myself pretty early. I guess it was survival mode. I pretty much cut my feelings off, you know? It was the only thing I could do to cope . . . I don't remember that me and mom had a very close relationship. I have a lot of good traits from her. Obviously, I love her. I think it makes a difference when it's *your* mom who is drinking."

* * * * * * *

Even though Aunt Doreen had serious issues with alcohol, it does not define who she was as a person or as a mother. Nor did she always drink. I asked my cousin Tina about her life with Aunt Doreen and she said, "Mom was normal and would do her thing. She always took care of us. Dinner was made, the house was clean. She would drink for a few days and then just stop—not have another for a long, long time."

Aunt Doreen didn't graduate from high school, and instead took various jobs working in restaurants, often right alongside her mother. It was at one of these places that she met a man named Ralph Freeman II. He was her first boyfriend, and Doreen was twenty years old when they got married. Her first daughter, Carrie, was born one year later in Minneapolis, Ralph Freeman's hometown. Together they had four kids, all of whom were born in the Twin Cities: Carrie (nicknamed Pougie), Ralph III (nicknamed Little Man), Susan, and Gayle.

In the early days with Ralph, Doreen was learning how to be a mother and a wife without the luxury of outside help or a solid foundation on how to build a marital relationship. Her own role models were less than reliable, and so she was on her own in a lot of ways. Regardless of Doreen's struggles, Ralph's own shortcomings were impossible to ignore, and their little family got off to a rough start. According to Sue, "My dad had bought mom a new house. He would go off drinking and drugging and stuff and the utilities and water were turned off because he didn't pay the bills."

Ralph was not good at staying home and got into all kinds of trouble in the bars, including with other women. This was before Aunt Doreen drank liquor, and having a drinker for a husband was undoubtedly too much like being a kid and watching her father raise holy hell because he was drunk. She had four little kids to take care of, and no way to make money or get a job outside the home. When Doreen finally left Ralph II, they moved to what Sue calls "the white house" in Duluth.

The kids were all really young during the split and Sue doesn't remember a lot about her dad, except he used to tell her that she was "his favorite." Sue acknowledged that "it's easy to play favorites when your parents don't live together." All throughout this time, Doreen never filed for divorce, and Ralph persistently tried to get back into Doreen's good graces. At some point Doreen moved from the white house to a duplex in West Duluth in a low-income housing development that Sue calls "the projects." Doreen shared a unit with Gloria, her younger sister, who lived upstairs. Gloria was also living as a single mother, and the two sisters both had to work jobs outside the house and raise their kids alone, which was made somewhat easier all together, since the two of them could help each other and look out for one another.

Ralph II stayed in contact with Doreen and would send Sue and the other kids birthday cards and gifts when they lived in the projects, including "a purple sting-ray bike" one time. She also said that she and her brother, Ralph III ("Little Man"), once went down to Minneapolis to stay with their dad who lived on Nicollet Avenue. She remembers that he played Jim Reeves and Bill Cosby records for them, which was one of the lasting connections between Aunt Doreen and her first husband. As Sue said, "She always liked to flip around and dance. She loved Jim Reeves, because Ralph Freeman loved it. She liked almost anything with a beat. She liked Elvis Presley. She liked so many songs."

And even though Sue didn't know her father very well, "He was my dad. I liked him. He was good to Mom sometimes, but then

Eleanor Godfrey would come by." Eleanor was "the other woman" in Ralph II's life. He went back and forth between Doreen and Eleanor for quite a while, but Sue said that's ultimately not why Doreen left him for good. "It's because he drank and didn't take care of bills and stuff." Ralph II stayed with Eleanor after that, but he died as a relatively young man, a few years after Doreen and her four kids moved to Duluth.

****

Sue remembers that when they moved, "My older friend was teaching me colors and things, so I wasn't in school yet when we lived in the duplex with Aunt Gloria." At this same time my dad, Francis, was working for North Shore Jobbing out of Grand Marais and he had to drive a delivery route to and from Duluth every day. He would regularly go to his two sisters' apartments and drive them both to the store to get groceries, since neither one of them had a driver's license. He remembers hauling bags of groceries up to Gloria's apartment and down the steep staircase into Doreen's apartment, both spaces full of his little nieces and nephews. After they made the move to Duluth, Doreen was working at Grandma and Grandpa Drouillard's restaurant in west Duluth. It was a breakfast and lunch counter called the Grand Café. The family story is that in 1957, after all their kids were mostly grown (Aunt Diane, the youngest of seven, was a senior in high school), Grandma Lola had finally had enough of Fred's drinking and she decided to leave him for good. She moved into a tiny cabin in downtown Grand Marais, where she tried to break free of Freddie's abusive behavior. Fred would have nothing of the sort and tried every manipulation that he could think of to win her back. He was incorrigible—on the verge of self-destruction—and begged her to come home to him.

In his last-ditch effort to woo Lola back, Grandpa Fred took a radical step and did what he had always wanted to do—he bought his own establishment. He had heard about a restaurant that was for sale in West Duluth and he swung a lease deal with the owner. He convinced Grandma Lola that she would finally get everything she ever wanted. She could cook her delicious food, something she had been doing her whole life, and he would manage the place—in other words, be the charming host of the café. He put everything on the line to make the deal, and Grandma Lola, bless her heart, stepped back into the marriage, this time with the added stress of running a restaurant. This decision would make her even more codependent on a man who she knew, deep down, was an unreliable protector of her heart. No one really knows for sure why she took him back and decided to throw her life back into the difficult job of managing a kitchen. But like Grandma Lola and Aunt Doreen, I also know what it feels like to be at a critical turning point in an abusive, untrustworthy relationship and still choose the path that goes backward instead of forward. Sometimes it's because you've convinced yourself that the problem is yours—that you need to learn how to forgive someone and that maybe this time, that person will change. That it's *your* fault somehow, and now you need to show that person some mercy and grace. Or sometimes it's out of fear or worry that your abuser will hurt themselves or hurt you if you choose to take the forward path and leave them behind. This was a likely scenario with Fred, who had already shown Lola he was capable of violence. And it's also possible that Grandma Lola chose to go in deeper with Grandpa Fred because on some level, she still loved him and craved whatever it was about him that attracted her as a young woman. She's not here to tell me about it, so we'll never really know what was in her mind and heart at the time. In the end, Grandpa's ploy worked and Fred and Lola became entrepreneurs.

Their lives were exciting and productive for a little while, but circumstances at the Grand Café would end up being yet another nightmare for Grandma, because Grandpa wasn't ever willing or able to change. In fact, with the added stress of running a business, Grandpa's drinking got even worse. Sue remembers being at the restaurant a lot when she was a kid. Doreen worked full-time, waiting tables out front and in the kitchen helping Grandma Lola. She said that "Grandma Lola was always the same. She'd be in her kitchen. They'd be working and just happy, and then at lunch Grandpa would take money out of the till and probably go to the Kom-On-Inn bar or something. It was always a nice atmosphere until Grandpa was there."

So, Grandma would work herself into the ground and Fred would show up in the middle of the day and help himself to the money she made, all the while acting like a big, important man at the bar down the street. I wasn't born when this was Grandma Lola's reality, but it makes me angry for her, and for the broken spirits of my aunties and cousins who had to watch that happen and keep their mouths quiet about it. The harsh family circumstances caused by Grandpa's drinking were not really talked about when we were kids. Doreen never talked about it with her own kids, and our dad never shared the worst of their childhood experiences with us, although he did confide in my mother about some of the hurtful things that happened, living under the thumb of an alcoholic and abusive father. Fred lorded his drinking and controlling personality over them all, even though they were grown women and men with kids of their own. I'm not sure any of them have ever escaped it. My aunt Gloria, who is eighty-nine, sometimes talks about it now. She'll refer to him as "Daddy," and then she'll call him something profane in the same breath. Those words and feelings have been banging around inside her mind for almost ninety years—which is too long. And it's an unfair burden for her or anyone else to carry.

After moving from the duplex (what Sue calls "the white house"), the two sisters, Doreen and Gloria, moved to "the projects," a low-income housing complex. My cousin Cathy, Gloria's oldest daughter, remembered that "this is where the single women lived who had kids. There were a few men there, but mostly women with loads of kids to play with." Doreen lived on Seventy-First and Aunt Gloria lived on Sixty-Seventh. Life in the projects was a daily struggle for Aunt Doreen, who was a single mother with four kids to raise all by herself, with the emotional residue of a failed marriage and a full-time job to keep up. How on earth did she manage it? As Sue said, "I never felt poor. I guess Ralph did. He remembers having empty cupboards. At Christmas, Mom couldn't have had any money. But Ralph and I both got these little bikes. And she made this big, papier mâché Christmas ornament. She dipped it in gold glitter and it had a red ribbon on it. I remember popping a balloon on Christmas. I remember thinking it was kind of amazing that Mom made that. She never was really crafty."

Even though they were poor, their life had a certain degree of adventure. Because Aunt Doreen had to work during the day, the kids were left on their own with Pougie, who was about thirteen, as their babysitter. Their apartment in West Duluth was within four blocks of the Duluth Zoo and close to the train tracks. Sue said that she and the three other kids would leave the apartment and "jump the trains and jump off at the zoo. We'd go to the train station and they'd give us paper and pencils and stuff. The train went around the zoo and so you wouldn't have to pay to get there. It would let us off by the bear dens. We'd play in there every summer. And back then, behind the bear den it's all open. We never had any bear encounters, but we'd run all over in there! We'd go swimming down in the creek there. They would let us feed the snakes little white mice and play with the monkeys. We even got to feed the tigers and feed the babies with a bottle. It was wonderful there! And we would try to help too. A lot of people were mean to the big hippo—people were mean and would throw rocks in its mouth. So, we'd stand guard."

* * * * * * *

The instinct to stand guard over hippos or your younger siblings came honestly to Aunt Doreen's kids, because that's what Doreen did her whole life. She stepped into her role as protector at a young age—a characteristic that is also related to a person's ability to work hard and take care of things. This very strong work ethic is really prevalent in my dad and in all of my Drouillard aunties and uncles. They watched both of their parents work very, very hard, and in turn, all their kids learned how to work hard at a very young age. Aunt Doreen was no different and learned the basics of running a restaurant kitchen from her mother. Working in a café is grueling, and if it's a family-owned place, it's always all hands on deck during the breakfast and lunch rushes. And if you have emacifeeder tendencies, like Aunt Doreen did, the good work of feeding a hungry crowd often leaves the cook, the waitress, and the dishwasher too tired to eat, or perhaps even turned off by food.

One afternoon after a long shift at the restaurant, Doreen went out for a drink after work. One drink turned into many drinks, and still Doreen did not eat. Her kids were alone, wondering where she was and why she hadn't come home. My stomach aches thinking about the precarious situation she put herself in that night and how it made her kids worry. It is one of the places in Aunt Doreen's story where, if things had gone just a bit differently, she may not have made it home to her kids. If she had fallen, or if it had been a bit colder out-side, or if a bad man had decided to follow her out of the bar and down the tracks—she made herself vulnerable to so many terrible possibil-ities that night. Sue remembers it as a turning point for their family: "Mom decided to take the railroad tracks back to the apartment. She was drunk and she wasn't dressed warm enough, just in nylons and her work clothes. We were glad to see her get home safely and we tried to warm her up and made her some cream of mushroom soup. She said she wanted to read the paper and ended up tearing the newspaper into pieces, like it was crackers and putting it in her soup."

After feeding people all day, both literally and figuratively, Do-reen was incapable of taking in nourishment for herself. She just didn't want to do it. She likely had every intention of having one cock-tail and going home, but that's not what happened that night. And while binge drinking might be a form of self-medication, it might also be seen as a gateway to feeling loved and accepted. I've seen this play out with a lot of people in my life, and I've felt that way myself. A lot of people really loved Aunt Doreen. She had many good friends, and having lots of people around her always made her feel loved and valuable. At heart she was a very social person and she genuinely liked to laugh and dance and cut loose, especially after a hard day's work. Having grown up with her as my auntie, it's really easy for me to see how she could so easily start out as the life of the party and then gradually fall into the dark and comforting fix of a whiskey binge. I talked to my cousin Tina about this part of Aunt Doreen's personal-ity that existentially takes in emotional nourishment by taking care of and feeding others. The part of her that would work up a frenzy to make sure that everything was perfect and then afterward, sit back and watch everyone else enjoy the party that she had lovingly prepared and placed beautifully on the table. Tina felt that "[it wasn't] a matter of her trying to be independent. It's a matter of being loved from lots of people. There's power in numbers. She loved chaos and being in a big group. She was the cook. The one cooking for everyone. It really made her feel good. Storytelling, laughter, reminiscing. And yet, she was capable and independent. She wouldn't ask for it from others. She would create it all on her own, and then just watch it all happen."

I watched Grandma Lola do this when I was a little girl. She would be staying with us at the house and would bake all morning, lining up pans of rolls and loaves of bread on top of the vent in the bedroom floor, which was positioned directly above where the woodstove was in the basement of our house. And this was delicious bread in a variety of sizes and shapes—perfectly round buns, golden-topped loaves and sticky caramel rolls that she would decadently top with melted butter while they were still warm and put on a plate for whomever was there that day. But I can't honestly say that I ever saw Grandma Lola eat a caramel roll herself. I think she would put the caramel rolls out for others and then sit down at the table and smoke a cigarette. This trickiness with feeding others as a way to nurture ourselves is something my sister, who became a chef and also owned a catering company, and a lot of my Drouillard cousins inherited from Grandma Lola and Aunt Doreen. We like to feed people. It makes us feel needed and somehow complete.

* * * * * * *

It was 1962 when Doreen served up a hot turkey sandwich at the counter of the Grand Café and ended up embroiled in a love affair. Soon after, the Freemans became a family of five. Aunt Doreen named her baby boy Bruce, and he was perfectly handsome. She guarded him like a mother bear when he was little, and when she talked to him, even as a teenager, she always had an extra amount of tenderness in her voice. She fed him well, like she fed all her other kids, and he grew up alongside his brother Ralph and older sisters.

It was New Year's Eve when an out-of-control car driven by the mayor of Duluth crashed into the front window of the Grand Café. He was with a woman who was not his wife, and so a coverup about the accident was concocted. The mayor was determined to keep the incident out of the news. My aunt Gloria Martineau said no authorities were called and no report was filed. By preventing them from making an insurance claim, one powerful person caused Fred and Lola to lose their restaurant and any hope they had of retaining an investment of their own. After that, they made an ill-fated attempt to open a new restaurant. It was called the Tourist Café, and it was also in West

Duluth. According to my cousin Cathy, "Grandpa drank the restaurant away." After they lost their second restaurant, Grandpa started working at the Chun King factory in Duluth and Grandma Lola took a job cooking at the Gopher. Grandpa suffered an injury at Chun King and was physically unable to work. He went on disability and, feeling totally without purpose, continued down his backward and treacherous path.

In spite of all that, Sue remembers it as a relatively calm time for their little family, even though Aunt Doreen worked a lot, with Pougie having to babysit all of the younger kids. She shared that on special occasions Aunt Doreen would "get out the frying pan and slice potatoes really thin and make potato chips, which was always a treat." Sue continued on: "We didn't have too many family gatherings besides the holidays. We had to go to Grandma and Grandpa's and Grandpa was kind of scary to me. I didn't trust Grandpa. He tried to kiss me one time. Men in that age-group, a lot of them were like that."

Sue was about eleven or twelve when that happened, and she never told her mother about it. She also said that "Grandma was always walking on eggshells every time he was around. I don't remember him hitting her, but he was just rough."

I asked Sue if she thought Aunt Doreen was afraid of Grandpa. "Yes," she said. "[Mom and Grandma] would both straighten up when he came around."

There was part of Grandpa Fred that "walked on water," in the eyes of his kids and other people who knew him. As Sue said, "There was a part of him that was a magnificent person." But as his alcoholism got more and more advanced, his mind began to get away from him. My mother has theorized that Grandpa was an undiagnosed schizophrenic who used alcohol to self-medicate his ailment. He would sometimes hear voices or have unexplained encounters with worlds that only he knew. There was one incident when he decided to paint all the walls, furniture, and everything in their apartment stark white. According to Sue, "When he [Grandpa] started losing it, when he painted everything white and got paranoid, Mom had Ralph stay there to kind of watch Grandma and make sure Grandpa didn't do anything crazy. Grandpa thought someone was coming after Grandma Lola," which was not grounded in reality at all. So, Grandpa's drinking combined with mental illness would continue to affect the people in the family in very difficult ways, as everyone tried to sort through what to do when the family patriarch begins to lose his frail grasp on reality.

I suspect that both Aunt Doreen and Aunt Gloria, who lived in Duluth at the time, were fully aware of his declining mental state, and they both did what they could to protect Grandma Lola. This was something they were all conditioned to do from the time they were little kids. But they had their own families, and no one could be there every minute. Gloria's daughter, Cathy Ann, said that things got very, very bad for Grandma Lola. She said that she and Grandpa Fred were living in a house on Raleigh Street, and "every morning, a cab was there to pick up Lola and take her to work, and the driver always had a bottle of whiskey for Fred. Lola never knew what she might find when she got home. One time she came home in July and the house was decorated for Christmas. And another time she came home, and he had painted the whole kitchen bright purple."

This was the midpoint of Grandpa Fred's mental decline, which would get much worse as time went on. Miraculously, Grandma Lola continued to work full time so that the two of them had money for the rent, because work was what she knew best and it got her away from Fred.

* * * * * * *

In 1965 a tall man with sharp, angular features began to frequent Anton's Restaurant, where both Lola and Doreen worked at the time. He was in town on a construction job and took a liking to Grandma Lola's cooking. The man obviously knew a good thing, especially when it was topped with homemade gravy, so he became a regular. Grandma liked to cater to him and would make him something special on the days he came in. Eventually she introduced him to her daughter Doreen, and the two of them hit it off immediately.

Al Voce was born in Eveleth, Minnesota, on the Iron Range. A first-generation Italian American, Al had never been married and did not have any kids of his own. Grandma Lola's purposeful introduction that day would be the start of something brand new for him, as well as for Doreen and Doreen's children. Looking back, Sue says, "To this day, I don't know why he married a woman with five kids. He loved her. He took us all on like we were his own kids, you know? He treated us like we were one of his—gave us all the same opportunities and everything. Like a saint." She then shared another formative moment for their family that also involves a carefully made meal, "I remember he was coming to our house for dinner when we were living in the projects. Mom made a chicken for dinner. And there was Al sitting at the table, making noises and sucking on the bones . . . We'd never had a man in our house, and we were all just staring," she says, laughing at the memory of their first dinner with Al, who clearly enjoyed the dinner very much.

Aunt Doreen wasn't exactly forthcoming with some key details about her life when she and Al first started dating. Bruce was barely two when they met, and initially she only told Al about her oldest four kids. But as Sue said, "He came over for dinner, and there we all were!"

Apparently, her failure to disclose all five of her children didn't matter that much, and Al and Doreen got married in Duluth during the month of April, not long after she had him over for chicken dinner. Doreen was thirty-four years old and Al was thirty-eight. Sue remembers that "Grandma and Grandpa were at the wedding, but they didn't have a ceremony or anything. It was just Grandma and Grandma. And then Tina was born."

Her full name is Catherine Doreen Voce. The family nicknamed her "Tina" because she was so tiny, and my dad has always called her "Tina Jolena." She is named after Catherine Voce, whom they all called "Grandma Voce," an immigrant from Italy who came to settle on the Iron Range as part of the first wave of Italians in northern Minnesota. According to Tina, "Grandma Voce learned English and went back to school. Grandpa Voce wouldn't speak English but understood it and only responded in Italian. Grandma Voce wanted her own children to learn English," adding, "I think she was more progressive in that way." Their son Al didn't speak fluent Italian, but he did know enough to communicate with both his parents. A man known for his healthy appetite and good sense of humor, Sue and Tina remember him telling them at the dinner table: "*Mangia, mangia,* come and eat!" Uncle Al would teach Aunt Doreen how to make real Italian spaghetti sauce and an authentic loaf of Italian bread, and she would teach him how to make our family's old recipe for white bread, made with scalded milk and basted with melted butter. Knowing this tidbit about the two of them makes me very happy—they experienced love at a perfectly set table with a platter of spaghetti and two kinds of bread.

Before moving to Eveleth, the Freemans and Voces lived on Third Street in East Duluth. Aunt Gloria had moved to a house on London Road, and Grandma and Grandpa Drouillard still lived in Duluth as well. Grandpa Fred had a particularly close bond with Tina, because they shared July as their birthday month. This was significant to him, and he used to say she was the only one of his grandkids born in "his" month. After Tina was born that summer, the following winter months of December and January were bitter cold with terrible blizzards and windstorms, even by Duluth standards. The story Tina tells is that "Grandpa came to the house in the evening, knocking on the door unexpectedly. It was nasty cold. He came into the house and said, 'I need Tina.' He was going to take me out to the porch. Mom wrapped me up and Grandpa held me, just pacing the porch, back and forth, all the while talking to me in Ojibwe. He walked up and down, up and down for a long time, just talking to me. Finally, he came back in the house and said to Mom, 'She just saved my life.'"

Was it the unforgiving cold air and unrelenting wind that sent Grandpa over the edge, or something else that made him seek out Tina that day? Perhaps it was a feeling of being trapped in the city, far away from the deep woods, that caused him to panic. On some level he knew he was about to snap, like a caged and desperate wolverine snared on one of his winter traplines. If something similar had happened in the Burge family, they would say that Grandpa was calling on the magic of babies to try to cure what was ailing him. Perhaps it was his own way of "bringing the baby home," in order to save himself from the darkness.

My cousin Cathy also said that when Grandpa was losing his mind, he "would walk over to the Good Shepherd Catholic Church to make his confession and he would talk in Chippewa to the Irish priest." The priest, of course, didn't know what Grandpa was confessing to, but the fact that he needed to come clean and ask for penance in his first language says a lot about who he really was. As Cathy said, "He was so afraid of losing his Ojibwe language." The idea of total assimilation into the mainstream was never possible for Grandpa. The notion that you can somehow erase the essence of a person through force or coercion is an exercise in cruelty and is always destined to fail. His upbringing in Chippewa City and close connection to the earth never left him, even when he was living in Duluth. Tina remembers that he used to sing to her "all the time in Ojibwe," the way his own mother sang to him. And now before we go on, it's important to confirm that my cousin Tina is a completely rational and down-to-earth sort of person, who isn't inclined to make up stories. Acknowledging that fact makes what happened between the two of them in Duluth even more powerful. Tina went on: "He would tell me to do things as I was growing up, but not with words."

One day at their house in Duluth, Aunt Doreen went upstairs and caught a preschool-age Tina carefully drawing on the white wall behind her bedroom door. According to Tina her mother got very upset, since drawing on the wall was a naughty thing to do, "She was going to spank me and then the phone rang. It was Grandpa. He said, 'What are you doing, Sister?' Mom said, 'I was about to spank your granddaughter.' And Grandpa said, 'Don't spank her, Doreen. I told her to draw the fish on the wall.'"

Tina remembers that Grandpa "told" her to draw a fish, even though he wasn't in the room with her, or even in the same house. It was a telepathic transference between the two of them, something unexplainable, but knowing my cousin and knowing what I know about Grandpa Fred, this story is completely plausible. I've found that it's important to set aside some preconceived ideas about our ancestors, especially if we are to ever truly know how very gifted and complex Grandpa Fred was. While he was likely schizophrenic, some of his kids and grandkids, to this day, recognize that Grandpa had the ability to do things outside of our conscious world. He had the ability to walk in dreamscapes and send messages to people in extraordinary ways, sometimes to life-changing effect.

Grandpa visited me in a dream the night before I was to start teaching a basic Ojibwe language class to seventh graders. I was really nervous about it, and that night, in a very deep sleep, I dreamt I was in a classroom full of kids and I was staring blankly at the chalkboard, unable to remember the words I wanted to write on it. Grandpa Fred appeared standing next to me at the front of the room. He was wearing an old-timey Pendleton wool plaid shirt and his black hair was perfectly greased back away from his face. He gently took the chalk from me and began to write words from my lesson plan on the board, spelling them out phonetically, just as I had learned them. When I woke up, I felt Grandpa's presence close by, and I knew that he was giving me his permission to speak.

Tina has also had Grandpa visit her in her dreams at different times in her life. After it happened, she would tell her mom about something Grandpa said to her from the dream world, and it would be in Ojibwe or would be something only Grandpa would know. As Tina said, "Mom would stare at me like, 'What the hell is going on?'"

Tina maintains that she never experienced anything other than love from Grandpa Fred. She said, "There's always been a close bond between him and me. Mom never said anything bad about him. I have a different view of him because of that. I never saw the raging part."

Someone who did see and experience Fred's very complex personality was his wife, Lola. He tormented her, and yet she loved him and stayed with him through some very dark times. Cathy tells the most frightening story: "One time, Grandma came home, and he grabbed her and tied her up and threw her in a closet. He grabbed his gun and sat out on the porch, waiting for 'the posse' to come and get him." It makes me boiling mad, knowing that Grandpa treated Grandma Lola like his hostage. It's clear he was mentally unstable, but I'm not sure if he was ever properly diagnosed. Any treatment he received was when he was sent to detox or, on more than one occasion, taken away to the mental hospital in Moose Lake. My dad was the one who had to have him committed. It's not something he ever talked about to us, only to my mom.

Given Fred's dangerous and unpredictable situation, the Drouillard siblings did what they could to protect Grandma Lola. She would stay with Doreen and her family regularly. It's not really surprising that Aunt (Lola) Doreen had a very strong relationship with Grandma Lola. She was named for her, and they were very much alike in a lot of ways. Because they worked side by side together for so many years, they became more like sisters, rather than mother and daughter. Tina agreed with this observation: "I remember Mom and Grandma being like best friends together. Mom held Lola in high regard. They used to drink at [Mom's] restaurant, the Happy Fisherman. Grandma was always there. She helped Mom all the time. Grandma worked at the Harbor Inn too. She was always a loving parent. Mom and Uncle Hank Amyotte and Grandma would play three-penny-ante poker in the back room with a jar of pennies. They always just had a community pot of pennies, and they would play on days when the restaurant was closed. The three of them would smoke and drink whiskey and 'talk smart' and do the 'soft-shoe.'"

That was what Aunt Doreen called their spontaneous bouts of dancing around the back room. Grandma Lola never drank when the kids were young. She was known to have her share of cocktails as she got older, but never to the point of no return. She was usually happy after she had a few, but sometimes she would cry, and then Aunt Doreen would cry too. And sometimes my dad's cousin Lois, Grandma's niece from the Linnell side, would be there, and all three of them would be dancing together, or crying. If one started, they all followed suit. They had a lot to cry about.

****

The Happy Fisherman was Aunt Doreen's restaurant in Colville, just across the highway from Lake Superior. The Colville beach is one of the few level beaches on that stretch of road. It's where beach rock piles up gently, creating a blanket of pink stones, perfectly round basalt pebbles, and an unimpeded view of the horizon. Aunt Doreen and Uncle Al moved from Duluth to a stretch of land just across the highway from the beach in 1970. They bought an already established supper club that came with a restaurant, a house where the family lived, and what they called the "hacienda" which was a little white house down from the restaurant that they would rent out to snowmobilers or summer visitors. All these buildings sat on top of beach gravel, because before the highway was there, the beach went right up to the bluff that overlooked the restaurant. They bought the business from a man named Al Crow, and the fish house across the highway, which is now in ruins, was still used by a local fisherman, who would supply fresh trout, herring, and menominee to the restaurant.

Tina was still very young when they made the move, and she

remembers learning how to bring cups of water to diners when she could barely see over the counter. It was a family-run place, so Sue, Ralph, Gayle, Bruce, and Tina all helped out while Aunt Doreen ran the kitchen. Uncle Al still had a full-time job working for a construction company in Eveleth, so he was gone during the week and would come home to the North Shore on weekends. That left Aunt Doreen in charge of operations, which was a brave decision, since she had watched her own parents struggle to run two cafés in West Duluth. She knew very well where the traps and minefields of running a restaurant were, but there were people to feed and parties to cater, and Doreen was always up for the challenge.

Tina remembers that "when we first got in there, we were open a lot." The Happy Fisherman was a full-service kind of place, with a lunch counter and rustic wooden tables tucked into alcoves with windows that faced the lake. My mom agreed to waitress there for three weeks, to help them get the restaurant up and running. She said it was pretty rough at first, but she committed to three weeks, so she stayed on to help. Aunt Doreen, of course, was the cook. Ralph did the dishes and helped in the back. Sue also waited tables, but Gayle was often at home next door, babysitting her younger siblings Bruce and Tina. Aunt Doreen's oldest daughter, Pougie, was already married by that time. She lived in Duluth and had her own son, Castle, to take care of.

Aunt Doreen's menu was impressive: broasted chicken, jo-jo potatoes, slow-roasted ribs served with BBQ sauce from her own recipe, steaks that were cut from sides of beef right at the restaurant. Both Aunt Doreen and Hank (Alfred Henry) Amyotte would be on the band saw cutting steaks before service. Uncle Hank, as Tina called him, "would help all the time."

Hank Amyotte lived in a little stone house just west of the Happy Fisherman that is still there. A World War II veteran, he had been recruited to serve with Merrill's Marauders, a special operations unit trained for long-range jungle combat. Hank was awarded a Bronze Star, a Presidential Unit Citation, a Rifleman Badge, a Victory Medal, and a Good Conduct Medal. According to his brother Bill Amyotte, "Henry was behind Jap lines in Burma for a hundred and twenty-eight days, I think. They had to drop their supplies to them. That was really a rough go there."[5] My dad remembers Uncle Hank telling stories about his experiences in Burma, reliving how the men had to kill and eat monkeys to survive. Hank and Aunt Doreen were great friends, since the Amyottes and the Drouillards have a shared history going all the way back to the Chik-Wauk days on the Gunflint Trail. Hank worked there before he went off to war, and there is a wonderful family photo of Grandpa Fred, Uncle Hank, Tempest Powell, and Irv Benson that was taken just outside the resort. He was considered part of the family, and Tina recalls that "Uncle Hank's sister lived in Duluth and they would stop and see her" when they were passing through.

Because they had known each other all their lives, Doreen and Hank considered themselves cousins, and Hank spent a lot of time at the Happy Fisherman, sometimes sleeping in the back room. Some of Tina's best memories of him are when she and Bruce "would sleep on the beach and cook bannock over the fire and he would sing in Ojibwe and tell us stories."

An Anishinaabe man and Grand Portage tribal member, Uncle Hank knew about the old ways and traditional medicines; he once rendered bear grease from a small bear to heal Gayle's psoriasis. According to Tina, "It stunk to high heaven, but it worked," and Gayle's skin cleared up, just like Hank said it would.

In 1972 Grandpa Fred died of a brain aneurysm. I was five years old when he died, so I have only fuzzy memories of that time. My mother said the whole Drouillard family came to our house after the burial. She remembers the kindness of our family friends Dick and Lou Anderson, who brought a fifty-dollar check over to our house to help with the funeral expenses. My mother said it made such a big difference to them, and it stands out as a significant part of the day for her. From my mother's point of view, the day of Grandpa's funeral was a sad and drunken affair, with all of Fred's kids ending up downtown at the bar, while a few of the women stayed back at our house with what must have been a whole pile of Drouillard cousins. I'm not sure where Grandma Lola ended up that night. I can only hope someone had the wherewithal to take care of her. My mother referred to it as "a mess," and I'm sure she is right about that.

Grandpa's death didn't help matters when it came to his eldest daughter's compulsion to drink too much. My cousin Sue was in high school when he died. It was at the height of Auntie's efforts to run the Happy Fisherman, and Sue remembers that "Mom was drinking a lot. I would have to go to the restaurant and do prep. The laundry would pile up. A lot of times when it was cleanup time at night at the restaurant, I would just leave and then come back in the morning to do it. It was an easy, efficient place to run, really. And a pretty popular restaurant. But Mom would drink so much. She'd be in town at 5 p.m. when we were supposed to open. She would hang out with her friends Tita [Fern] and Muriel and Joy. They'd all be there drinking. They were being harmless . . . just having a good time. And yet somehow we managed to get supper out."

Aunt Doreen got her driver's license after she moved to Grand Marais, because the kids needed to get to town for things, and there were a lot of errands to run for the restaurant. Al was in Eveleth most days, so there was no one else but Doreen to run the restaurant, see that all the kids were fed, and that everything was taken care of. Getting a license would be an ill-advised decision for Doreen, who would go to town on errands, decide to pop into the bar for a drink, slip into too many lowballs, and then get stuck in town. It's important to note that Grandma Lola, Aunt Doreen, and Aunt Gloria never had their driver's licenses as young women, or in some cases ever. And let's just say that driving a motor vehicle was not any of their fortes, even if they were stone-cold sober. In the Drouillard family, the men were the drivers, at least until Aunt Diane, Doreen's youngest sibling, was in school. In one very telling instance, Aunt Doreen called her house from town, unable to drive. There was no one there except Bruce, who was just nine or ten years old, and he hitchhiked to town to pick up his mother. Those years, trying to run the Happy Fisherman and stay afloat took a big toll on Aunt Doreen and, by extension, on her kids. As things spiraled more and more out of control, so did her reliance on alcohol to get through it. As Sue explained, "I did move away from home my senior year and lived at Gopher Cabins [in Grand Marais]. And then Gayle moved in with me. She was still in high school but ended up not going to school. It was very dysfunctional by then. Al was working on the Range. He would come home over the weekend and he and Mom would get into it."

I wasn't there to see any fights or gain a real understanding of why Uncle Al and Aunt Doreen would fight. Given that Sue and Gayle left home early due to Aunt Doreen's disease is a good indication that Uncle Al had had enough as well. With Al still keeping a job on the Range and their four older siblings out of the house, the youngest two, Bruce and Tina, forged what Sue calls "quite a relationship." Bruce had to learn to take care of things at a very young age and was really protective of his little sister, something Sue also noted: "He was always her big brother," acknowledging that she was not there anymore to help. "I was in California at the time. I hitchhiked there and wrote Mom a postcard from Wyoming."

****

With the older girls gone, the workload at the restaurant fell harder on Aunt Doreen, which in some ways caused her to fall harder, in a metaphorical sense. And she fell without asking for a net, which is also terribly sad. This precarious existence continued for another year, and in 1973, everything came crashing in, much like the windows at Fred and Lola's Grand Café when the mayor's car hit it on New Year's Eve. But Aunt Doreen's life didn't crash for the reasons you might think. It wasn't a car accident or some other outside calamity. The restaurant didn't go bankrupt, and no one was served a bad piece of fish. Everything changed forever when Aunt Doreen had a heart attack, which was shocking to her friends and family because she was only forty-two years old. While recovering from this initial bout of heart trouble, she was at the local hospital undergoing a stress test when she suffered a second heart attack, which was much worse than the first one. Aunt Doreen lost consciousness, slipping in and out, and she was hospitalized in Duluth.

She stabilized, thankfully, and stayed at the hospital for a week or so. And, true to form, even though she was very sick, Aunt Doreen was still able to concern herself with the aspects of raising kids, and making sure that, on the outside at least, everything seemed shipshape, like making sure the food was served in pretty dishes, even if everything else was falling apart. Tina shared that "Dad brought Bruce and me to see her. We got dirty, somehow. And Mom was sleeping in her room, and I got up on the bed, you know, sitting with her. She woke up and said to Dad, 'What the hell is up with these children?' And she got up out of her hospital bed and started washing our faces. Kids had to be clean!" Tina laughs at this memory, and I do, too, because I can just see Aunt Doreen's little nightgowned body, popping up from her bed and out of a deep sleep, trying to fix things up so everything was nice. "What would the nurses think?"

After Aunt Doreen got well enough to go home, the Happy Fisherman was open only on weekends, which in turn, made the restaurant less and less profitable. Her older kids were no longer at home to help, and the delicate matter of Doreen's overall health made life in Colville quite stressful for everyone involved. Faced with the threat of financial or physical ruin, Uncle Al and Aunt Doreen decided to abandon the restaurant business entirely, and in 1975, Uncle Al moved Aunt Doreen, Bruce, and Tina to his big yellow house in Eveleth. They still owned the property in Colville, so they rented the restaurant building to a local man, who, according to Sue, "left fish scales everywhere." The whole building burned down in an accidental fire not long after the family left for the Iron Range. Uncle Al divided the property and sold it in chunks for much less than what it was actually worth. Sue thought that Uncle Al just wanted to be finished with it, which makes a lot of sense. It's a long way from Colville to Eveleth.

Their house in Eveleth is where Aunt Doreen made us "chocolate mustache" for breakfast with her homemade buttered toast. I remember that the floors were all carpeted with rich red carpeting and the place felt old and drafty, like a relic from the boom-and-bust years on the Mesabi Range. We visited them just a few times when Aunt Doreen lived there. I was in junior high by then and Tina was in high school. I remember one visit when Tina came home from school dressed in a traditional-style, pale-blue dance outfit, with a long skirt and a fancy fringed shawl that her mom gave her. Aunt Doreen encouraged Tina to dance in the powwow circle, even though Doreen was never taught to fancy dance. But it's really easy to imagine her out there in the sun with a fresh pair of moccasins on her little feet, and her shoulders wrapped in a robin's egg blue fancy shawl. It's a sunny day, the grass is still damp with dew, and she is lined up with her friends and cousins, her arms crossed in front of her chest and smiling a closemouthed grin. The dancing starts, but instead of a more traditional dance step, she would be doing her own version of the "soft-shoe," done to a traditional drum beat. I wish Grandpa hadn't purposefully kept her and the rest of his kids from learning his Anishinaabe ways. I understand why he did that, but I can't help but wonder how Aunt Doreen's life may have been different if she had danced in powwows instead of in her own kitchen. She would love to know that her daughters often signed up to feed the dancers and powwow dignitaries at the annual Rendezvous Days in Grand Portage over the years. She would be so proud of them, making big pans of wild rice, scrambled eggs, and sausages to feed dancers of all ages on the Saturday morning before the start of the Grand Entry into the circle.

****

Following her heart attacks, Aunt Doreen quit smoking, and drinking alcohol became less and less a part of her life. She was only in her fifties when she moved back to Eveleth, but she had successfully earned the status of mindimooyenh in some ways. When I asked Tina about moving to Eveleth and being the only daughter left at home, she told me about how her mother talked to her "differently" than her older sisters. She would sit Tina down and answer all her questions about life and how to do things in this world—how to take care of things. According to Tina, "She never shirked those conversations with the younger ones. Not so much with Pougie or Sue. Mom was very insightful. She was not a chatterbox, but she was very, very funny."

She offered up her advice to Tina's friends and our other cousins too. "She wasn't afraid of the big conversations," Tina said. "She didn't know how to talk to Pougie about things, but she learned how to later."

Once when Aunt Doreen stayed with us overnight, I got a bloody nose out of nowhere and she helped me take care of it. That night she was the first adult to talk to me frankly about getting my period, and what "being a woman" meant in terms of carrying around the burden of monthly pain. When she talked to me about this, she was matter-of-fact and very caring. She was able to normalize it for me in my mind, and she granted my new physiological reality an element of power, rather than shame. That's a great gift to give a young girl. This is another reason why Aunt Doreen had such a loving impact on my life, and on the lives of many others in our family.

For Aunt Doreen's generation, the nurturing of things always fell on the girls. This was not forced on them but was more of "a given," in terms of the way things were. The girls were responsible for bringing warmth to the home—hauling in firewood, cooking meals, hauling water, washing up, and making sure everyone was happy and healthy. All of my Drouillard aunties watched Grandma Lola work herself to the bone, and then come home and take care of her seven kids and her husband too. Following Grandma Lola's lead, Aunt Doreen learned how to cope and do good, even though the waves were high and the customers never stopped coming in the door.

In the same way that she cooked for others and carried her knowledge of baking and feeding a crowd to the next generation of women in the family, Aunt Doreen also carried our family Anishinaabe history from her generation to the next. The value of that family history was never lost on her, and she carefully passed her strength of identity along to all her kids and to her nieces and nephews too. She was always proud of it and was never apologetic about the times in her life that she had to fight for herself or others, to defend who we are as a family. This was an expectation placed on her by her father, which she lived up to, to the best of her ability, but it was also something she learned from her own aunties, her grandma, and her friends, like Uncle Hank Amyotte.

When I asked my cousin Sue if there were any specific life lessons she learned from her mother, we talked about the grandmas and aunties who came before us and she said, wisely, "We come from these women. We are part of them. They made us, good or bad." Then she told a story about how Aunt Doreen taught her a lesson about taking responsibility for herself: "One year I got an F on my report card. I thought, 'Oh cripe, what's Mom going to do?' I thought about changing it, but she saw the F. I waited and waited, and she didn't say anything about it. I said, 'Mom, what do you think of that F?' And she said, 'What do you think about it?' I thought that was a good way to deal with it. You've got to know yourself what's good and what's bad."

* * * * * * *

Just two years after the Voces moved to Eveleth, Grandma Lola was diagnosed with pancreatic cancer. Doreen took Grandma to Eveleth for a while, and she stayed there with them until she had to be hospitalized at the Care Center in Grand Marais. Tina remembers that her mom did whatever she could to keep Grandma Lola comfortable, caring for her not out of duty, but out of love. Aunt Doreen, in spite of her weaknesses, never stopped wanting to protect the people she loved from pain. But who tried to protect Aunt Doreen from her pain? I asked Tina this question and here's what she said" "We all tried to be there for her. Ralph tried to take care of her. Gayle did. Dad did, but it took him awhile. Uncle Hank did. Grandma did. Aunt Joyce took care of her. She would never ask for help. She always had people around her, and they helped her."

Of course, Aunt Doreen never asked for help. In her mind, she lived for and was perfectly capable of managing a full restaurant, cooking Sunday dinners, throwing big family gatherings, and raising hell on a Friday night with her girlfriends. She had lots of friends. She had a lot of family. And truth be told, it took a village to take care of Aunt Doreen when she was drinking, but everyone loved her through it anyway. Her daughter Sue reflected on their relationship, now that her mother is gone: "She gave me a lot of good things. She made her life. She was a wonderful mom as far as being a provider. I think I have a lot of her traits. Her sense of humor. I still say some things she always said. I know she was a kind person and had a big heart. But we didn't have that kind of relationship. I know she had it with other people. It is what it is. I can't undo anything, so I have to accept everything I did. I have to live with it."

Starting as bad cells in her cervix, Auntie's cancer was in the advanced stages when they diagnosed it. She stayed with Pougie in Duluth for a year while the doctors treated her with radiation implants. She went into remission, which lasted about a year, but then the cancer moved into the base of her spine as well as other bones in her body. She was in a lot of pain—excruciating pain. A blockage developed and they did surgery to ease the symptoms. The last time Tina was with Doreen, she spent the day in her room at the hospital. She said, "I knew that was going to be the last time. Before that, when I left for Eveleth, she would always say, 'OK, honey,' but that time she called me by name."

Sue was also able to spend some time with Aunt Doreen when she was sick. She stayed at her house in Grand Marais for a few days.

Doreen was very sick, but she still wanted to be there. Sue's daughter Teri was really little and wanted to try on her grandma's long nighties, which Aunt Doreen thought was so cute. I asked Sue what Aunt Doreen was like toward the final days of her life and she said, "She was mom to six kids. She always enjoyed having her kids at home . . . and all of us kids were at the hospital. She had a blank look on her face and I couldn't tell what that look was. I was more relieved when she passed. Because I wouldn't have to worry about her anymore."

Aunt Doreen's struggles with alcoholism were a part of why Sue worried about her mom. When I talked to Sue over the phone about her mother's life, Sue felt that "she must have been in some type of turmoil or pain that she couldn't deal with. That's why people drink like that . . . [When she died] I didn't think of myself. I was thinking of her. I wanted her to be at peace. To just let her go."

* * * * * * *

In the Ojibwe language, if you add *iban* to the end of someone's name, it indicates that they have died and you are missing them. *Inzigos Doreen-iban*. And so, we are missing her and we all cry for her, like my dad did on the day of her funeral. Is it any wonder that our hearts are broken when we think of Aunt Doreen? Watching the dirt pile up on top of her grave was such a cold, helpless feeling. It didn't feel right to just bury her and walk away. It's been thirty-six years and I still miss her. We all do. Uncle Al missed her too, and every year before he died, he would make the drive from Eveleth to St. John's Catholic Cemetery in Grand Marais to put fresh flowers next to Aunt Doreen's headstone, which is right next to Grandpa and Grandma's shared grave marker. He would sometimes drop by my parents' place afterward for coffee, but he never stayed very long. My sister remembers that after Doreen died, Uncle Al gathered up a few things to send with her on her journey, including her comb and her favorite paring knife.

If Aunt Doreen were still with us, she might be in the kitchen cooking Sunday dinner right now. February 2021 would have marked her ninetieth birthday, and her daughter Tina once confided that "I've now lived longer without a mother than when I had a mother."

The namesake of her own mother, Aunt Lola Doreen-iban was of the earth. She fought with her hands, fists, legs, and wit. She watched her own mother be victimized by her father, and yet she still looked up to him. She found a way to forgive him. And she would cry about him, like we cry for her. She was a mother to Pougie, Ralph, Sue, Gayle, Bruce, and Tina, and if she had grown older, she would have been able to meet more than a handful of grandchildren. She would have loved them and been so proud of them all. At times, she needed mothering herself, but as she would say, "Never mind, I can take care of myself." And then she would steel her jaw, give you "the look," and that would be that.

Because she spent her whole life feeding other people but often missed feeding herself, it's time now to create a magnificent feast for Aunt Doreen. It would be held outside on a sunny day. Everything would be homemade in the grand tradition of the Drouillards, with fresh bread, frosted cinnamon rolls, and caramel rolls like Grandma Lola used to make. There will be chocolate cake with chocolate frosting, chocolate chip cookies, and homemade apple pie. Nothing would come out of a box, and the food would be served in pretty bowls or on platters, just like Aunt Doreen would do it. There will be a big platter of fried walleye with tartar sauce, pork steaks, buttered wild rice, corn gravy, and mashed potatoes—because Aunt Doreen made the best mashed potatoes! I would ask my cousins to bring some slow-roasted ribs, like the kind she used to make at the Happy Fisherman, to be served with the secret BBQ sauce her customers used to drive ten miles to enjoy. There would be authentic Italian spaghetti served with Italian peasant bread from Uncle Al's recipes. And for dessert, of course, we will serve up hot cups of "chocolate mustache" topped with whipped cream, along with perfectly buttered toast points on the side. At the center of the table there will be a huge vase of yellow roses with sprigs of cedar boughs mixed in, and napkins the color of wild roses. After all the food is set out on the table, I will hold a bit of tobacco in my left hand, because its closer to my heart, and offer it to the biggest tree I can find. Then we'll fill a plate with a little bit of everything, and set it down at the head of table, to make sure Aunt Doreen is able to eat first. Only then will the rest of us be welcome to join the feast.

She Taught Us: A Poem for Doreen

She taught us
how to feed a crowd,
with fried fish
buttered toast,
jo-joes
and bannock bread.
She taught us
that love sometimes
comes on a plate,
with chocolate cake,
pork steak
clover rolls
and corn gravy.
It's our job now,
to stay full up;
to keep feeding each other
like she taught
us to do.

Gloria

MY AUNT GLORIA'S HOUSE is full, literally and figuratively. Like three queens and two jacks in a hand of poker, she is a full house. Not just fully situated and planted, like the carefully tended shade perennials in her backyard garden, but plentifully stocked from top to bottom with the trappings of her long life. Her given name is Gloria Faye Drouillard, and she was born on Christmas Day 1932. My dear auntie is still with us on this chilly day in February 2021, as I cozy up in a wool blanket the color of the sun to write through my memories of her, even though she's only a few miles away. Visiting her is not possible at the moment, because our local Care Center has been on lockdown for more than one year, to keep the elderly residents safe from a microscopic sickness that weighs nothing but has outweighed anything in modern history. The last time I saw Aunt Gloria in person, I had dropped in to visit, and her eldest daughter, Cathy, was there, too. The three of us sat at a table in the dining area just down the hall from her room, and we reminisced about life and how to live it. Auntie Gloria still knows me well, even though she can't remember a lot of things these days. For someone with dementia, history is created two seconds behind what the mind brings forward, and the past is anything that isn't standing right in front of her. Her memory loss is exacerbated by poor eyesight, and now hearing loss, but she is still here, and I love her very much. Her roomful of memories, unlike those of some of my other aunties, is full to the brim, just like her actual house used to be.

One of the best things about moving back home was that I got to know Aunt Gloria much better than I did when I was a kid. She lived in Duluth when my sister and I were growing up, and we didn't get to see her very often. Her life was ridiculously full with the day-to-day duties involved in raising her kids—six of them, just one shy of the number her own mother raised. At different points in her life, Gloria was married, then not married, and then married again . . . repeat. Once my mom and I were having coffee with her and we were talking about women-related things like love and marriage, and Aunt Gloria muttered under her breath "all my stupid husbands." The way she said it, growly, with a bit of a laugh, was her way of admitting that she had lived a lot of life and made it through the tough times, without much help from the men in her life. And this, it turns out, is an understatement. My aunt Gloria is a survivor. She hides a multitude of injuries that she incurred in the womanly wars she fought, and in spite of the pain she's experienced in the past, she is just about as cute and funny as a person could ever be.

I was still in high school when she moved back to Grand Marais after living in Duluth for many years. At that time, she was married to a man named Jim Martineau ("stupid husband" number three). My cousins Roberta and Matt (not related to Jim) were still in school and the four of them moved into a house that directly faced Grand Marais Harbor. The house once belonged to the Sobanja family, and later it became the Loafer bakery, then Chez Jude, and after that, the Harbor House. Before it was converted into a bakery, that house was really neat inside, with lots of original woodwork, bright, south-facing windows, and a big kitchen at the back of the house. I loved to visit Aunt Gloria there, because her houses were always so very well put together. There was a lot to look at, and it was always sparkling and clean.

When I was working on my first bona fide writing project, I got to sit down with Aunt Gloria several times and ask her questions about what it was like for her when she was growing up and things about the family that related to Chippewa City—research that eventually became a part of my book *Walking the Old Road*. The house she lived in then was on the west side of Grand Marais, on a quiet street that ended on a cul-de-sac leading into the woods. There were always deer running around back there and sometimes bears too. Aunt Gloria loved to feed the birds, and there were often a variety of sparrows kicking around on the ground, woodpeckers and blue jays clinging to suet balls, or flocks of pine grosbeaks who came to rest on the apple tree in her front yard. Grand Marais proper is really just a paved grid of roads on a hill, set in the middle of the forest, and that's where she felt most at home, close to the woods and not far from Lake Superior. Her house was like her own frilly nest, and she loved it when anyone came over to visit. She always had a pot brewing on her Mr. Coffee machine and she loved to just sit and talk. Oftentimes she would want to show me something—like a book she was reading or an old piece of family ephemera she had found in a box somewhere. Her house in some ways was like our private family museum. There were lots of photos of her kids and grandkids and old pictures of Grandma Lola, Grandpa Fred, and her sisters and brothers, including my dad, Francis (Pooty) Drouillard. She had framed newspaper articles about Grandpa's days as a fishing guide, or pictures of him and Grandma Lola that were taken inside their café in Duluth. Her basement was chock-full of things to look at, and almost everything had a story to go along with it. She remembered where everything was, and most often, where she got it and what she paid for it. Her great-grandson Cameron has very good memories of visiting her at that house when he was little. He remembers that "she cared a lot about her things and that she had 'crazy antiques' in the basement, set up so perfectly." The basement had a bedroom, storage spaces, laundry machines, a bathroom, and a central room, which was filled from ceiling to floor with coordinated displays of her collected curios.

There were mounted deer and moose horns on the wall, including pairs of horns that my dad gave her, and some from a deer that Uncle Bruce shot. Everything was always impeccably clean and in its place—and there was a roost for everything, no matter where she lived. In addition to family history, Aunt Gloria also collected chickens—not the live, clucking kind, but the ceramic and porcelain kind. There was a chicken in every little nook and cranny that she had room for. And if she ran out of room, she'd have my dad or her son Matt build a shelf high on the wall in the kitchen, or in a little spot here, or over there, so that she could fit in a few more. I can just see her standing in her kitchen and pointing at the specific place where she thought a new display might fit.

This wonderful house is where I was able to interview her about her childhood and get the story of it in her own words, not anyone else's. I first asked her about where she was born, and if she knew anything about that day. She said, "I was born at home. It was Christmas. And I think Lucy Caribou was there and my mother's sister Lois. I guess Daddy wanted to name me 'Barbara' and mother wanted to name me 'Tallulah' after the actress Tallulah Bankhead [she and I both laughed heartily at this]. Lois Cogley is the one that named me Gloria. The priest was there too. And he said, 'Gloria in saecula saeculorum.' So that's why Lois named me Gloria. I wouldn't have minded Tallulah . . . I think that's kind of cute." (We both laughed some more at this.)[1]

Having Lucy Caribou there to help Grandma Lola during the delivery is a good indication that Aunt Gloria was born in the little house in the woods that was about a half mile from town and a half mile to Chippewa City. Lucy was their closest neighbor at that time, which was before there was any kind of road to speak of. There was a path through the woods to her house, which was located just across from where the Catholic church parking lot is now. Aunt Gloria remembers that "Lucy was our neighbor for as long as I can remember. It was about a block away. The Free church is close to there now. The house we grew up in is still there, but it has been moved several feet."

The Drouillard place was right at the bottom of the road that goes up to the current school garage. That's where they all grew up. I asked her what the house was like inside and she said, "There was one bedroom us kids all shared—it was called 'Gaag's Bedroom' because an old lady named Gaag once lived there with her son." My dad, Francis, said that they would terrorize each other at night in that bedroom by whispering in a low, scary voice, "Ghost . . . skeleton . . . bear . . . GAAG!" *Gaag* is the Ojibwemowin word for "porcupine," which doesn't really seem that threatening, unless it was an old woman who had the ability to shape-shift into a giant, quill-throwing porcupine, which is actually quite scary—especially if she is hiding behind the door or under the bed. Yikes!

* * * * * * *

As we talked that day, Aunt Gloria took me through each room in their old house. She said there was a living room and a kitchen with a wood-burning cookstove in it. She told me that Grandma Lola always kept a can of grease on top of the stove to use for frying. My dad said that he remembers Grandpa Fred slathering grease from the can on his bread, which was usually a mix of bacon fat, lard, and bear fat. There were just the two small bedrooms, one for the kids and one for Grandma and Grandpa. When they got a bit older, she said her oldest brother, Monty, would sleep on the couch in the living room, and "the other six of us slept in Gaag's bedroom in bunk beds. Doreen and I slept on the bottom with Gale and Diane, and Bruce and Pooty slept on the top bunk."

I asked Gloria how well she slept, having her brother's and sisters' feet in her face all night and she laughed about it, thinking back on how all four of them fit together like a puzzle. My uncle Stormy (Gale) has also joked about what that was like, with one kid or the other accidentally peeing the bed and how it would get "nice and warm . . . and then cold . . . and then warm again." They all laughed about this, because that's how it really was. Back then, you had to take the warmth wherever you were able to find it, I guess.

Times were very lean for the Drouillards and other Native families on the North Shore in the late 1920s and 1930s. Aunt Gloria was born during the height of the Great Depression, which affected everyone in northern Minnesota to one degree or another, but especially the Native families who lived both on and off the reservation. At that time, Anishinaabe people were effectively cut off from a lot of the traditional and seasonal ways of life, where hard work was collaborative and the products of the work were shared within the larger community. Working together to prepare for the winter with the goal of taking care of each other—that's how the people survived the very long, cold winters before northern Minnesota was colonized by people from outside of the tribal tradition. As Aunt Gloria said, "Well, I think back then everybody was poor. And I remember in the winter it would get so cold that we had to block off the kitchen and Gaag's bedroom and we would all kind of stay in the living room and Mom and Dad's room. Just certain times you know, when it got so terrible cold." According to my dad, their bedroom was so cold, Grandma Lola would store the meat in the corner of the room.

In the 1930s Anishinaabe families who lived off the reservation in Grand Marais lived in separate households on separate pieces of land and it was up to each family to ensure that they had what they needed to feed their nuclear family, instead of pooling resources together as a clan-based society would have, like Anishinaabe families did before the Reservation Era. The Western concept of single-family home ownership was imposed on people who culturally were taught to live together, not apart. The dire circumstances faced by my dad's family, living in the woods fairly far away from the next house, was that if something went wrong, you did not have extended family members there to help you—at least not like it was when extended groups of family would winter together where there was good hunting, fishing, and access to plentiful fuels in the surrounding woods. In Grand Marais, Grand Portage, and Chippewa City, once you harvested all the trees on your "property," you had to go farther to get more, or have the money or goods to buy or trade for it. Aunt Gloria told me what that isolated feeling was like for their family, who lived mostly independently from others. During one brutal cold snap the family had to divide their already small house in two in order conserve wood fuel and stay warm. She said, "I remember one time when we had to block off the kitchen, Mom's butter and potatoes froze solid. She felt really bad about her potatoes getting frozen because they all went rotten."

When you have seven hungry kids and your entire winter potato supply goes rotten, what does a mother do? I imagine Grandma Lola found a dignified way to make up for it. She was very proud and so was Grandpa Fred, who often let his pride get in the way. A French and Anishinaabe man who grew up as the grandson of an "Indian" agent, he was, I suspect, acutely aware of the stigma that surrounded the people who grew reliant on government subsidies to get by. It was his grandfather, Nelson Drouillard, after all, who was the first government agent at Grand Portage, the man charged with "instructing" the people how to farm on what is perhaps the rockiest and most thickly clay land in all of Minnesota. What an impossible thing to balance, being the son of a Frenchman whose father was assigned to "acculturate" the people of Grand Portage and also the son of a traditional Anishinaabe woman who never learned to speak English. Based on the stories I've heard about him, Grandpa worked very hard to avoid toppling over, like a turtle on its back, in his attempt to balance the starkly disparate worldviews he was born into and had to traverse his whole life.

Grandpa Fred was born in Chippewa City in 1907, the youngest of twelve children. His father was John Drouillard, a Frenchman who moved to Grand Portage when he was a young boy. His mother was Elizabeth Anakwad, a 100 percent Anishinaabe woman who was born in Chippewa City in 1864. Their twelve kids were all baptized at St. Francis Xavier Catholic Church—the little church that is still standing, not far from where the first modern-style Anakwad house was built. When Aunt Gloria was growing up, she would walk to "Chippewa" three or four times a day to visit her friends. "It's didn't matter how many times," she said. I asked if they ever went to church there, and she said, "I never went to the little church out there. We played in it. But we'd go out to Chippewa City and see Leona [Morrison]. And I remember Charlie Newton lived out there. I remember his mother. And then we'd go down and play on the lake, on the lower road down there. We'd pick berries. We'd walk on the Old Road down to Chippewa City at night and pick pussy willows. In the evening, Mother [Lola Drouillard] used to take us for a walk all the time. And we'd go to Chippewa City . . . and there were all kinds of marsh marigolds down there. Mother liked to go for a walk at night and she'd take us down there. I remember that very well."

* * * * * * *

The Old Road was walked by many people over the years. Walking was how people got places, because most people did not own cars, and most of the roads were little more than overgrown dogsledding trails carved through the woods. When Grandpa Fred was growing up, the kids from Chippewa City went to school in Grand Marais, a mile's walk from his house in Chippewa City. Aunt Gloria said, "Dad went to school until the fourth grade." And, after leaving school he worked as a hunting guide in Canada at the age of ten. She also said, "He bought his first home for Grandma Drouillard when he was fourteen." I asked her who taught him to hunt and be a guide at such a young age and she said, "He always thought of himself as 'self-taught.'"

Grandpa Fred's pride in being a self-taught hunter and fisherman, as well as someone who was able to provide a house for his own mother at such a young age, created some grandiose expectations that ruled over his psyche for most of his life. Based on what I've learned about his life, as the father of seven kids, his personal sense of pride prevented him from ever asking for help or appearing vulnerable in any way. This rigid view of his own exceptionalism was something he also placed on Grandma Lola and their children, even though the family struggled to rise above abject poverty. He wanted his kids to be independent and tough, and a lot of them tried very hard to fit his expectations, including his three sons and Aunt Doreen, his oldest daughter, who tried throughout her life to be fearless. People like Fred didn't ask for handouts of any kind. Aunt Gloria said that "back then there was 'Relief,' where you could go and get food and clothes if you needed something." Her childhood memory is that "only once . . . my dad would never let my mother get something from Relief. We went to the Courthouse and mother picked out winter coats for us. I remember when we got those—they were heavy, wool winter coats. Daddy would never do it. She wanted to, but he wouldn't let her."

When Gloria was born, job options for Ojibwe men on the North Shore were built around the harvesting of natural "resources" like working as pulpwood loggers or fur trappers or signing on as laborers to work on road building or the various infrastructure projects. These jobs offered either a weekly wage or intermittent payouts based on the number of trees you felled or number of animal skins you were able to bring to market. Trapping wild animals was how Grandpa made money when his kids were very young. It required him to leave home for months at a time, often with just one pack on his back and a pair of snowshoes, essential to make his way through the deep snow, many miles away from other human beings. As Aunt Gloria told me, "He always said the stars were his blanket. And he would tell us about how warm he stayed, sleeping under the snow. When you think about it, they didn't have the nice fabrics back then or anything, Staci—think how cold they got! And then to go out there and he would be gone, like, for a month. And just living out in the woods and making camp.

And when he would come home—what I remember were his eyes, they were just dark. I didn't want to look at his eyes. He'd get just like an animal. When he'd come home, I was scared of him—I didn't want to look at his eyes."

Her feeling that he had to become like an animal to do the work of trapping places him firmly inside the wild and brutal nature of survival in the north woods. It's something you can't ignore if you live here, because wild things and human things often cross paths, which sometimes results in a violent ending for the wild thing. For a hunter and trapper like Grandpa Fred, it's either kill or starve to death. And as an Ojibwe man, killing animals was not something he would have taken lightly. The strong belief that you only kill what you can use fully was instilled in us from the time we were kids. Our dad learned it from his dad, and every deer season you might find a deer heart boiling on our stove, which dad would slice and make into sandwiches, because he was taught not to waste anything. The conflict inherent in trapping animals like foxes, wolves, and martens that were not traditionally eaten as food is something that must have gotten under Grandpa's skin and possessed him like a shape-shifter.

****

I was thinking about Grandpa Fred just the other day while tramping along the snowshoe trail behind our house. Not far along the trail, one of our dogs started scratching at some snow alongside the path. There was a patch of blood there, left behind by a rabbit or squirrel that met its end in a bobcat's mouth. I knew it was a bobcat because there was just one, round track floating on the crust of snow close by. The sight of blood in the snow is always a trigger for me because of the day I found the place where wolves had killed our dog Katagon. We had a dog sitter that night—it was New Year's Eve and we had planned for a night of fun with friends in Duluth. Not long after we got there our sitter called to tell us that our two dogs had run off into the woods and only one had come back.

A fluffy white dog with one big black spot on his back, Katagon was our little protector, and even though we were not there when it happened, he still felt it was his duty to be brave and keep our territory from harm. There was an ice storm that night, and so we thought it unwise to drive home in the dark. Neither one of us slept, worried about our little dog. By the time we got home the next morning, a layer of fresh snow had covered up the place where he was killed, but it was very apparent what had happened. There were wolf tracks that circled around his own little tracks and something dark hidden under the snow that I still can't unsee. It's taken many years to try to reconcile what happened and I still haven't resolved how I feel about the wolves that killed him. But one thing is certain—when you live in a wild place, you are at the mercy of the forest, and it will take things from you if you are not careful.

Continuing our snowshoeing up to the ridge that passes through a stand of sugar maples, I imagined Grandpa Fred slowly making his way along his winter trapline. I have a pair of his old bear-paw snowshoes that my dad gave me—they are the traditional kind, made of light, flexible ash wood, tough sinew, and a double-stitched place at the center that would have held his leather bindings in place. It's hard to imagine how many miles he put on them and under what conditions. The dead creatures he found in his traps and the suffering, still-living creatures he had to kill in order to make money from the skins would have left bright-red bloodstains behind in the snow. He had become hardened to it—to the violence of it—and I understand why it would be very difficult for him to leave it behind when it was time to return home. I think Aunt Gloria probably sensed that her dad was not the same person who had left the house a month before, ambitious and light on his feet. He carried back with him the sounds a trapped pine marten makes when it knows it's about to die and the scream of a snared wolf who was hunting in the wrong place and at the wrong time. Those are the kinds of screams that rattled around inside Grandpa Fred's mind—the ones Aunt Gloria could see lurking behind his eyes every time he came out of the woods.

Grandpa Fred was sometimes the hunter and sometimes the prey. At a time when families starved if they didn't procure enough animal skins to sell at the Johnson Trading Post in Grand Marais or at posts in Duluth, Grandpa did what he could to make his forays into the deep woods as profitable as possible. Given the toll it probably took on him, every animal life had to count for something. Aunt Gloria said the local game wardens always had it out for him—it's not clear why. Perhaps he went over his limit, or maybe he was trying to avoid paying fees or taxes on the money he made as a trapper. She told me that at the end of one season, "He had all his furs and he didn't know how to get them down the [Gunflint] Trail. And so, he said to the game warden—they were at Chik-Wauk Lodge [at the end of the trail]—that he had a box of clothes to send to town and he couldn't find a way to get them down. So, he asked the game warden if he would take the box of clothes down the trail. And here it was his furs in there! The warden brought them down and delivered them right to the house!" (*Laughs.*) And then she added, "Yeah, he had a really tough time."

She claimed that most everyone had a tough time when she was growing up, but I asked her about those who weren't poor. She explained that "some were a lot a better off than we were. Like the game warden's daughter, Gertrude Allen. She took a shower in the morning before she came to school and I asked her, 'Weren't you cold?' and she said, 'No, it's nice and warm in our house.' I was so used to being cold. [*Laughs.*] We were always getting dressed around the stove!"

****

I asked Aunt Gloria what downtown Grand Marais was like when she was growing up and if the houses were different there. She said, "Grand Marais was a heck of a lot smaller than what it is now, of course. And the buildings were a lot smaller. There are a lot more tourists now. There were very few streetlights back then. [*Laughs.*] Some houses had running water—but not all. I think I was eleven years old when we got electricity. I think it was available, but we didn't have it until then [1943]. And we never got running water."

She said she remembered living with just one light source at first: "I remember the living room light when you came in the door. I remember we only had, like one bulb too. I remember Dad got mad at us one night and we had one light on the ceiling and he took the bulb away, so it was pitch black."

I asked her, "So, did you ever get it back?"

She said, "I don't remember getting it back! I remember being without it a long time."

The Drouillard kids spent the bulk of their time outside, except when it was very cold. They were all used to walking to school or walking downtown to Mable's Café, where Grandma Lola worked, and just heading out into the woods for the day. The boys had shotguns for hunting rabbits, and the girls played house in the thick woods surrounding their cabin. Of course, a plethora of woodland creatures lived in the woods, and as Aunt Gloria told the story, "All the years we lived here, there were gobs of deer and bear. They never bothered us. One time we were going up the trail and Pooty ran into a bear with his bike. Me and Jack Netland were behind him on the trail and the bear ran right past us and rubbed our legs as it went past. [Laughs.] It was pitch black!"

I asked her, "Did the bear make a noise?"

And she said, "Well, when Pooty hit it, it went 'ugh.'"

She and I laughed pretty long and hard about that story. And then she said, "Now I'm scared to death. I'm scared to walk home at night from downtown. But we were told they would never bother us, and they didn't."

She also told me that bears would come in really close to their house, because their family would just throw tin cans and other items out the kitchen window and into the woods. Back in those days, people would often just toss their old things in a lake or drag them out into the woods. Out of sight, out of mind. Apparently, the garbage heap would grow quite large and so would the number of neighborhood bears, digging around in the pile and perusing the refuse for an easy meal.

****

By the time Aunt Gloria was six or seven, the local economy on the North Shore was in full transition from being resource dependent to the tourism-based economy that it is today. New restaurants opened downtown, and lodges and resorts along the North Shore and on the Gunflint Trail welcomed visitors from faraway places like Chicago, Milwaukee, and Minneapolis. This meant that Grandpa Fred's skills as a woodsman were needed to help guide fishermen from the big city who made the long trek north for an extended stay at Chik-Wauk on Saganaga Lake. This would become his main job every summer, something he was known for in the adventurous Northwoods tales of those who were lucky enough to share a boat with him over the years. A lot of Grandpa's regular clientele were doctors or lawyers from big cities far across the Great Lakes. I asked my aunt Gloria if she thought Grandpa ever felt exploited, being 50 percent Anishinaabe and hired to take rich white men on outdoor adventures. She said, "I bet he did. But he was good friends with all of them. They all just loved Dad. I don't think Daddy ever forgot he was Indian. He was proud. Axel Haavesto [his fellow worker] used to say about going into the woods with Daddy, 'You could go in the woods with him—you'd turn around and he'd be gone.'"

Sadly, Grandpa Fred didn't take much time to teach his own sons how to disappear into the woods and come back with dinner. That was something they had to learn on their own, and most of them did learn, in my Dad's case, very well. Grandpa expected them to do it on their own because that's how he learned it. As Aunt Gloria remembered, "He never taught the boys about being in the woods. He was mean to his boys." And then she offered this story about being a little girl and experiencing what it was like when the screams rattling around behind Grandpa's eyes came to the surface: "I recall twice my dad spanked me. One time he hit me so hard I peed the bed. And he was going to spank both Doreen and me—only I was the one that got caught—'cause we were peeking at our presents. It was Christmastime and he caught us and we ran and hid under the bed. Doreen got way under the bed—up against the wall—and I got grabbed and he gave me a crack. But a lot of times he didn't have to spank us, he'd usually just look at us and that would be enough."

Gloria told me that one of her most awful memories stems from when her oldest brother, Monty, was in high school and wanted to play on the basketball team. For some reason, this really irked his father, who strictly forbade him to join the team. Grandma Lola, in a valiant effort to give Monty an opportunity to play, secretly let him go to practice and covered for him by asking [two of his brothers] to do Monty's chores after school. That way Fred wouldn't know that Monty didn't come right home. Aunt Gloria remembers that "[Pooty] and Bruce were doing Monty's chores—back then, we had to go out and drag our own birch logs home. And that's the time the axe glanced off that tree and split Pooty's kneecap."

Dad was about eleven, and the ax did a lot of damage to his knee, at a time before telephones, when the local doctor was far away and sometimes wouldn't make house calls to "Indian" families. One of the kids ran over to Lucy Caribou's house, and Lucy and her daughter Marjorie came to the house and doctored my dad's knee so that he wouldn't bleed to death while waiting for certified medical help, which may or may not come. Aunt Gloria summed up the story by saying, "That's how Dad found out that Monty was at basketball practice. And Daddy raised holy hell."

No one really talks about what Grandpa did when he found out, but my guess is that it was pretty bad. So bad that when Uncle Monty left Grand Marais after finishing high school, he didn't come back to visit for more than twenty years.

****

A more truthful retracing of the family history is necessary to understand what life was like for Aunt Gloria and her siblings at their house in the woods, because the people and events that shape our childhoods also shape the decisions we make when we are older. The poet Muriel Rukeyser once asked, "What would happen if one woman told the truth about her life?" Her answer: "The world would split open." If our intention is to make peace with the past, then getting as close to the truth as we can, without causing further pain, is how we will be able to break the cycle of violence within our families. But telling the truth is usually uncomfortable at best and terrifying at worst, and so we don't tell. And then more people get hurt. So, what happens in Aunt Gloria's later life relates directly to what happened on the day Grandpa found out that everyone was hiding something from him and he raised holy hell because of it.

Because I love my Aunt Gloria, I find it impossible to simply gloss over Grandpa Fred's destructive and unpredictable behavior, like when he painted everything white at their apartment in Duluth. Fred's behavior shaped every day and every future day's life for his wife and all his kids, forever. If we truly are to understand the lives of our mothers, aunts, and grandmothers, and the parts of them (good and bad) that got passed along to all of us, then we must be brave enough to hear the unvarnished truth about the men who made us too. *Debwe*—the truth—is that Grandpa subjected his family to fear, intimidation, and sometimes violence, especially when he had been drinking and things didn't go the way he wanted. And drinking is always complicated. To further confuse things, Aunt Gloria said there was never alcohol in the house and Grandpa never drank at home, but he certainly did drink, and he also bootlegged liquor for a time to make extra money.

There was just one time in particular she remembers having liquor in their house, and it wasn't on purpose: "Ma and Dad never kept anything in the house. My dad drank, my mother in later years, but all the while she was raising us, she didn't drink. I only remember one time there being anything in the house. That's when us kids got drunk. Pooty, Bruce, and I did. Because we wanted to play bartender to use that cute little shot glass. I don't remember who had been there—some friends of Mom and Dad had left a bottle of whiskey, and we thought it would be fun to get drunk. That's when Bruce fell through the porch and split his eye open right here (showing me a place above her eye). If it wasn't for Marjorie Caribou, Lucy's daughter, Bruce would probably have bled to death. I remember laying on mother's bed and I was just drunk. I don't remember what happened to Poot. He got drunk too. We were just little. And from that day on, Daddy said, 'There's never going to be another bottle of alcohol that comes in here.' It seems to me it was Aunt Eudora and Lloyd Brown that came to the house. They lived in Superior, you know. And it seems to me that it was them that came that day."

The disease of alcoholism was not something Fred inherited from his own father, but other ruinous things got passed along to him. From a Drouillard family history that Aunt Gloria had placed out on her kitchen table one day when I was visiting her, she read aloud the biography of John Drouillard, Fred's father, who was the lighthouse keeper in Bayfield, Wisconsin, for a time. He was first married to a woman in Bayfield named Mary, and they had two children. John then left his family in Bayfield to work on the North Shore, where he met and "married" Elizabeth Anakwad, a woman fifteen years his junior.[2]

According to the family archives, John was a teetotaler: "Never used tobaccos nor tasted intoxicating liquors . . . and he once saved a deer from three large timber wolves." I don't know if Great-grandma

Elizabeth knew about John's other family, or if his white wife, Mary, knew about his family here on the North Shore. Mary's fate is unknown, but we do know some things about Great-grandfather John. He died in 1928 before Aunt Gloria was born, so she never knew him, but she did remember some stories about his life. I asked her if she knew how he died, and she said, "Well, I understand that he killed himself. In fact, the way my dad told it, is—his dad told him to go get his straight razor to shave himself and he cut his own throat. And I guess he lived for three days after that. And Daddy always said, 'And I'm the one that brought the straight razor to him.' I don't know why he did that. Because gee—he was quite old. Those papers there say he was an octogenarian, which means he was over eighty years old. Daddy said he cut his own throat. Maybe he had cancer or something. Because he never drank. I don't remember Grandma Drouillard drinking either."

Great-grandpa John's death certificate says only that he died of "old age." This is not to say that he didn't cut his own throat, but there is some question as to whether Fred was making up a story, or if John Drouillard actually did ask his youngest son to bring him a razor and used it to commit suicide. If the story is true, what a terrible burden to place on your son. I would think witnessing his own father's bloody death, and thinking he helped him do it, would have orchestrated a whole chorus of screams in his mind. It should be noted that Grandpa Fred, as a larger-than-life part of our family, was sometimes known to be an unreliable narrator of history, especially when he was drinking, which sometimes placed his word in doubt and, more often, had his whole family walking on eggshells.

And eggshells, the real ones, were what Grandma Lola was cracking by the hundreds, at one of her many kitchen jobs in downtown Grand Marais. Aunt Gloria confirmed that "Mother cooked in every restaurant in town. Daddy, he raised us when we were younger, by guiding and trapping and hunting. And then he started working for Nunstedts up at Chik-Wauk Lodge and he wanted Mom to come with him. So, they boarded us out. Usually, I stayed with Lucy Caribou and sometimes with Helen Dahl, Uncle Willie's daughter."[3]

****

Grandpa was always very jealous about Grandma, and Aunt Gloria's theory is that he wanted Lola to be with him at Chik-Wauk because he didn't trust being away from her. And of course, she was a very good and efficient cook whose skills were also needed at the busy resort. But when they made the shift to summer work on the Gunflint Trail, they made the decision that their very young kids would have to spend summers with extended family or neighbors close by. This was a mixed blessing for the kids, because they would be away from Fred's unpredictable behavior, but were essentially being shipped out to live in other people's homes, one or two at a time, something that could be risky for them, depending on where they ended up and who they ended up with. Grandma Lola's sister Ida would often host them, and sometimes the kids would get farmed out to different places.

Aunt Gloria was seven when she and her sister Doreen were sent to live at Lucy Caribou's house, just a little way through the woods from the Drouillard house. For Gloria, spending those very formative summers at Lucy's house taught her a lot about women's self-sufficiency and the Anishinaabe way of being in the world. She remembered the intimate details of life at Lucy's: "Lucy hooked rugs—that's how she made a living. She hooked rugs and hand braided rugs. She went and got maple syrup all the time and maple sugar candy. And her rugs were just absolutely gorgeous. Her whole kitchen was filled with boxes of rags, and she had a great big loom on the table all the time, spread out when she was hooking rugs. And she didn't have any running water or anything. But Lucy had a nice, clean, little house. And we stayed there a lot when Mom and Dad would go up the trail. She used to take in boarders, and she fed them and took care of them."

Occasionally Lucy's sister Philomene Evans would come to visit for long periods of time. My dad spent whole summers with Philomene at her house in Grand Portage when he was just eight years old, which was a very formative time in his life. Philomene also left quite an impression on little Gloria. "Philomene had a dog named Katagon," she said. "If I ever had a dog, I'd name it Katagon. It was a great big dog. You couldn't get near it. We had to throw the food at it. She'd say, 'Just throw it. Don't get near him, he'll bite you.' I guess Katagon killed wolves and everything."

This story about Philomene's dog was the reason my partner and I named our own little dog with a black spot Katagon. *Katagon* in Ojibwe is rooted in *katagoonce*, which means "he (or she) is spotted," like a little deer. Sadly, our little Katagon didn't prevail over the wolves like big Katagon did. I worry that it was my fault for naming him Katagon in the first place.

Aunt Gloria continued by saying, "I suppose Lucy was a 'citian' Indian. Philomene, she lived up in the bush all by herself, and there wasn't anyone around her. She roughed it. Anyway, Lucy scrubbed all her clothes in tubs on the back porch. And she had a daughter named Marjorie. We all really liked Lucy."

When I interviewed Aunt Gloria about her childhood, and specifically Chippewa City, she talked about our family being part of a larger community of people who were mostly separate from the non-Native families who lived in Grand Marais. Their house was a stopping-off place for friends and relatives from Chippewa City, and a lot of what she shared with me became part of *Walking the Old Road*. That Old Road was a main thoroughfare for a lot of years. Gloria said, "I remember, of course, everybody walked back in those days. Georgie would stop in and have a cup of coffee if he needed a rest. He'd visit with Mom or Dad. Us kids would visit with the people who stopped by, talk to them." She was referring, of course, to George Morrison, perhaps the most famous modern artist from the state of Minnesota and her friend Leona's older brother. That's how it was back then. She remembers people playing music on the road, including her cousin George Drouillard, Uncle Willie's son. She said, "He could play a Jew's harp—he used to come walking up the Old Road playing a Jew's harp and he'd sit on the porch and visit with us."

The Old Road went both ways, of course, and Aunt Gloria spent a lot of time on it, either by herself or with her mom. "I visited the Morrison family," she recalled. "Joe Morrison and Jim Morrison lived together at the time. Jim had a daughter named Leona, and she was my best friend. So, I'd go to Chippewa City to visit Leona. Or we'd walk out to Aunt Alice [LaPlante]'s—she lived a little further, you know . . . Loretta LaPlante and I were friends." She continued, "Another thing I remember about Chippewa City is that down there, on the north side of the road, it was just covered with sunflowers. And I used to walk down there and get a big bouquet of sunflowers. There were always so many wildflowers over there."

****

A more frequent visitor to their house was Great-uncle Charlie Drouillard, Grandpa Fred's brother. He had his own little house close to where they lived, on what is now County Road 7. He worked a lot of odd jobs and knew how to fry homemade doughnuts in bear grease. Aunt Gloria said that "Uncle Charlie was our favorite uncle. I visited him once when he was in the nursing home. He was the first one to go into the nursing home—he'd had a stroke and he was in there a long time. Daddy would go visit him and talk Chippewa all the time. He was comical and he could jig like you couldn't believe. And he would get drunk and jig for us. He really liked my mother [whom he called "sister Lola"]. He used to get sent away to the work farm all the time, 'cause of fines and getting in trouble. And one time he broke into the old Northern Lights [bar]. He was just going to get a drink, but he stayed in there all night and got drunk, and when they opened up in the morning, there was Uncle Charlie sitting at the bar. And he got sent away to the work farm. But he'd come home and we'd say to him, 'Where have you been, Uncle Charlie?' And he told us he was at 'agricultural school.' Because he was in charge of the potatoes on the work farm. You know, they had to grow all their own stuff. He called it 'agricultural school.' It was in Duluth. I wonder sometimes if he didn't do it on purpose so he'd have a place to live in the winter."

Charlie never got married or had a family of his own, so knowing that his nieces and nephews were fond of him, in spite of his relatively harmless transgressions, says a lot about him and about the Drouillard family, in general. Life was difficult, and it seems like forgiveness and understanding were easily won, especially if you were a good dancer.

Before the modern incarnation of Grand Marais, a functioning town with sewer and water services, city utilities, and exactly one streetlight, the kids who lived here and at Chippewa City enjoyed a nearly endless range of woods and lakeshore for playing. I try to imagine what that was like before the paved highway came through and the woods crept right up to the lake shore in most places. This brand of north woods–style freedom was one of the bright and shining memories from Aunt Gloria's childhood. Learning how to be at home in the woods has always been one of the best things about growing up on the North Shore. The Drouillards and Anakwads are of this place, and having a homeland where the bones of our ancestors are buried is one of the only things that provided ballast for a lot of our relatives, who struggled financially, experienced great loss, and were in many ways marginalized by history.

****

Being in the woods or working outside in the garden have always been Aunt Gloria's favorite things. And now, when you visit her in the Care Center, the first thing she will do is ask you to take her outside or take her for a drive along the lake. And sometimes she begs, as if fresh air is the only thing in the world that will be able to save her. Even if there's a brisk wind, she prefers to be out in it instead of being inside. And so, when she was telling me about the places she used to play, she told me about their expansive childhood territory, including one spot on the shoreline not far from where Great-grandma Anakwad used to live. As kids, Gloria said, they gravitated to this place, but were told specifically not to play there: "All the little trails that used to be down there—where the sewer plant is—there were all these neat little trails and big jack pine trees. And Mother used to tell us, 'Don't play down there—that's where the Little People live . . . Now don't you go down there, I mean it,' she said. 'That's where the Little People are. There are other places to play.'"

This is just one of the stories that Auntie told me that might make some people roll their eyes and dismiss her tale as mystical hogwash. And that's fine. But according to the old stories, the *bukwadji* or *bagwajininiwag* (the Little People) appear in person and in stories all across Anishinaabe country. These beings are known to be diminutive, "knee-high or even smaller." Their name literally means "person of the wilderness," and they are the spirits of the forests that we live in. Sometimes known as *pukwudgies*, the Little People have magical powers, such as, "the ability to turn invisible, confuse people or make them forget things, shape-shift into cougars or other dangerous animals, or bring harm to people by staring at them."[4]

Wistfully Aunt Gloria added, "It was really neat down there. The ground was really soft and nice and stuff. We did go down there and once in a while you got kind of a funny feeling—kind of scared. We never went down there at night. But on a nice, sunny day, you know, it was nice down there."

So, sometimes the spirits of the forest are benign, and sometimes they are malevolent, depending on the circumstances. This is something Grandma Lola and her kids knew very well. Grandma Lola was not Anishinaabe, but she was married to an Anishinaabe man, and so she learned to speak conversational Ojibwemowin and heard and experienced cultural stories and life events that other white women didn't. It was part of marrying in. As Aunt Gloria says, "I remember Daddy knew the medicine man up in Grand Portage. Daddy called him 'Stump.' When he first started going with Mother, she didn't believe in the medicine man. So, he took her to Grand Portage and Stump had this wigwam and he literally made the wigwam dance. And after that mother believed in him."

Aunt Gloria grew up seeing the land in a different way than kids from other families did. She said that "Chippewa City was all part of the Grand Portage reservation. The little town of Grand Marais was 'Indian.' And when the white man came, they kind of moved the Indians and that's where Chippewa City is. There's a lot of Indian burial grounds all over in town."

* * * * * * *

The Drouillards had relatives living all over the place, including Fred's mother, Elizabeth Anakwad Drouillard, and a number of his sisters, who owned a cluster of homes on the east side of Grand Marais, not far from the east bay. Aunt Gloria said, "My aunt Carrie Paro lived in town about a mile away from Aunt Alice's. We used to visit Aunt Carrie all the time. She had such beautiful daughters. Carrie and her husband, Frank—they're my godparents. I remember Aunt Carrie always being in the same house. And that's right over there where the Aspen Lodge is now."

I asked her what she remembered about Great-grandma Elizabeth, Chi'zubet (Big Elizabeth), who lived in that same cluster of houses where the Aspen Lodge and credit union are now, on the south side of Highway 61. She described her grandma as looking "really Indian" and said that "Grandma Drouillard's house was real small. And Grandma was crippled. I don't know how she got crippled, but she had a cane and we'd go down there and scrub for Grandma and she'd sit in a chair in the middle of room and scrub the floor close to her chair. She had, like, a kitchen and little teeny living room and then her bedroom. I remember it was really clean and neat and she had a bunch of neat stuff. Grandma had lace curtains—and that's what caught on fire. Grandma, she was stern, she was really stern. I was a little bit afraid of her."

When her lace curtains caught on fire, there was no one there that day to extinguish the flames. Aunt Gloria continued with her story: "I remember when Grandma died. The wake was at Aunt Josephine [Zimmerman]'s house. I think I might have been seven or eight [she was eight]. I remember being at home that day. And I remember seeing Daddy run downtown—when he heard the fire whistle. I remember when he ran. He was playing with my brother Bruce on the porch, and Bruce was so cute, he couldn't leave Bruce."

This was the third fire that Great-grandma Anakwad experienced in her life, something that apparently made her youngest son, Fred, very nervous. As Aunt Gloria tells it, "And otherwise, every other time the fire whistle rang, Daddy would always run down to his mother's house, just in case there was a fire. And that was the only day he didn't run down there—the day her house burned down. Aunt Carrie had pulled her out and Aunt Carrie was burned, too. And Grandma died—I think three days later she died."

And then she said, "I think he always kind of blamed Bruce. That was the third house she lost to a fire. And every time, he'd run down there except that time. Bruce was the baby [he was four], Pooty was five or six. Grandma is buried in Chippewa City and her funeral was at the church. I only remember going to the wake at Aunt Josephine's. I remember coming in the front door and she was right there. The casket was right there."

Of course, Grandma Lola cooked a feast to feed everyone who attended the wake and the funeral. She did this for a number of other Chippewa City relatives and friends too. Aunt Gloria confirmed that "whenever there was a wake for any Indian that Dad knew, Mother would cook just everything. All the Indians really liked Ma. And Mother could talk Indian pretty good. Some of it she really could understand good."

And then she told me about when Great-uncle Charlie died, the man who used to get shipped off to "agricultural school" in Duluth. She said, "Back then caskets weren't wood—they were made of this thick gray felt—I remember when Uncle Charlie died, I went to the Chippewa City cemetery. They lowered the casket down and everyone would throw a handful of dirt on there. And when they threw the first shovel of dirt on there, the casket broke. Daddy said, 'Oh well, that's all right.'"

She turned to me and said, "Sad, ain't it? They were all just that cheap felt with white inside."

****

As Aunt Gloria got older, she was expected to take on more duties at home. Aunt Diane, the youngest of her siblings, was born in 1939. That was right around the time Grandpa and Grandma left most of the kids in town all summer to go work at Chik-Wauk. During the fall and winters, when their parents returned to Grand Marais, the kids had to go to school and were also expected to contribute to the household. The boys would work washing dishes in the restaurants downtown where Grandma cooked, and the girls stayed at the house, helping to take care of the family. As a product of the ubiquitous and far-reaching morbidity of motherhood tradition, the oldest girls were expected to take care of the younger kids, plus do a lot of the cooking and cleaning and other indoor work. This left very little time for them to be kids, especially when they got a bit older. As Aunt Gloria said, "We were at home so much. We just didn't have the kind of social life we have nowadays. We were in bed at eight o'clock and we worked after school."

I asked her what school was like for her in Grand Marais and she said, "I quit in eleventh grade. Mainly, I didn't want to quit school but I couldn't keep up on my studies because I had to help out at home and Daddy made us go to bed at eight o'clock every night. By the time I got done cooking, washing dishes, and having to go to bed at eight o'clock—I couldn't keep up. I remember that so well. I remember

Mother was working at Mable's, and I had to run downtown after school, find out what we needed from the store for supper, run to the store, run home, start the supper, cook it, wash the dishes, and then it was time to go to bed. And that's basically why I quit school."

With just one year left, she was forced to drop out at the age of seventeen. In 1950, Grandpa Fred brought a man home he called "McCloud," but his real name was McClure. Fred had met him downtown in one of the bars and they became drinking buddies. Thomas McClure was a serviceman housed at the Grand Marais Coast Guard station when it was still occupied by Coast Guard personnel. A man in a uniform, he made a big impression on Gloria, who was now eighteen years old. Thomas, whom everyone called "T.J.," was also impressed by Gloria.

There's a black-and-white picture on my parents' shelf that was taken in the woods, when my dad was about two years old. He's in the background, just next to Grandma Lola, who is wearing a summery skirt and sleeveless blouse. She is sitting on a bench next to four of her children (the youngest three hadn't been born yet). On the opposite end of the bench, there is Uncle Monty, who looks to be about seven. Next to him is Aunt Doreen, who is peering at the camera with impatience. Her little hands are clenched and she has a fierce expression on her face. Right next to her is Aunt Gloria, who was about four at the time. She is in a simple little dress, and her face and hands are softly poised and feminine looking—the opposite of her sister Doreen. Auntie Gloria has always been pretty, with strong, high cheekbones and thick straight hair that is always smoothly in place. When she was young her hair was really dark, and even now at almost eighty-nine, it's not completely gray. She likes to wear pretty headbands or pull her hair back from her face with little clips. She has blue eyes that smile in tandem with her mouth and is blessed with exceedingly long eyelashes—a feature she has passed along to all of her kids. So, when Grandpa brought T. J. McClure home that day, I'm one hundred percent certain Gloria was beautiful and unforgettable.

Aunt Gloria's eldest daughter, Cathy Firth, Cathy's grandson Cameron McClure, and I met in February 2021 to talk about her mom's life. She shared what she knew about the early days of Gloria and T. J.'s relationship and helped to fill in some of the details about her dad's life. Thomas "T. J." McClure was born in Roosevelt, Oklahoma, in 1929, but his home was in Stockton, California. When they met, T. J. was about to go back to California, where his parents lived, because he had aspirations of joining the air force. According to Cathy, "Grandpa Drouillard got mad after they started dating because he felt he wasn't good enough for her."

T. J. made it clear that his intention was to marry Gloria, and so Fred and Lola tried to intervene by forcing her to go to Chik-Wauk for the summer to help her mother in the kitchen. Cathy said, "She had a nervous breakdown while she was there, and she remembers riding down the Gunflint Trail in the back of an empty pickup truck."

The trail was a dirt road back then, which meant her ride was rough and dusty. When she got back to Grand Marais, she stayed with her aunt Ida Kimball for a little while. Aunt Ida is Lola's sister, and she used to live right next to the cabin where Aunt Doreen was born, a stone's throw from the Grand Marais harbor. Not long after she got there, she was able to reach T. J. and he promptly sent her a ticket to California. She got on the bus at the old Jackson's Café in downtown Grand Marais and didn't get off until it reached Stockton. As Cathy explains, "Three days later they were married in Las Vegas. He paid another couple who was getting married to act as witnesses, and on their wedding night, T. J. and the other couple got drunk and Mom was sober, sitting all by herself with the three of them passed out in the car."

I wish I could talk to Aunt Gloria about that day and tell her how similar her and Aunt Lila's wedding nights were, with both of them ending up newly married to men they didn't know very well, being left basically alone and stone-cold sober while everyone else around them was passed out, drunk. Poor aunties.

Aunt Gloria lived with T. J.'s parents in Stockton because he was called up to fight in the Korean War. Gloria worked at a drugstore while her husband was gone, and she once told her daughter Cathy that "Granny McClure was the oldest woman I ever knew." This assessment is likely related to the fact that this antiquated woman, her mother-in-law, took issue with Gloria's 1950s-style brassiere, and she "made her bind her breasts" by wrapping her torso with a tight cloth. This was fully thirty years after corsets disappeared from the dressing rituals of American women. For more perspective, Granny McClure imposed her own medieval views on women's bodies and sexuality on her eighteen-year-old daughter-in-law's body in 1951, which was just two years before Betty Grable, Lauren Bacall, and Marilyn Monroe starred together in How to Marry a Millionaire. Thankfully, T. J. did join the air force and Aunt Gloria was able to get away from her mother-in-law, who had some strangely severe ideas about modern womanhood.

T. J. was first stationed in Big Spring, Texas. Aunt Gloria told Cathy that they had a good time there, and all was well. And then with laughter, Cathy shared that "they liked to set anthills on fire just for fun. They were broke, you know—and T. J. would yell 'This means war!' and then light the gas on fire." After that, T. J. was relocated to Wright Field (which is now Wright-Patterson Air Force Base) in Dayton, Ohio, which is where Cathy Ann was born. Cathy was her mother's confidante throughout her life and has clear memories of her childhood and the things her mother told her about their lives together. Wright Field in Dayton was home to the infamous "Project Blue Book," a government investigation into UFOs that took place from 1951 to 1969.[5] The story is that after the rumored crash of an alien spacecraft in 1947 in the desert around Roswell, New Mexico, the broken craft and the bodies of the aliens were secretly transported to Wright Field and stored in a place called Hangar 18. So, Cathy laughs about this as being the place where she was born, adding, "Mom always used to say to me, 'Your real parents are in Hangar 18.'"

The little family spent a bit of time in Minneapolis before T. J. was stationed in St. John's, Newfoundland, where they lived for three years. Aunt Gloria talked about their time in Newfoundland a lot. She's my only aunt, to the best of my knowledge, who ever lived outside the United States. Cathy said it was a very happy time, and she inherited a lot of photos that were taken during those three years. She says, "He was handsome and she was so pretty." They met friends there and lived in a house that was built up on stilts so that the cows could pass under it. It was on the Labrador Sea close to where the Titanic went down, and was similar to the North Shore, where Aunt Gloria was born, in that it was situated on the rugged shoreline of a big body of water. Cathy told a story about living in Newfoundland when she was little. She said she "was giggling, poking my little toy broomstick at a hole in the wall." When her mother came over to investigate, she discovered that "there was a rat inside the wall that would poke its head out and go back in when I stuck the broom in there."

They returned to the United States in 1957, and T. J. got a job working in Mountain Iron, Minnesota, where their second daughter, Bridgette, was born. Another beautiful child, with eyelashes a mile long just like her mother's. They were now a family of four. The decision was made to find housing for Gloria and the two kids in Duluth, because T. J. got his orders that he was to serve far away, across the ocean in England. And so, Aunt Gloria and her two little daughters were left alone in Duluth while he was away. When a woman married a military man in the 1950s, it was guaranteed that she would move around a lot. As a military wife, you were reliant on him sending money home so that you could pay the bills and keep your children fed. This arrangement worked out for a while, and the little family was able to stay afloat, but just barely. During this time, T. J. was sent home on furlough to Duluth and then . . . Aunt Gloria had another baby on the way.

After his break, he went back to England and the money he was sending home to Gloria just dried up. So, there she was with a five-year-old, a three-year-old, and another baby on the way, with no means to make a living and no one there to help her. It makes me feel blue, thinking of how desperate she must have felt. And hurt and angry, too, because Aunt Gloria discovered that the reason T. J. stopped sending money home was because he had taken up with another woman in England. Someone Aunt Gloria succinctly referred to as "the red-headed woman." Left with no other choice, Gloria had to call her husband's commander and report that T. J. was an adulterer who was shirking his financial duties and that his family was suffering. As Cathy says, "They were destitute."

Cathy was attending kindergarten at Jefferson in Duluth and they lived on Ninth and First Street East when Aunt Gloria's water broke. She remembers the three of them, Gloria, herself, and Bridgette, walking hand in hand, the few blocks to St. Luke's Hospital so that her mother could get medical help. She shared that "Social Services took Bridgette and me until Mom came home from the hospital."

When Thomasena was born my parents, Joyce and Francis, were living in Grand Marais and he was working as a truck driver, making trips up and down the North Shore. On the day they were discharged he picked up his sister Gloria along with her new baby girl and drove them home, making sure they had groceries and some things she would need for her baby. He tells the story that "we were in the elevator at St. Luke's, and Gloria had Tommy all wrapped up in a little blanket and some people in there said to me, 'What a beautiful baby,' and I said, 'Thanks, but she's not mine.'" Everyone always laughs at this, because, of course, she wasn't his. Named for her father, Thomasena joined her two sisters and her mother to make a family of five, minus T. J. McClure, who missed the day she was born but wasn't finished taking advantage of his wife's good graces.

This is the time period when a number of the Drouillard relatives lived in Duluth. Grandma and Grandpa were in the restaurant business at the Grand Café. Aunt Doreen and her four kids had also moved to Duluth, after Doreen left her first husband, Ralph Freeman, in Minneapolis. The two sisters shared a duplex on Central Avenue in West Duluth, and Grandma and Grandpa lived down the street from them. They shared this joint living arrangement for three years, from about 1960 to 1963. Cathy was in first grade and remembers that right after they moved in, she and Pougie, Doreen's eldest daughter, were sent to stay with my parents, who were living in Grand Rapids. This was just one of many times that my cousins from Duluth would be sent to stay with their Aunt Joyce and Uncle Poot.

When Cathy, Cameron, and I sat down recently to discuss her mom's life and our shared history, she talked very frankly about how hard things were for their family at that time. She was just a little girl, but she "felt like I was expected to be like an adult when I was seven." There were a number of destructive influences at work within the family in the years when Doreen and Gloria lived in the duplex together, and Cathy and Pougie ended up babysitting their little sisters and brothers at a very early age. Cathy said, "I was made to be responsible for my sisters and I had to watch them, alone, when I was seven years old." Because of this dynamic, Cathy felt more like she was her mother's friend than her daughter. She sees that there was some good in this, saying that, because her mother treated her as a friend, "She told me a lot—I was the one she talked to as a friend, and it was like that for many years." Cathy admits that because she had to help raise her sisters, "it affected how I raised my own kid and grandkids. I feel fortunate to have gone through that—it shaped my life."

* * * * * * *

Listening to Cathy explain what this was like for her and recognizing that she was one of many women in my extended family who were forced to learn to become mothers long before their bodies and minds were ready to have their own children, I've concluded that it's a common pattern in some families and should be recognized with a name. And so, I'd like to call this exclusively female phenomenon **moth·er·sis·ter·ing.** *Verb:* 1. Acting as surrogate mother to one's younger siblings. 2. Acting as surrogate mother to one's own mother. *Also:* **sis·ter·moth·er·ing;** the act of two sisters mothering each other. *Use:* "The oldest sister of six children, Cathy Ann stepped in to mothersister her younger sisters." *Also:* "Her teen years were spent mothersistering her younger siblings while her parents were away at work, forcing Gloria to forgo her own education to make sure her family was cared for."

As the eldest Burge daughter, Auntie Faye was an expert at mothersistering. On the Drouillard side, Aunt Doreen and Aunt Gloria were too. As young girls they were all expected to sacrifice their own childhood needs and teenage years of exploration to the care of their little brothers and sisters, because their own mothers were absent in some way. The pattern of mothersistering would continue in the families of almost all of my aunties—particularly the ones who had a lot of kids and not a lot of resources to care for them. As Cathy aptly puts it, "big, poor families."

While living on Central in West Duluth, a lot of times Cathy would be the only one at home with her little sisters when her mother was gone. She said she once went out looking for her, and "I remember walking down to the Kom-On-Inn and finding Mom and Doreen sitting on their bar stools with rollers in their hair." Knowing and loving them both, it's mighty easy to picture the two sisters side by side, talking intimately with drinks in hand, while smoke from their cigarettes hangs lazily in the air. For them, it was a show of caring sisterhood, which should never be confused with mothersisterhood, because that's another thing entirely.

****

Enter T. J. McClure, who was back in the United States after being served a general discharge from the air force. He must have said some interesting things to Aunt Gloria to convince her to take him back, but the facade didn't last very long. He was working at Gamble's hardware store in Duluth, and one night the manager drove by and saw the lights on in the store even though they were closed for the day. The manager went inside, and he interrupted "McCloud" and a young woman, in a state of, well . . . you know. After that, he wasn't welcome back in Gloria's house. She was now truly alone, with three kids, going on four.

The two sisters moved out of the duplex they had shared for a time and into different apartments in what Sue, Doreen's daughter, calls "the projects," where a lot of single women with kids lived in Duluth. Cathy remembers this as a relatively fine and secure time for their family—which, it turns out, would definitely be the calm before the storm. Away from neighborhood bars, and with a growing support network of friends who lived in the apartment complex, things stabilized for them. By then, their family had grown to four daughters, plus Gloria. And things were relatively good for a while. But then, in Cathy's words, "One day Mother brought this guy home. He had a grocery bag full of popped popcorn and we thought that was the greatest thing we ever saw."

His name was Robert, but everyone called him "Bronco." He wasn't a tall man, and he wore his hair in a crew cut and had a full-time job at the Duluth Steel Plant. He was divorced, so as Cathy joked, "he was quite a catch," being legitimately single and with a job. Cathy remembers that he was nice to them at first, but then alcohol was brought into the mix, and everything shifted. Gloria and Bronco dated casually at first, but casual turned to serious, and the couple got married in April 1966. When they got married, Aunt Gloria was trying to pay off a debt she owed to the Cash and Carry, a convenience store around the corner from their apartment. Cathy said, "One night Bronco came home with a shoebox full of receipts, and all of them had my little, seven-year-old signature on them." This was the result of Cathy being placed into the role of sistermother to her little siblings. She was doing the only thing she knew how to do, in order to make sure they had food in the cupboards on the days she was left in charge of her sisters. That's a lot to expect of a seven-year-old. In an outburst, "Bronco threw the box at Mom, and shouted, 'What are you doing to your kids?!'" He ended up paying off the debt, which appeased the store owners, but it meant that Aunt Gloria was now indebted to him. So, it was just a deferral, in a sense, and it was something she would pay mightily for, and with significant penalties.

While Gloria was with Bronco, they had a baby girl, and now they were a family of five girls plus the two adults. They named her Roberta, but most everyone called her "Bobbi." Up until this point in Aunt Gloria's life, she had had to struggle through and overcome difficult times, and she somehow managed to keep things together. When Cathy got to this next part of her mom's story, I listened carefully and took many pages of notes about what happened in their house after Bronco stopped being nice. Cathy bravely recounted what she and everyone in their family experienced when the storm hit. And that storm hit hard and it hit often. After reading through what she said, I cried a lot, thinking about how much pain my auntie has suffered and how much I didn't really know about her. I took all my handwritten notes and burned them in the woodstove—sending them up the chimney as prayerful wishes for healing. My intention in writing about all of my aunties is to help ease the pain of the past, not bring new pain into the world. But because it's an important part of Aunt Gloria's life, I'm going to try to sum up what happened as carefully as I can. I do this to acknowledge the deep impact domestic violence has on families, and out of love for my auntie and all my cousins who had to live through it.

When Bronco stopped being nice, he hurt Gloria physically, and in permanently damaging ways that sent her to the hospital. He put her children (and his) in peril, and he left behind the ugly marks of brutality on my beautiful aunt Gloria's body and mind, including one occasion when he hit her so hard he broke her jaw. And she tried to get away. The first time she left him, he had gone to work at the steel plant, where his shift was scheduled from 11 p.m. to 7 a.m. Cathy remembers that night clearly: "As soon as he was gone, Aunt Diane and Jim [Gloria's youngest sister and her husband] drove a U-Haul around the corner and we moved everything into the moving truck. He came home the next morning to an empty house."

Aunt Gloria didn't tell any of her kids about the planned, middle-of-the-night escape, only her sister Diane. She was free of him for a while after that. Cathy was finishing seventh grade at Hoffman High, and she said that things were relatively calm for the family. They got their first dog, a Basenji named Barnabas, who was named after a lovelorn vampire on the TV show *Dark Shadows*. She says, "We watched that all the time. Mom used to love it." And then one day she came home from school and Bronco was sitting at their kitchen table, almost like he had never left. The welfare office in Duluth had given him the address where they were living and according to Cathy, "He wooed [Mother], and tried to get her back."

If you think of family history as a 33 ⅓ rpm LP vinyl record, this is where your favorite song on the album gets scratched, and the record begins to skip, over and over, until someone intervenes to make it stop. Gloria had watched her own mother get tossed around, tied up, and dumped into a closet by her father. Her feminine role model, Grandma Lola, was perpetually diminished by a man who said he loved her, but his actions were the opposite of love. Love, it seems, can be a hiding place for violence, like prettily colored buttercream roses on a cake that's full of razor blades. Learning about love, and how love can sometimes be bad for you, was not something Gloria was equipped to sort out at the time. In the Drouillard house when they were all growing up, they witnessed danger and domination inflicted under the guise of being in love. Gloria saw it happen to her mother, and now her kids were watching it happen to her. And whether our families are happy and healthy, or damaging and dysfunctional, one thing is for certain: the kids are always watching.

That fall, when Cathy was just starting eighth grade, she came home from school and her mom and all the other kids were next door, sitting on the neighbor's sunporch. Aunt Gloria was pregnant at the time, and the circumstances were explosive. As Cathy tells it, she asked her mother, "'Why are you out here?' And Mom said, 'The door is locked and he won't let us in.' So, there was a window on the front door and I busted the window open with my boot. I went upstairs into my room, picked up my typewriter and threw it at him at hard as I could. I yelled, 'Don't you ever touch my mother again!'" This is when sistermothering gets turned on end and children are made to feel that they are responsible for not only the protection and safety of their siblings but also the well-being of their own mother. A few months after the typewriter incident, Cathy said she came home from school and her mom was sitting at the kitchen table with a cup of coffee and a cigarette: "She had her sunglasses on, which she wore pretty often, because she would have bruises and black eyes." And here's where their situation reached a turning point, stemming from Cathy's nonchalant response to her mother's circumstances. She said, "I didn't say one word. And that was when Mom said to me, 'I need to make a plan— it's starting to affect you.' She was worried that I would lose my sympathy for her. I was starting to believe [the situation] was normal."

Whatever it was about that day gave Aunt Gloria the incentive to take the song off repeat. But it didn't happen immediately. One night Bronco got really violent and Cathy watched him shove her mother while she was holding her brother Matt, who was just a tiny baby. She grabbed her little brother out of Gloria's arms, went upstairs, and called their neighbor, a woman named Rivia Lutzka. And Rivia called the police to report that a crime was being committed downstairs and that children were in danger. It finally ended, and this time, it was Aunt Doreen and Uncle Al who helped Aunt Gloria and her kids move. "Bronco never came back after that," Cathy said.

* * * * * * *

In the summer of 1972, the older girls were pretty grown up, and Cathy, who was eighteen, was expecting a baby of her own. Grandpa Fred was very ill, and in keeping with the double standards that exist around the morbidity of motherhood, in which women are expected to have lots of kids, but only when the time is perfectly right, Gloria tried to keep Cathy's pregnancy hidden from the rest of the family. She was sent to Monticello, Minnesota, to live with Aunt Diane for a few weeks, and then, fully pregnant, was shipped off to Texas to serve as babysitter for a couple whom Aunt Gloria had met through the Baptist church. (Gloria attended the Baptist church for a number of years, but Cathy was a confirmed Catholic and has stayed a practicing Catholic her whole life, saying, "The Catholic Church is my refuge.")

When I interviewed Aunt Gloria back in 2001, she confirmed that Grandpa Fred was also a devout Catholic who always kept his Bible next to his bed. The family did go to the Catholic church in Grand Marais (the current location of the Grand Marais Art Colony) regularly when they were kids. Gloria said, "It got pounded into us. Mother taught Sunday school at the Congregational church for seven years. And then—a couple years before Dad died, he made mother turn Catholic. So, she went and took lessons and turned Catholic and they were remarried at the Good Shepherd Church in Duluth. So, Daddy really was religious in many, many ways, and he read his Bible every night. I've got his Bible here. It was on his bedstand there, all the time."

True to form, Fred used religion as another way to diminish Lola, who preferred the kinder, gentler doctrine of the Congregational Church. According to Aunt Gloria, "He always said mother was 'a heathen.' So, she converted for him. And one time, you know in the Catholic church bulletin, they named the members and how much they gave, and that just turned my mother off. You know, to print how much you gave to the church."

Grandpa died in October 1972, and Cathy remembers mother-sistering all of the younger ones so that her mother could attend his funeral at St. John's Catholic Church in Grand Marais. After her dad died, Gloria's life, as well as Grandma Lola's, settled down a lot. Around 1974, Gloria got a full-time job cooking at the Lakeshore Lutheran Home, which is also where her daughter Cathy was working. Cathy lived at home with her little son Jason, and sometimes Grandma Lola lived with them too, one big family of mothersisters and sistermothers.

****

Sometime in 1975 Grandma Lola got sick and was diagnosed with metastatic cancer of the pancreas. She lived at Aunt Doreen's in Eveleth for a while, until things got really bad, and then she was admitted to the hospital in Grand Marais. In 1976, the year before Grandma died, Aunt Gloria and Aunt Diane drove home to visit her. Gloria did not have her license, so Diane was the driver. They stopped at the Green Door in Beaver Bay, an infamous halfway point, which seems rather ridiculous now, but that's what a lot of people did back then, stop for a beer midway between Duluth and Grand Marais. While they were at the bar, a man asked Gloria if he could buy her a drink and she said yes. And then he asked her if she wanted to dance, and she said yes. While they were dancing, he said, "You don't remember me, do you?"

She said no, and he reminded her, "I'm Jim—I'm the manager who caught that cheater T. J. McClure at Gamble's that day."

The man at the Green Door was Jim "Bugsy" Martineau, the same man who caught Gloria's first husband having an affair at the hardware store in Duluth. This fateful meeting would lead to her third marriage. Incidentally, my cousin Cathy said that "she never paid for her own divorces. The next husband always had to do that." And that's what Jim did. He now worked at Reserve Mining in Silver Bay and would commute to work from Duluth, where they lived. Aunt Gloria later confessed to Cathy that Jim Martineau was the only man she was ever in love with. Which is both happy and sad, because Jim also had a lot of troubles, including the kind with alcohol. But he loved Gloria and that was the incentive he needed to try to get better. So, he checked into inpatient treatment at Miller Dwan. Cathy shared that the family would go to visit him for "family nights" and that Aunt Gloria went through the AA program for codependency to be supportive of her new husband. She quit drinking, and aside from one or two isolated episodes, she never drank alcohol after going through the program.

When he got out of treatment all six kids still lived at home. Cathy was grown, of course, and lived there for financial reasons. She was a single mother, and she worked and helped her mother out financially. In turn, her mother would babysit her son Jason when Cathy was at work. When Jim came home after being in the hospital, Aunt Gloria asked Cathy to move out, "for the sake of her marriage" with Jim. So, she and Jason moved out, even though it would be financially hard to manage living on her own. Jim fell off the wagon, and Gloria kicked him out. And then she asked Cathy to move back in again, which she did. And then Jim made another effort to get clean, and he moved back into their house on London Road, struggling all the while to stay off alcohol. It was at this point in their marriage that they made the decision to leave Duluth completely and move to Grand Marais, in an effort to make a truly clean start.

****

In October 1979, Gloria, Jim, and the two youngest, Roberta and Matt, all moved into a house in downtown Grand Marais, just steps away from Aunt Ida's house, the place where Aunt Gloria had stayed before getting on a bus to Stockton, California, to be with Tommy McClure, her first husband. She had come full circle. They first lived in the old Sobanja family house across from the Harbor, which Aunt Gloria told me was haunted. She said she was upstairs in her bedroom one day, and she lay down for a minute to take a nap. She felt someone sit down on the bed near her feet and she thought it was Bobbi. She said something to her daughter, but no one answered her, because there was no one there. That was just one of the interesting things that happened in that old place.

After leaving the haunted house, they moved to a place in Creech-ville on the north side of town. I remember visiting them there when I was in high school. My cousin Roberta always had beautiful clothes and a very chic haircut. We were all into the Esprit line of clothes, and no one wore it better than Roberta. Roberta went into the military when she was a junior in high school and she did very well in the service. She is now married with kids and grandkids of her own. In every house she has ever lived in, Aunt Gloria always had Bobbi's official portrait prominently on display. Her daughter in uniform— she has always been so proud of Roberta's accomplishments. Bobbi's younger brother, Matt, has always been handsome, quiet, and kind, and he's still that way today. The only boy of six kids, he took really good care of Aunt Gloria when she was living in her house on First. He would do repairs, make sure her mower was always in good working order, take her to the store, and do other things for her. She's always loved him a lot—her only son.

It was the 1980s and as it goes with the mining industry, Jim Martineau got laid off from Reserve Mining in Silver Bay after which he went to work construction in Beulah, North Dakota. It was when he came home from Beulah that he told Gloria he was leaving their marriage, which came as a shock. As Cathy tells it, "He walked down that dirt road carrying his suitcase and she was running behind him crying. He was the one man she was really in love with."

Aunt Gloria was so sad after that—losing the only man she ever loved was a massive blow to the heart. A year or so after he left, Jim died of his own massive heart attack, which happened on the dock in Silver Bay. He was with his current girlfriend, who had bought a fancy speedboat with money she acquired through a bizarre medical settlement. Apparently, she had undergone some kind of surgery, and the doctors accidentally left a sponge inside her. This strange fact never failed to make Aunt Gloria's hackles go up. "They left a sponge in her!" she would exclaim every time she rehashed the story of Jim's death. When Jim died, Gloria's girls took her to his funeral. Even though they had been separated for a few years, he was still technically her husband, so they all went together. Cathy remembers that they sat in the very back of the church and during the service Aunt Gloria whispered to her, "That son of a bitch. Look at all these women crying for him."

* * * * * * *

In a show of ultimate fighter strength and grit, Aunt Gloria has now outlived all of her "stupid husbands." She liked to sum up her roller coaster of romances by proclaiming, "I married the same guy three times—he just had a different face."

Oh, Auntie Gloria, how did you survive it all and still have the ability to make us laugh?

Something she told me back in 2001 gives some insight into how she made it through, and it directly relates to the relationship she had with her own father and mother, and her generous and loving ability to show them grace, while recognizing that they were fallible human beings. She said, "I think growing up affected each of us. You know, we'll talk amongst ourselves. But I'm glad I was raised the way I was raised. I think everyone does the best they can at the time. I know that's true for my mom and dad. I think my dad did the best he could. What kind of life did he have? When you stop to think about it, *what kind of life did he have?* My parents went through a lot of hardships. Just like Daddy's knowledge of the woods and what he did to get by. Look at the hard life he had."

She continued to talk, revealing one of the deeply buried truths about her father, Fred, and acknowledging how hard life was for her mother, Lola: "I wish Daddy would have told us kids more. There's only sometimes, when he'd have some drinks or something, that he'd tell us some things. Mom said that Dad never wanted children and then she had seven. 'He never wanted kids,' she said. My mother went through hell too, because of my dad's drinking. She loved him. She had a lot of love to give. She sure did."

My auntie and her brothers and sisters often put Grandpa Fred on a pedestal, because they learned to value hard work and were taught to show respect for those who are no longer here to defend themselves. But shouldn't respect also be shown to the women and children in this world, or the world to come, who had traumas inflicted upon them? In writing about Grandpa and how his own trauma affected Grandma Lola's life and the lives of their kids, I respect and understand why a lot of people in our family have sidestepped the treacherous crevices that run through the glacial ice of our shared history—divisions and impasses that continue to threaten our family's health.

When glaciers melt, the rivers of water begin to flow underneath the thick ice, and these rivers get bigger and more powerful, as the ice of thirty thousand years begins to soften. The traumas that remain trapped and frozen inside will soon be dislodged and swept away by a twisting and turning stream that stays hidden from sight—a hydrological conduit with the power to carry our painful memories and moments of violence away, drop by drop. As the ice disintegrates underneath the surface, the power of the sun begins its divine work from above, and the glacial rivers move faster, until they are raging and free. This is where the healing starts. If our collective history is like an infinite river, telling the truths of our collective past has the power to send our shared traumas forever downstream.

I've come to believe that the process of telling the truth is as essential to our collective and long-term well-being as the warmth and light of the sun is to a field of sunflowers. *Giizhatay*—the sun is shining warmly. As the daylight tracks across the sky from east to west, every individual blossom follows it, turning their shaggy heads with devotion, like an audience follows the lead singer on stage. Sanctity of truth. Sanctity of love. Ideals that are held in high regard, but are often hard to uphold, especially when truth becomes trapped and frozen and love is used as a means of control, jealousy, and possession. As Aunt Gloria said so beautifully, Grandma Lola "had a lot of love to give." And is there any greater source of sunlight and warmth than love? The sanctity of love, in the truest form, is like the sun. After the glacier has disappeared, and the icy water has been transformed from liquid into air, the rivers of melt water leave behind serpentine eskers, like raised scars on the surface of the land. And these are the places where new roads are built.

* * * * * * *

When Gloria and Jim moved back to Grand Marais in 1979 to find a new path of their own, Gloria's eldest daughter, Cathy, was also breaking new ground. That same year she fell in love with and married her husband, Mike. She said, "Mom loved Mike—she knew that I liked him, which I did." Since then, their family has witnessed many, many hockey games, both lost and won. And now Cathy has four grandchildren of her own, Cameron, Cassie, Connor, and Cooper. They all miss their grandpa Mike, who passed away just a few days before Auntie Gloria was admitted to the Care Center. Cathy is a survivor, too, and I'm proud to know her and call her mindimooyenh— someone who has held a lot of things together and has a lot of love to give.

Almost everyone who ever visited Gloria at her house on First would likely agree that she was the happiest when she lived there. All her kids and grandkids were able to spend a lot of time with her at that house. Cathy's son, Jason, and his kids knew it well, and so did Melody and Macie, Melissa's two daughters. Bridgette would visit, and so would Tommy and her family, and Bobbi's family too. Matt and his daughter Kayla knew the inner workings of everything in her house, and almost every day for a number of years, Aunt Gloria would make lunch for Matt on his lunch break. I witnessed this ritual a number of times, and I was always very touched by it, her cooking for him, and his gracious acceptance of whatever it was she made for him that day. She now has twelve grandchildren plus thirteen great-grandchildren, and every single one of them has a place in her heart, and has graced the space on her wall or on her refrigerator.

Gloria's little house was a labor of love, and she fussed over it. Her daughter Thomasena initially helped her with the down payment so that she could buy it. It would be the first time she ever owned her own house and was able to pay it off. This was always a big source of pride for her, and she talked about that a lot. She always worked full-time, and sometimes more than full-time, to make sure everything was well cared for. She worked at Cobblestone and cooked at the hospital for a time. And she also cooked at the Senior Center for a little while, but the job that most people remember her for was as a checkout clerk at the Municipal Liquor Store. She didn't drink liquor herself, but that didn't matter to her at all. And if you had stopped in to buy beer and she liked you, she'd call you "Honey." Auntie worked at the liquor store until she was almost eighty, and if you are one of the people who reached "Honey" status, consider yourself lucky.

****

Aunt Gloria had to come back to her home on Lake Superior before she was finally able to settle down, which is something she and I have in common. One of the places where I lived after moving home was a little cabin that was never meant for the winter season. On those bitterly cold nights when the northwest wind pummeled down the hillside, the old gas furnace in the middle of the living room would make a small "whoosh" before the heat came on, and my two cats and I would sit in front of it on the floor, trying to stay warm. Our yearly family ritual was always to visit Aunt Gloria on Christmas Eve Day. Sometimes she would make a batch of homemade Tom and Jerry batter and we would have a drink in her kitchen, at the antique table in front of the window. She would spike ours with a dram of rum and then she would sit down and enjoy a "virgin" version without liquor. We would talk and eat cookies, and "ooh and aah" over her holiday decorations. She had a main tree in the living room, which was always impeccably decorated, and then little trees around the house, all with colored lights and sparkling tree ornaments. It was when she started losing track of her Christmas ornaments that we knew she was losing her memory.

The year that I was living in that cold cabin, I had stopped in to visit Aunt Gloria on Christmas Eve Day, just like we always did, and she had a big present all wrapped up for me. She wanted me to open it before I left, and inside was an electric blanket, soft blue and snuggly warm. I thanked her for it and then said, in a quintessentially Minnesota way, "You didn't have to do that, Auntie."

And she said, "Oh honey, I love you and I don't want you to be cold."

I hope Auntie Gloria is nice and warm today in her little room at the Care Center. It's not where she wants to live. She still wants to be back in her house on First, watching the winter birds land on the bird feeder in the front yard, the one my dad made for her using antlers from a moose he shot at Grand Portage on the Pigeon River. He would have shared some of the meat with her, too, because that's the way it's done. She might have fried some of it up for Matt's lunch or made a pot of stew with it. She was a good cook, just like her mother and sisters were, but her days of cooking for other people are over now.

Aunt Gloria has always enjoyed a treat. In fact, my dad's affectionate nickname for her was "Munchie," and so over the years I've often taken her something delicious to savor, because I know she appreciates homemade things. I once took her a perfectly baked chocolate croissant that was still warm from the oven. It was a beautiful, sunny summer morning and she was in her nightgown when I dropped in. I had perfect timing, because there was a pot of freshly brewed coffee in her Mr. Coffee machine. We sat at her table and ate our croissants and drank coffee together. She had a freshly cut white-and-purple bearded iris in a blue glass vase on her table, and I took a picture of it, and one of her, because both were so beautiful that day. After breakfast, and while still in her nightgown, she took me outside and gave me a tour of her gardens. It had been a slow spring, but the days had gotten warmer and now everything in her yard was green and frilly. In the backyard, she showed me a carefully planted and perfectly tended shade garden, with a variety of hostas and flowering perennials.

She took me to the bigger garden, which got partial sun, and there were purple catmint flowers blooming and a whole range of leafy and succulent greens, as expressive and artistic as an impressionist painting. She was particularly interested in telling me about the cedar tree behind her house. She had planted it as a small tree and mothered it along, making sure it got watered and that no other trees were allowed to compete with it. It was straight as a white pine and beautifully lush, and she had placed a birdbath underneath it, the lacy boughs reflecting on the smooth surface of the water. Over near her shed, she had planted a huge patch of rhubarb at the base of some old birch trees, and she situated the plant so that it got just the right about of sun to thrive but not too much, which would cause it to bolt prematurely. The rhubarb leaves were enormous, and she had put a little chair next to it so that she could go out and sit under the birch tree and bask in the glorious and peaceful beauty of the day. "Gloria Patri, et Filio, et Spiritui Sancto. Sicut erat in principio, et nunc, et semper, et in saecula saeculorum." To the Father and to the Son and to the Holy Spirit. And to the mother and the daughter and the auntie who is so named—Gloria.

Sunflowers and Sparrows: A Poem for Gloria

She brought home a whole armful of sunflowers,
that were growing in a ditch,
close to her friend Leona's house.
"Even birds can plant flowers," she said.
When the sparrows arrived,
kicking and scratching like chickens,
it was time to pick pussy willows—
the fuzzy advent of leaves,
and soon, marsh marigolds—
the harbingers of blackflies and summer.
Every year she did this,
or remembered that she used to,
whether she lived in the city, like a House Sparrow,
or in the woods, like a Song Sparrow.
Every year, until she didn't remember,
she brought home a whole armful of sunflowers.

Betty

WHEN I TOLD MY AUNT BETTY I would like to write a book about my aunties someday, she said, "Just don't use too big a words."

What Aunt Betty was lacking in big words, she made up for in her deep knowledge of people. When I interviewed her in 2016, the summer before she passed into the arms of her own Lord and Savior, she explained the inner workings of the Burge family to me in plain-spoken detail. I don't know if she was trying to help me find the right words, or if she was just completely confident that the truth would, indeed, set us free. So, when she was telling me her version of how they all grew up, she was really open about the emotionally fractured and at times highly dysfunctional relationships between her and her sisters—relationships that were planted on the Warba farm and blossomed later, as each of them raised their own families. And while her sisters may have struggled with false and untrustworthy narrators in their lives, Betty's true north compass was always set on the cold, hard facts, according to Betty.

Our Christmas auntie, Betty lived her life as a devout, Jesus-loving Christian. She never balked at bringing Jesus into almost any conversation. She followed TV evangelists but was also active in the local Congregational church. She went to the Congregational church on Sundays, but as an extended family we spent our Christmas Eves at Bethlehem Lutheran, where the candlelight services would begin at 5 p.m. Those nights were very dark, the sun setting around four o'clock in northern Minnesota. And often, December 24 would be the time of the first real, rip-roaring blizzard, when the northwest wind would hammer down on the Sawtooth Mountains at thirty-five—gusting to seventy—miles per hour, bringing with it steadily falling, cold, crispy snowflakes that began to pile up just in time for the drive to church. Sometimes the wind would be so powerful we had to park the family station wagon facing downhill toward Lake Superior, so that we could open those big, heavy car doors in the brutal wind. Aunt Betty, Uncle Lloyd, and our cousin Cindy would drive from their house at the end of County Road 7. It was where the Larsens lived until a very old age, when Betty and Lloyd had to move to an apartment in town. After that, their daughter, Cindy, took over, living in that same house, where she raised her own little daughter, Andrea.

On those Christmas Eves in Grand Marais, we would brace ourselves against the wind and along with the other parishioners, file into the reception area of the church. There we would take off our heavy coats, hats, mittens, and scarves, before taking our seats on the mahogany pews of the church. We would all sit together: Mom, Dad, Dawn, Cindy, Aunt Betty, Uncle Lloyd, and me. Sometimes Grandma Burge would join us, during the short time when she lived alone in Grand Marais after Grandpa died. The choir would sing Christmas songs, Pastor Bob would give the welcome, and the story of Christmas would be read by one of the Lutheran devotees. Aunt Betty loved Christmas more than anything, and she would SING her LOUDEST and BEST along with the rest of the congregation. Our dad, a reluctant Catholic who never really liked to go to church, played foil to Aunt Betty every year. While she was SINGING "Silent Night," Dad would be play-singing it, making us laugh and further encouraging my sister and me to become skeptical of organized churchgoing in any form. Occasionally someone near us would fart, or Uncle Lloyd would let out a little belch, and all reverence would quickly deteriorate into a debacle Jesus would have been very disappointed by, and Santa Claus too.

In spite of that, we would all do our best to persevere through the readings, the sermon, and the singing, until the culmination of the ceremony began: the lighting of candles. This was the only part of the Christmas service that ever made any sense to me. In trying to pinpoint why, I think it's because my own experience with religion was as cold as that forty-mile-an-hour northwest wind pummeling against the stained-glass cross that was inlaid into the front wall of the church. The candles added warmth to an otherwise frigid experience, and when the flames got passed along, from one pew to the next, the lights would dim and the magic of Christmastime would finally arrive in my heart. And after that, there would be cookies.

Following church, our family would pile back into our tank of a station wagon and make our way to Betty and Lloyd's house to continue the holiday tradition. And there were, indeed, cookies. This is something we did as very little children and would continue to do until after Cindy, Dawn, and I had left home after high school. The house would be lit with old-fashioned strings of lights, and the Larsen tree was one Uncle Lloyd had cut down himself. A logger, Lloyd had professional experience cutting down trees, and yet he always chose a tree that was somewhat sparse, and not really the "classic" shape of a Christmas tree you'd see in the movies or on a Christmas card. The tree was always placed in the northeast corner of the living room, and Aunt Betty decorated it with multicolored lights, Styrofoam gingerbread houses and gingerbread men, old-timey ornaments she inherited from Grandma Burge, and miscellaneous tchotchkes collected over the years and brought out especially for the holiday. And right here is where Aunt Betty would scold me and say, "Staci Lola, what's a tchotchke? I told you not to use too big a words."

Sorry Aunt Betty, I really did try.

* * * * * * *

Aunt Betty was born in late September 1935 in Wood County, Wisconsin, not far from Wayauwega, which was one of the primary stops along the Burge family migratory route. As I mentioned in Auntie Faye's story, the family lived in Lawrence Lake on the Iron Range for about three years before moving to Warba, Minnesota, where Grandpa had a job working in the mines. The tale of their first night there was still clearly etched in Aunt Betty's mind, even as an elder so many years after. When they purchased the potato farm in 1939–40, the only existing potential home was the basement of a partially built house. The roof was what would eventually become the first floor of the farmhouse. When Freda and Bill moved their seven kids to Warba they all shared the rough cement basement area with a few corners cordoned off to serve as bedrooms. So, George, Faye, Lila, Pete, Betty, Carol, and Joyce, who was only two, all settled in, with the intention of building the rest of the house as soon as they had the money. At the time, all seven kids had to share one corner and Grandma and Grandpa had their own sleeping space in another.

That first night, they had just enough time to move their belongings and beds into the basement, have a quick supper of cheese sandwiches with tea, and crawl into their various blankets before the sun went down. I'm sure they were exhausted from the move, and being in a strange new place probably made it hard for many of them to fall asleep. At some point during the night, a booming rainstorm swept through, and Grandma and Grandpa and all the kids woke up to the sound of water pouring down the cement walls of their basement dugout. The rain kept coming, and the entire basement flooded, leaving their freshly transported belongings bobbing around in the muddy water. Freda, Bill, and the older kids gathered up the younger kids and took them outside to the barn, the only other semiprotected shelter at the time. Aunt Betty remembers Grandma crying and yelling and saying "aw quat tee saw," over and over again. The next morning the family walked into town so that Grandma could call Ed Nelson, the Norwegian farmer who had sold them the property. And, as Betty said, "she cussed him out." You see, Freda had gambled every penny of her mother's inheritance to buy that farm, and she felt she had been cheated and squeezed dry, like a nightshirt being forced through an old-fashioned wringer washer.

In reality, the Burges didn't have much time to waste on blaming old Ed Nelson for their misfortune. Winter was coming, there were potatoes to pick, and now a leaky basement to repair so that they wouldn't freeze to death when the snow fell. As part of his job, Grandpa Burge had helped demolish a building over in Virginia, and he brought several loads of scrap lumber home to the farm and set about building a proper house. Aunt Betty said that he was laid off a lot in the winter, and so after the upper floors were framed in and covered with siding, he used the winter to gradually finish the inside of the structure, eventually turning a dank, flooded basement into a two-and-a-half-story house. The boys George and Pete both helped Grandpa with the construction, and some neighbors helped them too.

One of the first things Grandpa did was get a pump for the basement, for when the next big rainstorm came. They added a kitchen with a woodstove, a dining room, living room, and a bedroom for Grandma and Grandpa just off the kitchen. The upstairs had three bedrooms and "high windows" to peer out of. Aunts Faye and Lila shared a room, the three younger girls had another, and Uncle Pete and Uncle George slept in the third bedroom. George didn't live in Warba very long, since he had graduated from high school and was about to go off to college in Virginia. So, for most of the time after that, Uncle Pete had his own room because he was the only boy. Aunt Betty said that when they lived in Warba she never had her own bed and always had to share one—first with Lila and Carol, and later with Carol and Joyce. She couldn't win in either case, because she said someone was always peeing the bed. Joyce was just three or four when the house took shape, and Faye was about fourteen or fifteen by the time the upstairs was finished and the hardwood floors were laid in the kitchen and living room on the first floor. The first bathroom was an outhouse, just at the edge of a line of trees. Aunt Betty told me that even though they had a very modest house, she was "always warm and was never hungry."

She remembers the night Grandpa had just varnished the new hardwood floors in the living room. Faye and Lila had been out after dark and they came home in the middle of the night and knocked the heater over, leaving huge scratches in the floor. I asked her if they got in much trouble and she said, "Dad loved Auntie Faye, so she never really got in trouble. But you know, Lila used to sass Ma, and one time my dad got his belt out and he spanked her. It happened just once. He never did it again and I think she took advantage of it after that. How could she be as nice as Faye was? Kids take the opposite road sometimes."

I asked Betty what their everyday life was like on the farm and she said, "Mom worked all the time, cooking and cleaning, so Faye was like the mother of the kids, in a way." All the kids had to help with the chores. Pete milked their one cow and helped outside in the garden.

Betty, Carol, and Joyce had to help in the kitchen and vacuum upstairs. Aunt Betty said they hated vacuuming the most, so one day, "they just plugged it in and they all laid on the bed with their butts sticking up in the air, pretending they were vacuuming." Grandma Freda, not easily fooled, "snuck upstairs and hit all three of them on their butts with the vacuum hose." This was not malicious hitting, just Grandma's way of making her point. Aunt Betty said that they all laughed about that incident for years and years afterward, thinking of how they all screamed when Grandma Freda started whipping the vacuum hose all around the room.

****

Though it was during World War II, George, the eldest Burge, had gone on to college to study engineering. So instead of coming home in uniform, George came home from college with some big new words in his mouth and bearing Christmas presents for all of his little sisters. This fond memory could have been the beginning of Aunt Betty's love of Christmastime. She remembered that George handed her a present wrapped in a roll of paper. "It was paper dolls. He took me in his arms and said, 'I love you.'"

When she told me this tender story about Uncle George, I got the feeling that Aunt Betty still held up George's kindness that Christmas as one of the purest moments of her childhood—a time when she knew for certain that someone loved her and cared about her. This was a gift he transferred to his little sister, and it became a gift Betty learned to share with others, all throughout her life. Anyone who knew Betty knew that her capacity for love was enormous, especially for all the kids who were lucky enough to have her as part of our lives. If I were to characterize this gift as an imaginary thing it would be **mo·ther·al·i·ty.** Noun: 1. Motherly conduct. 2. Using motherhood as a guiding principle. Use: "Her work as a teacher was driven by a deep-seated sense of motherality—always making sure that all of her students felt loved." Also: "Knowing her nephew was worried about his dog, Aunt Staci drew upon her own inner motherality and tried to talk him through it."

Aunt Betty knew better than anyone that motherly conduct didn't necessarily come from one's own mother. Sometimes it did, but in

Betty's case, she learned motherality from her older brother George and her older sister Faye. It was an inclination she learned to call upon when it came to her youngest sister, Joyce. When talking about what it was like to grow up with my mom as the youngest, Aunt Betty acknowledged that her little sister garnered both positive and negative attention in the Burge household: "Everybody loved her. She was so cute. The family doted on Joyce because she was the baby. Imagine six kids just doting on her! One year Grandma had to put away money for a doll Joyce wanted for Christmas."

My mother also tells this story as a formative event in her life: about seeing a pretty baby doll in the window of a store in downtown Warba and going to visit it every time the family was in town to do errands. She said she would stare at the doll and want to hold it, to smooth its crisp, white dress and hold the dolly's creamy, soft skin next to her cheek. She would dream about having it all to herself— her own little doll to practice motherality on. Then one day she went to town and the baby doll was gone. In its place was a pair of women's shoes. She went into the store and asked the storekeeper where the doll was, and he gently told her that "a woman from Wawina had come and bought the doll for her own daughter."

Little Joyce was devastated and went on believing that some other little girl was taking care of her baby doll. But on Christmas morning, Grandma Freda placed a daintily wrapped present in front of Joyce. She opened up the box and there was the baby doll with the soft, alabaster skin. Grandma, the storekeeper, and the rest of the family had been in on the secret, with all of them letting Joyce believe this sad little lie, which is also a part of the Christmas tradition that tricks kids into thinking they will get everything they want. In this case, Joyce got what she wanted and a whole lot more. Said Betty, "I remember making the doll a blanket for Christmas that year, so that Joyce could wrap up her new baby doll."

Grandpa Bill felt that too much fuss was made about the whole thing. Like the other kids, Joyce was made to be a pawn in the family game of playing favorites. Aunt Betty theorized that because Joyce got so much attention, "Maybe Dad did ignore her because of that—he maybe was trying to compensate for that. Joyce was scared of him because he would say things like, 'Shut up now. I want to listen to the news.' So, we would shut up. That's the way it was. Ma would make supper every night at five, and Dad would listen to the news."

****

It seems that everyone in the house took a turn at motherality. When Betty was in first grade the teacher sent her home because she wasn't making any progress in class. Grandma and Grandpa would send her back to school only to have her sent home over and over again. Her parents' utter lack of interest in why she was struggling so much in school resulted in Betty flunking first grade. This is not because she was stupid or had a learning disability. It turns out Betty couldn't do her work because she couldn't see the blackboard. She said, "I missed the first grade. I couldn't see and no one knew it. And so, I failed first grade. After that Carol and I went to every grade in school together."

After determining that Betty's eyes badly needed attention, it was Aunt Faye who took Betty to Minneapolis to get a pair of glasses. I asked her why it was Faye and not her parents and she said, "I don't think Mom and Dad had the money."

Now able to see the board and follow the lessons, Betty started to catch up in school, but she always stayed one grade behind. Because they were now in the same classroom, Betty and her sister Carol grew very close as sisters and friends. They were different personalities with different likes and interests, with Betty being quite talkative and Carol being more of a quiet animal lover, but the two of them grew up together on a daily basis and knew each other very well. And even though they were in the same grade, Betty was still two years older than Carol, so she also stepped in to take care of both Carol and Joyce when the situation warranted a dose of motherality. She told me, "I kind of mothered them but it didn't always work out. Like when we were kids, we were supposed to get dressed for church and I was in charge of getting them ready, but then took them to play in the mud. Your grandma just shook her head and said, 'Aw quat tee saw!!!' I had to wash all the mud off them and take care of them and get them ready for Bible school program that night."

When I was interviewing Aunt Betty those many years after she survived her Warba childhood she was very clear about the family flaws, and she had a good understanding of why Grandma and

Grandpa often went to war over their kids: "Ma would be mean to Lila and Dad would cover for that. Lila and Faye loved him and he loved them. Joyce and Carol were both scared of Dad, and Mom doted on Joyce and loved Carol—she was very protective of her." And then Betty said, "I think my dad only wanted Ma, and he didn't really want so many kids. He just loved her."

By the time Betty was a young girl, the mess created by the continuous cycle of the morbidity of motherhood proceeded to further enslave Grandma Burge, who had no way out of it. I asked my mother what it was like being the youngest kid of seven, and the toll that must have taken on her own mother. She said, "When my mom had me, she was crying. She didn't want to have another kid, but back then you would never have asked a male doctor about birth control. It was considered a woman's job to have children. That's why we were put on earth—to have children. That's what we all were taught. Well, after I was born, I guess a [female] nurse helped her so she wouldn't have any more babies. I bet you in the records, there was no such thing as a prescription for birth control."

* * * * * * *

Sifting through the Burge family history with Aunt Betty was always something of a revelation. She once told me, "I don't believe in keeping secrets just to make things look good." And so, when she explained things about Auntie Faye's life, and remembered certain truths about the lives of her other sisters, Betty was always a straight shooter, even if it wasn't always flattering. As much as we'd like to believe that our aunties were perfectly sweet and always did the right thing, the truth is that these women who made us didn't always overcome the traumas they experienced in the past. Much of the time, they were just doing what they had to do to get through it all. Part of having a sense of solid motherality as your guiding principle is accepting the fact that mothers aren't always perfect and that more often than not, the mothers in our lives have to live with a litany of mistakes and certain failures. As for her own mother, Betty was able to see with clarity how difficult the circumstances were for Freda, who had to balance life with seven children and a husband who, by most accounts, was a deeply dysfunctional person. Said Aunt Betty, "What a life Ma had. I love her dearly."

Back in Warba, the kids' school was located down on Highway 2, the main road that passed into and out of town. There were kids from Wawina and Swan River who went to school there, including other farm kids. Life in the country was rough for the poor kids and Mother remembers that on one occasion, "a teacher found lice on a little farm girl and the teacher humiliated her in front of my mother in the girls' bathroom." Because of Warba's history, I asked my mother if there were any Native American or Black kids at her school and she said, "No, all white kids." And then she shared this telling detail about life on the Iron Range back in the mid-1940s: "The first Black man I saw was in Minneapolis when I was with Faye. We were on the bus and I remember just staring at him."

Here is where I think it's important to tell some additional truths about the Stelter and Burge families, because as Betty has said, "I don't believe in keeping secrets just to make things look good." So, thank you, Aunt Betty, for giving us permission to talk about the not so nice side of the family. When I was going through the Burge treasure box of letters, I found a couple of telling passages in letters Grandma wrote to Grandpa. They are just a few words, but words that illustrate how racism and the fear of people who are not like us are lurking in the basements of all of our family structures, like mildew rotting away the bricks and mortar of the Warba basement. In a 1924 letter mailed from Eau Claire, Wisconsin, to her husband, Bill, in Cudahy, Illinois, Grandma Freda wrote, "My Honey Boy: Arrived at [her sister] Ida's about seven o'clock. I was not so tired, as I slept some. How did my darling get back? Did you sleep in the apartment and did you miss your mama some? Have you gone to the Federal already—any luck? It was 8:35 when I got in to [Rubbish] Junction. I never seen such a desolate place in all my life. I was the only female there. There was a rube sitting in one corner and a dirty Kike in another and the lights kept going off and on. Oh, it was real thrilling."

I looked up the word "rube," which is a turn-of-the-nineteenth-century slur for a gullible country boy. Its origin is similar to that of "hick." I also looked up the word "kike," which clearly stands out as a racial slur. Its origin is this: "The Yiddish word for 'circle' is kikel—illiterate Jews who entered the United States at Ellis Island signed their names with a circle instead of a cross because they associated the cross with Christianity."[1]

As someone who places a lot of value on words, discovering that these horrible words came from my own grandmother's mouth was really shocking to me. Could this be the same Grandma who made me blueberry buckle and sat on aces during family cribbage tournaments? But based on what I've learned about community-supported prejudice and the Indigenous history of the United States, there's really no reason to be shocked, when you consider that Grandma came from a German family who felt the most comfortable in a city or a bigger town, where they could live among pockets of people who looked like, prayed for, and believed in an America that was like them. They were supported by institutions and systems that favored people from their economic and social background, which is how the neighborhoods of America were carved out of history. In a letter that came soon after, there is even more evidence to support that some of the Stelters were involved in more outwardly racist activities. This letter is from Freda to Bill, also in 1924. She is still at her sister Ida's house in Weyauwega, Wisconsin, where she penned: "My Dear Billie, you are such a darling to write every day. I just love you more for it. Howard is feeling better some doctors say it is very serious and another it is not, so we do not know nothing definite as yet. Ida is so worried. Mrs. Hanson and I went down to see Juggs and Maggie in a play yesterday afternoon but it was rotten. I was so disappointed. Last nite they had a public Klans meeting here. Ida went down and I stayed home with the baby and Howard. What did you do on Halloween evening? Did you celebrate? I am so glad you did not go to that stag party. You are just a darling of a man. Won't you tell me something nice too?"

* * * * * * *

A teacher from Chippewa Valley named John Kinville published a book in 2020 about women who were involved with the Ku Klux Klan in the Chippewa Valley region of Wisconsin, including Eau Claire, where meetings were held at a clubhouse downtown. The book is titled *The Grey Eagles of Chippewa Falls: A Hidden History of a Women's Ku Klux Klan in Wisconsin*, and it details the strong KKK presence in Wisconsin, particularly in the 1920s, among women from towns all over the Chippewa Valley. Kinville even reveals that the first cross burning by the KKK in Chippewa Falls was on the hill behind Leinenkugel's Brewery, where there is now a cemetery.[2] Those Protestant white women were concerned with "the continuation of Prohibition, the importance of strong public schools, and the prevention of Democratic presidential candidate Al Smith, a Catholic, from reaching the White House in 1928."[3] According to Kinville's research, KKK members in the 1920s and 1930s were mostly "average" citizens of their communities, holding jobs and raising families, including women named Ida Stelter, my grandmother's sister and my great-aunt.

If we do indeed believe in telling the truth, then we must be willing to pull back the bed covers and expose whatever creepy-crawlies are living under there. This is something Grandma Freda believed was the right thing to do when it was her bed, or her children's beds, and as we've learned, she would have poured gasoline all over it and burned it to ashes if she thought the bugs would eventually burrow under her skin. And skin is what this is really about, isn't it? The "purity" of whiteness, unmarred by darkness, or in Grandma Freda's case, the fear of dirty bedbugs overtaking the clean white sheets of her bedroom. Grandma Freda was always trying to rise to the top, like cream floating on the surface of a pail of cow's milk. Both Aunt Betty and my mother have wondered out loud whether Great-grandma Polena's branch of the family tree had Jewish relatives hiding on it. Her maiden name was Wangerin, and indeed, Wangerin is known as a seventeenth-century Jewish community in what is now the city of Szczecin in northwestern Poland.[4] There is no real evidence, however, of Jewish culture or heritage within the Stelter family, and Grandma lived her life as a purely German, purely Protestant woman. This identity is boiled into the fabric of the Stelter and Burge family skirts, trousers, and coats, and kept my relatives in the precarious situation of always having to be better than, whiter than, holier than, more pristine than anyone else.

In reality, the Burges were a poverty-stricken farm family, and Grandpa Bill was an illegal immigrant who wasn't born in America. He snuck over the northern border and was allowed to stay and raise a family. The Stelters, and by extension the Burges, wanted to believe that their devotion to a Protestant version of God and Jesus placed them closer to heaven than other people. It didn't matter that Grandpa was dysfunctional and broken in a lot of ways. Or that Grandma struggled to find her own sense of individualism and happiness. When you are raised in a strict and narrow place, there's really no room to go anywhere else. And Grandma and Grandpa were in many ways trapped inside that narrow place. They were trapped in their economic situation, trapped in the societal limitations of men's and women's roles, and caught up in the belief that clawing your way upward required you to bring others down. It makes me sad for them and for the world we live in now, which is still trying to hide the blood-eating bedbugs that live where we sleep and emerge out of our mouths as racist taunts and hateful rhetoric.

* * * * * * *

My mother said that when Betty and Carol graduated from Grand Rapids High School, Grandpa Burge gave them each twenty dollars and they were "expected to sort of, disappear." The two of them moved to Minneapolis together, where they got some help navigating the big world from Uncle George and his wife, Elna, who had their own family in the Twin Cities. During that same time Lila and Leroy were also living in Minneapolis. That was when their second-oldest daughter, Loni, was born. Faye was living in Chicago and married to Bob Palmer, hoping they would soon be able to adopt Jimmy and Johnny.

In 1955 Grandpa Burge got yet another temporary job at Taconite Harbor, a newly built ore-processing plant near Schroeder, on the North Shore of Lake Superior. Like all his other jobs, this one would be a blip in time, but it came with company housing in a mobile home park set up just east of the plant, where other temporary workers were staying. My mother, Joyce, was going into her junior year of high school when they moved, so she transferred from Grand Rapids to Cook County High School in Grand Marais. She had to sleep on the couch in the living room of the trailer until they moved into one of Lind's cabins in Grand Marais a year later. That's where all three of them lived when Mom graduated from high school in 1956. It was during her senior year that Mom met my dad, Francis Odell Drouillard, who pursued her with great panache.

A handsome guy with an Elvis ducktail and a fast car, Francis worked relentlessly to sweep Joyce off her feet. Unlike Mom, Dad dropped out of school in the eighth grade; he was working full-time as a truck driver when they first met. During their courtship year, Dad took a job on the ore boats that ferried finished ore pellets between Taconite Harbor and Sault Ste. Marie, Michigan. Stored in the Burge box of memorabilia are forty-six letters that my dad wrote to my mother between July and October 1956, while he was working on the crew of the SS *Harry W. Croft*. That would amount to about eleven letters each month, sometimes more. I've not read these love letters, because they don't seem like anyone else's business. For now, they are rubber-banded together amid Grandma and Grandpa's love letters, written at a similar time in their relationship, when passionate love was what mattered the most.

After his stint at Taconite Harbor ended, Grandma and Grandpa Burge went all the way to New York, where Grandpa had another temporary job lined up. Their children were grown up and out of the barnyard, so to speak, so Grandpa finally had what he had wanted all along—to have Freda to himself with no kids around to take care of. My mother stayed here in Grand Marais and worked a full-time job, waiting tables at the El Ray Café. She was in love with my dad, who was scheduled to return home that fall, after his stint on the *Harry S. Croft* was finished for the season. During that time, Joyce would sometimes go to Minneapolis to visit her sisters, who after a few stumbles, had finally hit their stride.

By Betty's own account, Carol and Betty really cut loose in Minneapolis. They saved money and rented a little place in Northeast Minneapolis for fifty dollars a month. After a bit they moved to South Minneapolis, where they met two lifelong friends—Kitty and Patty. The four of them banded together with two more girls and rented an apartment that housed all six of them. As Aunt Betty said, "Oh my gosh, we had fun!"

Betty worked in the office at Grain Belt Brewery in Northeast Minneapolis, making twenty-five dollars a week. The job didn't end well when one day she accidentally "pulled out the telephone plug when the big boss was on the phone and I got fired. After that I worked at the Ford/Hopkins drug company." Aunt Carol worked as a waitress at the Flame Café and Nightclub on Nicollet Avenue in downtown Minneapolis, which was a fairly glamorous job because the Flame was where major country and western performers would play whenever they came to town. Betty was just twenty or twenty-one then, and she confessed that "we got kicked out of a lot of apartments." The sisters moved around a lot, occasionally attracting negative attention. According to Aunt Betty, it was an exciting time in their lives, "Some people would call the cops about noise—but there wasn't even a party! A lot of navy men would come over. They'd sleep on the floor and we'd go to our own beds. It was never a big deal. We used to drink cheap wine. I didn't drink that much. I did drink gin one time and I got sick."

Never much of a drinker, Aunt Betty was in it for the sociality. There's a picture of her taken around this time that really shows Betty's flirty personality. She's got classic 1950s vintage glasses on and she's playacting with a cocktail, pretending she's tipsy. In reality, she was just goofing around for her friend Kitty, who took the picture. I wasn't even born then, but it's so easy to imagine Betty and Auntie Carol laughing heartily with their friends about something silly. The two of them had a lightness together as sisters, something that their other siblings weren't quite privy to.

****

But all good things must come to an end, and soon the two sisters, Betty and Carol, finally decided to part ways. Betty explained that "Patty and Carol went to Seattle and Kitty and I lived together in Chicago." And then she added, "Oh shit—that's where I met my first husband."

In Chicago, Aunt Betty met a man named Tom, quickly got married, and then moved to the South, where he was originally from. "He was an asshole," she said. The place where he lived in Chicago had a dirt floor. She went on, "I don't know why I married him."

And then she followed up with the rest of the story, "We dated for a while. He was AWOL from the army. Stupid me. I gave him my car to go back to the army and I walked to work. Wasn't that stupid? I ain't doing that anymore!"

So, Betty moved from Chicago down to Tennessee and into a two-room house with her first husband: "It was a mess. To me, that was exciting, moving so far away. His mother was still fighting the Civil War. Right away, she was like, 'You're from the North.' She lived in a house that was on a river—it was by Memphis. But it was real hillbilly. He had a sister living there with two kids. We had bean soup every friggin' day and sometimes we'd have some baking powder biscuits."

Then Aunt Betty really exploded the story, right along with her first marriage. She blurted out, "And my father-in-law wanted to have sex with me!"

"How did you know?" I asked.

"I just kind of felt it . . . I just turned away from him," she said.

So, then I asked, "Did you ever tell your husband?"

Betty speculated that "he probably wouldn't have cared, I don't know. But, you know, I wasn't that innocent. I had been out in the world by then."

Betty followed her instincts and left Tennessee as quickly as she could. As she said, "Then I got tired of it all and I came to live with your mom [Joyce]. Thank goodness I didn't have a baby!!"

****

When Dad returned to Grand Marais after sailing on Lake Superior, my mother was right where he left her. They were married the following year, 1957, on the summer solstice. Joyce and Poot Drouillard lived south of Highway 61, in the little yellow house that was once next to Tommy Eckel's fish house. My aunt Diane also lived there for a time, about twenty years later. That house is still there and it's still yellow. Joyce worked at the El Ray Café, in downtown Grand Marais, where Louis Armstrong famously stopped in to have breakfast on his way to Thunder Bay for a concert performance. This is where Aunt Betty lived between marriages. "Your mom would work days and I would work nights," Betty said. "They were very good to me."

There was a lot happening in the lives of the other Burge sisters between the time Aunt Betty moved to Grand Marais and when she fell in love and married the man who would be her lifelong love. Faye, Carol, and Grandma and Grandpa were all living in Milwaukee, and Lila, Lee, and their four daughters were temporarily living back at the Warba farm. Grandpa Burge had run into some very bad luck while working in Milwaukee. As my mother tells the story, "Dad's eyesight was really bad, so he went to the doctor and had to have cataract surgery. Something happened in surgery and he lost his sight and he couldn't work anymore after that. He couldn't even get Social Security at the time. So, a friend in Warba, EvaLyn Carlson's dad, helped him get on disability assistance."

Back in Warba, and with no way for Grandpa to make money, Grandma Freda had to take over as the breadwinner of the family. My mother explained, "[She] worked at Fat's Café in Warba until she saved a thousand dollars, and then she went back to the farm and bought cows. That way she and Dad could have some income. Before that they were destitute."

And then Mom said, "Imagine how brave she had to be to do that. All she knew how to do was cook and bake. And so, that's what she did to get them out of that mess."

Betty shared the same story but added this detail about life on the farm: "So, she'd go out and milk the cows every day and sell it to the dairy man. She would butcher the chickens too—cut their heads off and cook them for Saturday dinner."

While Grandma was roasting chickens on the farm, Betty was working as a waitress at Mabel's Café in Grand Marais, where a man named Lloyd came in regularly for a breakfast of bacon, toast, eggs over easy, and black coffee. Lloyd Christian Larsen was born and raised in Grand Marais as part of one of the first Norwegian families to homestead here on the North Shore. His parents were Hans and Andrea Larsen, and my cousin Cindy related that her grandma Andrea arrived on the steamship America, which docked in the Duluth harbor, bringing settlers to the North Shore from every part of the world. A great number of the people who chose to homestead in Cook County came from Sweden or Norway. The ruggedness of the shoreline and the cold, unforgiving climate made them feel right at home.

Lloyd was a World War II veteran who was actually on his way to Japan when the atomic bombs were dropped on Hiroshima and Nagasaki. He worked as a logger from the time he was a very young man, along with his brothers, Roger and Hank. A man of few words, Lloyd was physically strong, blessed with a kind disposition, and as soft-hearted as his hands were rough and rugged. It seems like every day of the week Lloyd wore a white cotton T-shirt under a plaid wool shirt along with a pair of heavy wool pants held up by suspenders. He used a cotton bandanna handkerchief as an all-purpose wiper and blower, which set him apart from the other men we knew growing up. That red hankie was always half hanging out of his pocket, no matter the time or place. And almost every year at Christmastime, we would go to Joynes Ben Franklin and buy Uncle Lloyd a new set of bandanas for him to open on Christmas Eve.

Aunt Betty confessed that when they met, "Lloyd was married before too. I'm just telling you because this is how life goes. He met this girl. He liked her. I was so jealous of her."

"Who was she?" I inquired. And Betty said, "She used to split bills—where she'd take a counterfeit twenty-dollar bill with two sides and then cash them in for the bigger side."

I asked why I'd never heard that until now, and Aunt Betty said, "She had to go to prison for fraud 'cause they caught her finally. So, she went away to prison and then came back here. Lloyd lived with his mother, but he never divorced her. We had to wait for his divorce to be final before we could get married. I was living in Grand Marais, and my first husband, Tom, would call the house. If Lloyd was there, he would take the phone and say to him, "There's a lot of dead hillbillies up here.'"

****

Betty and Lloyd eventually did get officially divorced from their first spouses and got married on May 7, 1960. Theirs was a love story that reaches as high as the tallest white pine and continues to set a family precedent for how much love there can be between two people. Betty said to me on the day I interviewed her fifty-six years after their wedding, "I didn't know what love was until I met Lloyd." She and Lloyd were married at the First Congregational Church in Grand Marais, which was followed by a party at the Harbor Light where E. J. Croft played the piano, still a point of pride for Aunt Betty: "E. J. played at our wedding dance! I used to have a tape of him playing with his chopper mitts on!"

They first lived in a home in Johnsonville, a few houses up from her sister Lila and the Garners, just north of Highway 61 on Eighth Avenue. Not long after their wedding, Aunt Faye arrived with her little daughter, Jeannie. Just as Faye had once rescued Betty by buying her a pair of glasses so that she could go back to school, Betty in turn rescued Faye when her older sister was in a time of need. And even though they were newlyweds, Betty said that "Lloyd never got crabby, and Faye lived with us." All of Faye's sisters knew the story of Jeannie, of course. But the information was never shared with any degree of openness with people outside the family and Betty just accepted Faye and Jeannie without making a fuss about it. Betty and Faye would both suffer the indignities of women who have expectations placed on them by the morbidity of motherhood (a women's duty is to have babies), while still feeling the pressure of chronic femininity— the craven need to please men at all costs. Said Aunt Betty, "[Faye] didn't have boyfriends in Warba, and neither did I. She had different men when she left home. She was such a kind, kind person. I don't think she realized that people were icky. She got mixed up with stupid men. She wanted men. She wanted love. She was lovable. Bud Hauge screwed every woman in town and their marriage was annulled. That man was a philanderer. She always got herself into a bunch of shit."[5]

As for how Auntie Faye ended up with another woman's baby while never being pregnant herself, Betty simply said, "Faye told me about it. I just worshipped her and whatever she did was fine with me. So, Jeannie was part of the family and we loved her."

Faye stayed with Betty and Lloyd in Grand Marais that summer and worked at the Shoreline Inn cleaning rooms. According to Betty, Faye and her ex-husband, Bud, continued to have a very tumultuous relationship and she "went back and forth to him" a lot during the time they lived with her and Uncle Lloyd. My parents, Joyce and Poot, had left Grand Marais for Phoenix, and Faye drove off with Jeannie not long after that. Aunt Betty remembers that Faye's old car had a little potty chair in it for Jeannie, who was potty-trained somewhere between Grand Marais and Arizona.

For a long time, Aunt Betty thought she and Lloyd would not be able to have children of their own. She was worried that she was following in the path of her older sister, who longed for children more than anything in the world but was not able to get pregnant. Aunt Betty explains that "a gal I worked with at Mabel's Café was taking care of two brothers named Danny and Larry." Lloyd knew their mother—a local woman who was in the Moose Lake Mental Hospital, suffering with emotional problems. Betty and Lloyd decided to take the boys in as foster kids. She said, "We had them for two or three years and the state said, 'If you don't adopt them, we'll move them on.' It was the dumbest thing we ever did. I just thought love would fix it, you know?"

And here's an example of how the morbidity of motherhood plays tricks on women who are conditioned to believe that love, not preparedness or intention, is all you need to raise children. Aunt Betty thought her love, as guided by her own deep sense of motherality, could change the lives of two children who would have tested even the saintliest and best-intentioned foster parents. Aunt Betty theorized, "Maybe Auntie Faye put that idea in my mind—that love was enough."

I wish I could talk to Betty again and tell her that it wasn't Aunt Faye who put those ideas in her head. No, those expectations were the same ones placed on Faye, Grandma Burge, and Great-grandma Paulina. It's not Betty's fault that she believed having a good heart would be enough to bring about a miracle. And Betty, like Faye, would have to find this out the hard way. She said, "Things were good until the adoption. That's a terrible thing—to take kids away from their mother. Their mother still lived here but was back and forth to the hospital. And when she would come home, I would take the boys there to visit. It just didn't feel right to take them away every time."

According to her memories of that time, Danny and Larry's mother would come home for a few days and then one day, Social Services made the call—forcing the issue that either she and Lloyd would formally adopt them or they'd be sent away forever. I asked Aunt Betty if the boys knew what was happening and she said, "Danny [the younger brother] got very angry—maybe he would have anyway. And Larry—I don't know . . . it's just sad."

And then Betty reminded me of what Faye had experienced when the state of Wisconsin took Jimmy and Johnny away from her: "She loved kids. When Bob died, they took those boys away from Faye. That was one of the reasons she moved in with Carol and me. Jeannie came later. So, I can see why she would have taken Jeannie in after that."

* * * * * * *

Danny was twelve years old and Larry was thirteen when Aunt Betty and Uncle Lloyd formally adopted them in 1967. She and Lloyd had moved into a much bigger house by then—in fact, the same house they lived most of their lives in. It's on the very edge of the woods on the east side of Grand Marais close to where County 7 meets Highway 61. The house was relatively small, but they had a big backyard and a front yard with gigantic, old-growth white pines on one side of the driveway. The boys were raised Catholic, and Lloyd would take them to church every Sunday even though he wasn't Catholic. He bought them a yellow Ski-Doo snowmobile and pairs of bunny boots, so they could take off into the woods behind their house and be on the trail all day if they wanted.

Although Uncle Lloyd and Aunt Betty tried their best to bring a semblance of normalcy and routine to their lives, there were always indications that Danny and Larry were more than just troubled kids. Danny had an antisocial personality with a violent and unpredictable temper. Larry's disposition was less volatile, but he also struggled in social situations and was very vulnerable to the world. It was a hard time in the Larsen house, because it turns out that love is not nearly enough when your adopted sons both suffer from bipolar disorder in varying degrees. This, of course, is an inherited disease that is passed along from generation to generation, and given how their mother struggled, it's very easy to trace the source of their disorder. Aunt Betty said that during this time, "Lloyd was a little gruff sometimes. It was very frustrating. He just about hit me one time, but he hit the fridge instead. I tried my best to be fair to all of them."

It was only a short time after Danny and Larry were formally adopted that Aunt Betty learned she was pregnant. In early February 1969, nine years after they married, their daughter, Cindy Carol, was born. Betty and Lloyd were both over the moon about Cindy. For all of those nine long years they had thought they would never be able to have a baby, and then there she was—a moonfaced, blue-eyed baby girl. She was perfectly adorable and Aunt Betty and Uncle Lloyd's love for each other was compounded when Cindy was born.

Of course, Cindy was the focus of everyone's attention after that. And that meant a whole lot less attention for her much older adopted brothers. Larry had just graduated, and so he had gone on to college, but Danny still had a few years left before finishing high school. And here's where the story gets very dark. The family was getting ready to go somewhere and Cindy was really little. She was in the car in her car seat and Danny was outside in the driveway, waiting to depart. Aunt Betty came outside to find him holding the glowing cigarette lighter from the dashboard of the car in front of Cindy's little hands, trying to get her to touch it. Aunt Betty never trusted Danny after that, and it created an exponential amount of stress for her in particular. This didn't go over well with Danny, who was not well, and from the way Aunt Betty tells it, he was only getting worse the older he got.

In the end, something happened that caused Betty and Lloyd to give up on Danny for good. It's not for me to disclose any details (I promised Aunt Betty I wouldn't tell), but what he did was so destructive that she knew that he shouldn't be allowed to live there anymore. In retrospect, it's lucky their house never burned down. In her words, "I called Social Services and they took him away. I spent many years of guilt over that. He went to a halfway home in Duluth and they couldn't handle him. And then he went to Minneapolis." While he was a patient in a mental hospital in Minneapolis, Danny drowned in the Mississippi River. Aunt Betty said, "I still don't know if he jumped or fell into the river. It was not too long before my birthday and it makes me think he did it on purpose."

Lloyd, Betty, and Cindy stayed in touch with Larry, and they welcomed his wife and daughter to the family; they lived very far away but still considered Uncle Lloyd and Aunt Betty their surrogate parents and grandparents. Larry's disease took longer than Danny's to develop fully, but eventually it would put Larry into long-term care, where he still resides. He struggled mightily, his brain completely unmoored by paranoia and delusions, great and small. He got mixed up with an antiestablishment group known as the Rainbow Family for a while. He lost many years, and sometimes he would show up unexpectedly in Grand Marais, hitchhiking his way along Highway 61. Cindy said Larry's state of being was always unpredictable. Sometimes he was really out of it, and sometimes he would be there to help her when she needed an older brother. When Aunt Betty talked about that time and about the adoption, she admits that she was in over her head. It took her a long time to sort through it all—and she had the help of counselors and therapists who worked with her on forgiving herself for what happened.

* * * * * * *

Signing on to be a surrogate mother for Danny and Larry was very brave and also very naive. Possessing the gifts of motherality only got Aunt Betty so far, because what on earth can a surrogate mother do when a "natural" mother has gifted her sons with poison in the form of paranoid bipolar disorder? When you are watching your children gradually become unmoored, how can you possibly save them, in a world that is also rootless and shifting? The brutal irony that exists between Faye's and Betty's differing experiences involving adoption—with Aunt Betty choosing to give up two sons while Aunt Faye's sons were taken away from her—is a strange coincidence that intersects the lives of the two sisters. The pain of losing Jimmy and Johnny would forever change the trajectory of Faye's life. And the pain of discovering that love isn't enough to change the nature of children would also forever affect Betty's life. It was something that always haunted her, and it made her feel sad, almost like she had failed them and failed herself. On some level she wanted to believe that love in its purest form was best delivered to others as a motherly transaction, and that it would never fail.

She put this form of love into a lot of things, including the place where she lived. Auntie Betty's house on the edge of town at the edge of the woods was her castle. After Cindy was born, she and Lloyd bought a sizable piece of land at the end of County Road 7, which at the time was an unpaved dirt road. A two-story house was moved from elsewhere to their plot, and Uncle Lloyd added on a wooden front porch and a mudroom at the back of the house, where you entered the kitchen. The kitchen hasn't really changed at all since we were little kids. If you visit there today, the cupboards and general feel of the place are the same as they were when we were kids. There's a window that looks out into the side yard and a center kitchen counter where Aunt Betty decorated birthday cakes, placed cookies out to cool, or presented the feast on Christmas Eve and other holidays. My sister, who grew up to be a chef, sometimes pokes fun at the fact that Betty's electric stove caused her to burn a lot of things over the course of our young lives. Sometimes her bacon was perfectly crisp and sometimes it was charred on one side. And a lot of bacon was cooked on Aunt

Betty's stove, because Uncle Lloyd infamously had bacon, toast, and eggs over easy nearly every morning of his life. And lots of black coffee. That was Uncle Lloyd.

****

The Larsens' yard was visited by a lot of wild creatures. Deer wandered through regularly and more than once a black bear pushed its way through the screen door into the back entryway and raised holy havoc once it got in. Things like that happen when you live at the edge of the forest. The yard was really big, not quite a field, but definitely bigger than most. Aunt Betty loved flowers and her yard was always full of them. She planted shade gardens of hostas and bluebells along the east side of the house and sun-loving annuals on the south side. There were carpets of baby's breath all around the yard, old-fashioned roses and lilac bushes near the driveway, and an heirloom double peony that puts out enormous blossoms every June, exploding outward into shaggy clumps of porcelain pink and fuchsia petals. That was Aunt Betty. Uncle Lloyd dug a big potato patch into a corner of the backyard every spring, alternating sides each year to keep the soil balanced. He never fenced it off; his plants were always so rigorous and hearty, even the woodland white-tailed deer couldn't trample them down. More than a few times we were there to watch him carefully dig up a hill of dark red potatoes that were promptly washed, boiled, and mashed with butter for supper that night.

My sister and I spent an awful lot of time at Aunt Betty's house as kids, my sister more so, because that's where she stayed when our mom was hospitalized with her own mental breakdown. I was at Aunt Lila's house, trudging through sixth grade, and Dawn was at Betty's house, learning the ropes of second grade. Aunt Betty and Uncle Lloyd had a small room downstairs across from the bathroom and Cindy and Dawn slept upstairs, where Cindy's room was. I still have dreams about the staircase at Aunt Betty's house—it was strangely narrow and winding, with a window halfway up to the second floor. It's an interior part of the house that so many of us knew—the Garner cousins, Cindy's school friends, our cousins from Minneapolis. I'm sure any one of these relatives can tell you about that stairwell. Aunt Betty used to stand at the bottom and yell up at us, "Staci Lola! Dawn Marie!

Cindy Carol!" You see, Aunt Betty used to let us play upstairs as much as we wanted and pretty much whenever we wanted. It was the first time I remember being somewhere that was just for kids. Betty would mostly let us be, and we were able to entertain ourselves without much interference. It was a safe space for us, and that house has served as a safe place for many others over the years.

When I asked Dawn what she remembered about her time there, she said, "Aunt Betty was really nice to me, and Uncle Lloyd was never mean. I never heard him yell about anything." It took a lot to upset Lloyd, and when he was gruff, there was a good reason for it. The Larsen house was the site of many, many family cookouts, with everyone bringing dishes to share, hot dogs and hamburgers on the grill, and all kinds of snacks. The men would drink beer and play horseshoes, and the women would sit on the back porch and laugh and talk. Betty had inherited a four-person swing that Grandpa Burge had built, and we kids would play on it for hours, our little bodies piling up on each side, trying to get it to launch higher and higher.

At Aunt Betty's, our favorite games were Operation, Hūsker Dū?, Clue, and playing with Barbie dolls. We had suitcases full of them. Cindy and my sister and I, and sometimes Cindy's friend Muffin, would build a Barbie house out of anything we could find—these pretend houses were sprawling—and our fantasy Barbie lives would go on for days, especially in the summertime. Barbies were our first tour guides into the fantasy realm of chronic femininity, introducing us to body comparisons and the ridiculous expectation that every girl loves to wear pink. You could always tell Cindy's Barbies from ours because they had chewed-up feet. You know, the pointed Barbie feet that were much too small for her stature and designed only for stilettos? Some of them Cindy had nervously chewed, and some of them had suffered torture at the hands of her adopted brothers.

One summer when I was about ten, Cindy, Dawn, and I were deep into one of our Barbie marathons. We had taken over the entire living room at our house on Eighth Avenue. Our mom was trying to clean house—it was Saturday, after all—and we had converted every single towel and washcloth in our house into Barbie blankets or Barbie furniture or other such things. We were underfoot, oblivious, and causing Mother to go into a Kent III–smoking, Neil Diamond–playing frenzy. Exasperated, she ordered us to pack up our Barbies and "go to Betty's house!" We put all of our Barbie luggage in a red wagon, and the three of us headed to Aunt Betty's, which was on the far end of town, at little over a mile away along County Road 7. Mom called Betty right after we left to let her know we were on the way. Aunt Betty recalls that "pretty soon, there you were, plopping down the road, dragging a wagon behind you." This really struck her as quite hilarious, and she giggled about it for many years later. The poor little Barbies, both real and plastic, cast out and bumping down the road.

Aunt Betty's house and backyard served as our growing-up place in so many ways. Uncle Lloyd had built Cindy a playhouse out of wood, and we spent an entire summer in there, pretending it was our own house, tidying up the floor and putting the toy dishes away. We imagined we were the characters in *The Boxcar Children*, orphaned and forced to fend for ourselves. Of course, as soon as it started to get dark, we would head inside, where it was safe from the scary things that might be waiting for us in the woods behind the house. In a lot of ways, Cindy was like our middle sister because we were together so often, and we all lived through so many things over the years. She still feels like our sister, and her daughter, Andrea, is more like a niece than a second cousin.

****

Creating safe situations for people came naturally to Aunt Betty. Her house was a welcoming place where we could always be ourselves, and this idea of a safe space or being a "T" for others, like touching base in a game of hide-and-seek, is something that Aunt Betty liked to do. She served as confidante to a lot of people, including her sisters, friends, nieces, and nephews, and in many ways, she was like the emotional glue of the Burge family. Uncle George's kids were all close to Aunt Betty, even though they all lived many miles away. My cousin Sandy especially would often come and stay with Betty and Lloyd, as did her brothers, Bill and Mark. And all of Lila's daughters could tell their own tales about calling Aunt Betty on the phone when they needed motherly advice about something they didn't want to share with their own mother, or if they just needed an empathetic ear and wanted to talk.

In fact, Aunt Betty's phone number was the first one I learned how to dial: 387–2373. I would stand on a chair in our kitchen on Eighth Avenue and dial those numbers on the old rotary phone that hung on the wall. And every time I called her she would pick up. Betty never played favorites with any of us, and she considered us all to be special—but in our own, individual ways. One of her favorite things to say was, "Thanks for being you." She would tag it onto the end of a visit or on the phone, just as you were about to say goodbye. As she got older, sometimes she would cry talking about how special you were, and she really made sure you believed her. It's part of being a truth teller—which is something that characterizes Aunt Betty almost more than anything else I can say about her.

I've never really known such a teller of truths, and I think almost everyone who knew Aunt Betty would likely agree with that assessment. She was always right out with it, and sometimes it hurt a little to hear what she had to say, but then it was out in the world and everyone was forced to deal with it. Similar to when Aunt Betty added a healthy float of Diet 7 Up to my brother-in-law's family label Italian red wine at Thanksgiving. While Betty's sisters all struggled to hear the sound of truth over the din of unreliable narrators, the ones that whispered "Cover yourself up . . . lose weight . . . accept less than you are worthy of . . . eat that pie and you'll feel better," the unreliable narrators in Betty's life never gained a lot of ground. She seemed to know her own truth pretty early on, and when things got really bad, she got the hell out, or added a little fizz, as the case may be. Thankfully, she lived to tell the truth about a lot of things and stayed in control of the message right up until the day she died. What a truth warrior she was. I think that's why so many people loved her and trusted her.

* * * * * * *

One of the things I wanted to ask Betty the truth about was the story of Grandma Freda's brother Martin, and how Grandma finally was able to pull the Burge family out of the financial morass they perpetually found themselves in. Aunt Betty said flat out that her uncle Martin was gay but that it was never talked about. He was always very close to his sister Freda and would sometimes visit her when he was in town on business. In a letter dated Sunday, May 3, 1925, and addressed to Bill and Freda Burge, in Milwaukee, Wisconsin, Martin wrote: "Dear Sister and Brother: Will be in Milwaukee at the end of the week, perhaps Friday night. Please don't bother about lodging for me as I can stay with an old friend in Milwaukee who has a big flat. Hope to see you Saturday afternoon at the latest. Ours in a Hurry, Martin."

Great-uncle Martin was living in Chicago at the time, but he was also known to live in New York City and later on the West Coast. According to Aunt Betty, he had invested in the California Public Utilities Commission, based in San Francisco, where he lived for most of his life. And that investment turned out to be a very good risk. Because of his financial status, Martin was well traveled and comparatively metropolitan when you look back at the Weyauwega farm he came from. My mother, Uncle Pete, and Aunt Betty all remembered Grandma Freda staying in touch with her older brother throughout the years. He was never married and never had any children of his own, and based on family recollections, there was always a shared sense of mystery about their uncle.

It wasn't until much later that the Burges were forthcoming about Martin's sexuality. The story about how he fit in, or didn't fit in, to the Stelter family is very interesting because of what we know about the family's staunch Protestant upbringing and the narrow views that were kept about men and women. According to his obituary, Martin Charles Stelter was born in 1898 and died at seventy-two years of age in San Francisco. It was 1970, and Grandma and Grandpa were in financial limbo at the time, because of Grandpa's disability and the fact that they were growing older and couldn't take care of the farm all by themselves. When Martin died, he left his sister $100,000—a veritable fortune then, and a substantial fortune now. It was enough money for them to buy a little house in Grand Marais with a rental unit so that it would bring in some additional income. My aunt Lila was able to help them with the purchase agreement, which allowed Grandma and Grandpa to take their time selling the Warba farm. Because of Martin's help they were able to move back to the North Shore where their daughters Lila, Betty, and Joyce all lived. They would also be close to Silver Bay, where Uncle Pete and Aunt Marion lived.

The house they bought is still there—on the upper side of Highway 61 at the bottom of Harbor Light Hill. It sits back from the road, and there's a detached motel unit on the west side of the lot. Uncle Martin's bequest was also enough for Grandma and Grandpa to buy a trailer house in Tucson, where they planned to spend their winters. Grandma would never again have to spend another winter worried about the pipes freezing or fret about driving on icy roads. Because of Great-uncle Martin's generosity, Grandma and Grandpa were able to relax a bit and enjoy being close to their family, which included a growing number of grandchildren and great-grandchildren. This was a gift not just to them but also a gift to all of us, because now I would be able to get to know my grandma Freda on my own terms and meet Grandpa Burge as an older gentleman who was always kind and not scary, at least not to us.

After telling me the story of Grandma's windfall, Aunt Betty then shared that Great-uncle Martin is buried at the Maple Hill Cemetery in Grand Marais. Grandma used some of the money he gave her to buy burial plots for herself, Grandpa, and her dear brother, who took such good care of her in life and in death. I'm comforted to know that he is close by, and that his sister Freda never gave up loving him because of who he was. It's a good part of the Burge story, to know that he and Grandma were supportive of each other "no matter what," as Aunt Lila would say.

While they lived in Grand Marais, Grandma Burge would some-times take care of us. She was an avid reader and used books as her way to escape from whatever life circumstances she was in. I remember her reading huge, fat, clothbound novels with tiny type as well as pulpy paperback Harlequin romances, as many as she could fit next to her bed. Grandma was also someone who walked places, and even into her seventies she would walk from their house on Highway 61 and straight up Eighth Avenue, which is one of the steepest hills in town. Grandpa wasn't in such good shape. He wore Coke-bottle glasses, so thick they made his eyes seem like they were bugging out. And he was a big man—tall and stocky. He was not as able as Grandma, and so she would visit us on her own more often than not. They would sometimes host family picnics in their backyard, and I remember there being particularly tall spruce trees behind their house.

The kind of old trees that are hard to find around downtown Grand Marais now. She and Grandpa seemed perfectly happy together, even after so many years.

****

The winter we drove to California to visit Aunt Carol, Grandma and Grandpa were in Tucson for the cold season. The plan was for my mom, Aunt Betty, Cindy, Dawn, and me to drive there, pick up Grandma, and then go on to Los Angeles, where Aunt Carol lived. When we reached Tucson, Betty tried to call Uncle Lloyd from Grandma and Grandpa's trailer, wanting to check in with him and give him an update about how the trip was going. We were, of course, having fun and everything was fine. It was a memorable trip with so many firsts, including the first real tacos I've ever eaten, which we enjoyed somewhere between Grandma's trailer court and the sprawl of Los Angeles. Aunt Betty let the phone ring and ring and there was no answer. She tried again later that day, and still no answer. She was starting to get worried, but those were the days before cell phones or answering machines, so there really was no way for her to contact Lloyd, other than having someone go over to their house to check on him to make sure he was OK. So, she called her neighbor and asked her to run over and check on Lloyd, and when the neighbor called back, she reported that Lloyd wasn't home.

This sent Aunt Betty into full-on panic mode, imagining that the worst had happened. Maybe he went out in the woods by himself and got into trouble and froze to death. Maybe he went ice fishing on Northern Light Lake and something bad had happened and he fell through the ice and froze to death. Or maybe, just maybe, he had gone AWOL like when her first husband had disappeared from the army, or like her friend's husband had, when he decided to leave his family for another woman. Aunt Betty was really tense on the drive from Tucson to Los Angeles. She tried to conceal it, but she was really worried about Lloyd's whereabouts, and this may have been part of the reason why our car was filled with extra cigarette smoke, forcing Grandma to say "Aw quat tee saw," from the back seat while covering her nose and mouth with a frilly pink scarf.

Driving into L.A. was like entering another world. I still can't quite believe my mother drove us there. Aunt Carol lived on a skinny frontage road alongside an eight-lane freeway. For a girl from Grand Marais, where the only paved road is a two-lane highway in and out of town, Los Angeles was quite memorable. I remember us driving the Country Squire on a fast-moving freeway and seeing fires coming out of smokestacks on the horizon. There were really no trees to speak of, and the ones we saw were palm trees, but not like the lush palms we saw in South Florida, or the palm trees you'd see on *Gilligan's Island*. No, these were stranded soldiers struggling for oxygen in the smoggy L.A. basin.

We pulled up next to Aunt Carol and Uncle Earl's house and out came Carol, Earl, our cousins Ronny and Brian and—"aw quat tee saw"—Uncle Lloyd. Betty couldn't reach Lloyd because in a fit of loneliness and worry, he had driven to Duluth and hopped on a plane to Los Angeles. He had beat us there by a day. When I say Aunt Betty and Uncle Lloyd's love story is like the tallest tree in the forest, this is what I mean. He never had any intention of staying by himself, so he decided to join us in California. As a result, all of our activities included Uncle Lloyd. He went along to Knott's Berry Farm and trailed along with us at Disneyland. Bless his heart for loving Aunt Betty and Cindy so much. He couldn't live without them.

* * * * * * *

One of the things in Grandma Burge's box of letters and ephemera was Aunt Betty's high school graduation certificate. The general attitude was that because Faye, Lila, and Pete had all dropped out of school, it was imperative that Betty, Carol, and Joyce would all graduate. Aunt Betty's school career was particularly hard-fought, because she had to repeat a grade as a result of her poor eyesight and had to go through every class a year older than everyone else.

One of the skills Betty learned in school was typing, and that was a primary reason she was able to get office jobs in Minneapolis, Chicago, and Grand Marais at the local hospital, where she worked in the billing department for many years. She typed all her own letters, was familiar with computers before anyone else was, and because of this ability, was able to keep the Larsen family well organized. In keeping with her general sense of order, Aunt Betty would never forget your birthday. When I was going through my own boxes of keepsakes, I started a pile of birthday cards that Aunt Betty had given me every single year of my life, from when I was just one year old until I was nearly fifty. It's just how Aunt Betty was.

The most thrilling birthday for Betty was likely the day her granddaughter Andrea was born. It was in July and I was living in Duluth at the time. I got word that Cindy had gone into labor and that Uncle Lloyd, Aunt Betty, Dan (Andrea's dad), and Cindy's friend Jenny were all caravanning from Grand Marais and would be present for the delivery. Cindy had invited me to be there, too, and I was so happy and excited to be a part of Andrea's welcoming committee. As a woman who has never actually been able to picture myself as a mother of children (morbidity of motherhood be damned), being granted the opportunity to be a part of Cindy's most incredible feat on earth was somewhat overwhelming. But as soon as I got there and was able to see firsthand how everything in the room changed the closer we got to the baby being born, I was able to calmly be there for Cindy as best I could.

Labor takes many hours, and if you are responsible for being there as a witness to new life, the lights, the tiles, the scrubs, the sounds—all melt into a kind of blurry continuum where time as we know it ceases to exist. I will always admire Cindy's bravery that day, because it really was taking a long time, and it seemed like it really, really hurt an awful lot. And through it all, there was Aunt Betty, sitting in a chair at Cindy's feet, and there was Uncle Lloyd, in another chair with a happy grin on his face, not saying a word. When little Andrea was there to take her first breath, Betty and Lloyd were able to experience it with her—breathing along with their little granddaughter.

Thank you, Cindy Carol, for letting me be there with you, to see the circle of life in all of its nerve-racking, painful, and messy exultation. What a great honor. Among all of these musings about what it means to be a mother, and in an attempt to acknowledge the struggles of our own mothers and grandmothers, I've come to believe the old Burge adage that babies are indeed magic on earth, and that they can help ease some of the painful things that have happened to us in the past. Because what's more hopeful than a brand-new start?

In Betty's castle Cindy Carol and Andrea were her princesses, and Lloyd was her knight in shining armor. Their royal abode was a house with uneven floors, a narrow, winding staircase, and a big yard for a baby to play in. Around the time Andrea was two or three, Uncle Lloyd began to show signs of memory loss and a bit of confusion about what was going on around him. He still ate eggs and bacon for breakfast every day, but he was slowing down in a way that was concerning for Auntie Betty. She decided that it was time for them to move out of their house and into an apartment in town. Cindy and Andrea would live in their house, the one with the big yard, and the family would make a slow transition into whatever the next phase of life would bring. Aunt Betty did everything she could to make their apartment comfortable for Uncle Lloyd, who had not lived anywhere else since he was a young man, newly married to Betty. As I've come to know with my own father, a familiar routine is a friend to people with dementia, and so Lloyd struggled to understand why they were in a different place. It was a hard time for them, and Uncle Lloyd was never meant to live without Aunt Betty, even for a short time, as we learned when we tried to have a girls' visit to California.

****

We inherit a lot from our families. Whether it's a pile of money or an affinity for books, we also bring along the blood-and-guts trauma from the past within our physical selves. Sometimes we share the mannerisms of a grandma or the laugh of an auntie. Aunt Betty inherited a litany of health problems from Grandpa and other relatives. She had one wandering eye, which always made you question whether she was looking at you or the person standing next to you. And along with that was an early onset of nearsightedness, which is very much a Burge family trait. She also had trouble managing her blood sugar and was diagnosed with diabetes when she was in her thirties, which was earlier than others in the Burge family who inherited the same disease.

I mention these things not because I think they affected who she was as a person, but they did shape some of my memories of her. For example, she always had sweets and baked goods in her house, but she also had a bowl of sugar-free candy in a glass dish next to her bed, and one in the living room. In her later years, she had to inject insulin into her leg or belly before she ate a big meal. This would absolutely affect some people's choices about eating a meal in public, but Aunt Betty would just whip out the needle, pull up her shirt, and stick herself with the syringe right in the middle of a restaurant, or at the Thanksgiving table before we were about to eat. Diabetes would lead to some major health problems for her, but even as she and Uncle Lloyd slowed down, she made it clear that she would not leave this earth if there were still things that needed to be taken care of.

Aunt Betty's heart was weakened by diabetes, which eventually affects every part of a person's body. Nevertheless, it was still quite a shock when we heard that Aunt Betty had suffered a massive heart attack and was having emergency open-heart surgery in Duluth. My parents scrambled to her bedside, including one ridiculous night spent in the hospital waiting room, where they tried to sleep upright in the chairs provided, but Dad ended up falling on the floor in a fitful sleep. A cardiac nurse friend tried to warn us that people rarely recover from the kind of heart damage Betty had experienced, so when we went to see her, we were prepared for the worst. She had made it through the surgery, but her body was in a state of trauma and she was barely recognizable. Over the next five days, I was waiting to get word that Aunt Betty had left us. But that's not what happened.

My mother claims that Betty's sheer will to live was rooted in her love for Cindy, Andrea, and Uncle Lloyd. On some level, Betty knew that she could not leave Cindy alone with a little child and a father who was slowly losing his faculties to dementia. And so, she gathered up all of her Burge tenacity and she rallied. After a little time, she was taken off the machines that were keeping her systems in sync. And pretty soon she was sitting up in bed, and then was moved to sitting in a wheelchair. After a little while longer, she was transported to the hospital in Grand Marais to get her ready to go back home.

This was a long period of recovery, and Uncle Lloyd was starting to require constant supervision. Cindy and Aunt Betty made the difficult decision to move Uncle Lloyd to the Minnesota Veterans Home in Silver Bay. Cindy said it was the hardest thing she has ever done, and it breaks my heart that it had to come to that. Eventually Uncle Lloyd forgot that he liked eggs and bacon, he forgot that he drank coffee, and he forgot that he smoked a cigarette every morning after breakfast. He died the day before Cindy's birthday in 2010. A man who used to get drunk on beer and try to jump over the campfire, Uncle Lloyd was a person of few words, but he had an awful lot of spark. I can't imagine Aunt Betty would have ever married and loved a man who didn't possess a good helping of spark, and she certainly found it when she married Lloyd.

* * * * * * *

Aunt Betty stayed with us for a while longer. I guess she still had more to take care of. There were people who needed the safety of an empathetic ear and a place of respite, even if it was just a conversation at the senior center or a call that comes in the middle of the night from someone who was in grave danger and needed help. This world can be a scary place sometimes, especially for girls and women who know firsthand what it's like to be cornered in the barn, propositioned by your principal, or called names at school because you didn't fit into a neat little box. For a number of years, Aunt Betty served on the board of the local Violence Prevention Center and was on the call list for people who found themselves in an abusive and dangerous situation and needed help. This work didn't end when she got older and wasn't on the call list anymore. I believe Betty was witness to abuse on a number of levels, both as a girl and later, as a sister, an aunt, friend, and confidante for other women in her life. After Aunt Faye died, it was Aunt Betty who strictly forbade George Lindley's ashes to join the ashes of her sister Faye here in Grand Marais. Even in death, Aunt Betty was still protecting her sister—trying to keep her in a safe place, away from a predator, even if he was reduced to ashes. Her house was our safe space when we were growing up, and she was able to transform herself into a "safe space" for others, making room inside her emotional and spiritual life for other people's troubles, struggles, and trauma. Joy Harjo has said that "coming into this world, you're coming into a healing ceremony from beginning to end."[6] This is certainly true for all of my aunties, but Aunt Betty's story might be the best example of what it means to live your circle of life as a ceremony of your own making.

The autumn after I interviewed her about her life and the Burge family, Betty's health took a turn and she developed an ongoing infection in her body that was hard to combat because of complications from diabetes. On her eighty-first birthday she was in the hospital in Grand Marais, where she used to work. She had visitors all day and an ice cream cake. Anyone who entered her room had to cover themselves with fresh hospital gowns, caps, and paper booties over their shoes. We all gathered around her bed, looking like something from a future news story about the Covid-19 pandemic. My cousin Linda was there, Aunt Lila's eldest daughter; Cindy and Andrea were there too. Someone had brought in some balloons and Aunt Betty took at least two phone calls while I was there, one from my cousin Loni calling from Chicago and the other from a friend of Betty's from Grand Marais. She was in good spirits, joking about our ridiculous gowns, and Andrea sat right next to her the whole time, holding her hand and laughing at Betty's off-color jokes about spending her eighty-first birthday in the hospital. She ate a little bit of cake and I decided to get ready to go home. I said, "Happy Birthday, Auntie Betty! I'm going to head home now," and she said, "Staci Lola, thanks for being you." And I said, "Thanks for being you, Auntie Betty."

A few hours later my dad called to say that Betty had died. In true form, she waited until the party was over to make her exit from this world and take shelter in the arms of her Lord and Savior. I suspect it wasn't a coincidence that Aunt Betty's last day on earth was her own birthday. She had left all the sad questions behind about whether her adopted son Danny had purposely chosen her birthday to end his own life. In a way, it was like she was reestablishing control over her own birthday—reclaiming what belonged to her and casting away doubt. The arc of her life had made a complete circle, and she had safely landed in a place free of guilt, full of forgiveness, and with lots of flowers. And don't worry, Aunt Betty—in that place there are no big words to stumble over, just love, which is really the biggest word of all.

Safe Spaces: A Poem for Betty

We all need space to stretch out
to become human beings.
Like the tiny fist of a newborn
clinging to her mother's finger,
we must be allowed to reach out
and grab ahold of something solid.
Safe spaces are where we are free,
to be exactly who we are meant to be.
Transmissions through a telephone wire
or a carpet of words like baby's breath,
there is safety in peace,
security in love,
sanctity in forgiveness—
all spacious, human words
that give us endless room to roam.

Carol

CAROL HAD TO GO TO THE STORE to pick up a few things for dinner. She got in her cavernous, white Econoline van, eased it onto the freeway, and turned at the exit that would take her to the enclave of stores closest to her house in Los Angeles. She got out of the van, locked the driver's side door, and headed to the entrance. Moving through the automatic doors and past the nests of shopping carts, she proceeded to the produce section. While picking through the lemons, she realized she had left the house in her fluffy pink bedroom slippers. Mortified, she started walking with a pronounced limp, to cover for the fact that she had forgotten to wear shoes. A fellow shopper noticed her gimping down the aisle and thought, "Oh, poor, dear, there must be something wrong with her foot."

Aunt Carol was blessed with the ability to make everyone laugh, even if you weren't there to see it. Hers was the sort of laughter that lingers, like how this story still makes my mom throw her head back and cackle madly, as if it was something that happened yesterday. I remember when Carol was visiting us in Grand Marais one time, and something happened that involved her falling or stumbling out of our car in front of the liquor store, and my mom and Carol became incapacitated with laughter, like, for days afterward. This is partly about being sisters and partly about Carol being a ridiculously funny person.

It was her humor that saved her from life at the Warba farm, which was really hard on Carol in particular. She was born in Weyauwega, Wisconsin, in 1936, just fifteen months after her sister Betty was born. There's a pay stub in the Burge box of treasures dated 1937. It's from the Worden-Allen Company in Milwaukee, which paid Grandpa Burge $18.00 for one week's work. At that rate, he would have been on track to make a grand total of $864 a year. In 1937 the average annual income was $1,788.00, putting the Burges at a bit over half of the national average. Grandpa had to take work wherever he could find it, leaving Grandma at home with six kids, their ages ranging from twelve to less than one year old. My mother's first memory of her sister Carol is placed deep inside the old farmhouse basement in Warba. Mom was about four and Carol was six. "Oh, Carol would say funny things. That's how she got out of things with Mother. She could giggle and laugh." But Mom also admitted that her older sister "was always kind of a misfit." For reasons both seen and unseen, Auntie Carol was born into a life of struggle, and she worked very hard to break free of it.

With Grandpa often gone for weeks at a time, "Ma was always busy working and cooking and us kids were kind of on our own," said Joyce, the youngest Burge, who theorized that her mother "just blocked us all out. She was always cooking and baking and washing clothes and things." Grandma was often lost in her own world of things to tend to, including a lot of children to manage. Inevitably, something would go terribly awry and Carol would "just turn around and say something funny and Mom would start laughing."

When they were a bit older and Grandpa would be at home instead of away at work, Carol was always the first person to notice when his mood was about to turn. She would say, "'Uh-oh, Dad's eyes are turning green,' meaning he was getting mad." In fact, my mom remembers Grandpa always being mad. She said Carol in particular was fearful of his wrath, which rose above the surface often, usually because he was in no mood for having children in the house. For kids with any degree of sensitivity, his gruff and explosive manner was too much. My mother remembers an incident with Carol that set the tone between her and their father forever: "He grabbed ahold of her one time and she peed her pants. She never trusted him. Even when she was older. She had nightmares about Dad, even as an adult."

I asked my mom why Auntie Carol was so deathly afraid of Grandpa, which from the sound of it, was really quite debilitating for her. Mom said that when they were little kids, "[Carol] wouldn't even walk by his chair to go to bed. She'd try to stay as far away or stay as quiet as possible." And even if they made it upstairs past the volatile old ogre in the living room, he would sometimes yell, "Quiet down, or I'm coming upstairs!" My mom added, "I was scared of him, too, but not as much as Carol."

Based on what I've learned from my mom and other aunties about growing up on the farm, I was suspicious about why Aunt Carol was so terrified of her dad. Were there some dark and hidden family secrets being repressed or purposely buried in the family's collective psyche? So, I just flat out asked my mother about it, and she made it clear that "there was no sexual abuse from our dad." It was a relief to hear that, but I still wondered why Grandpa Burge was the source of such angst for Carol. His own childhood story provides some significant clues about why that may have been. A history that was long submerged by the family, the story of Grandpa Bill's childhood traumas is inextricably tied to how he treated some of his own children—traumas he passed along to his family like a bad case of swimmer's itch.

* * * * * * *

William Eric Burge was born in April 1901 in Winnipeg, Manitoba. The name Burge comes from Burgess, which is the old English and Irish family name before his ancestors came to North America. His mother, Eliza Jane Tufts, crossed the ocean from England on a passenger ship in the 1870s as a baby, along with her parents, James and Maria Tufts, who came from Norfolk, England. The family horror story about their voyage is that Eliza Jane's mother left her on deck for a brief moment and came back to find a rat chewing on her baby daughter's ear. A harbinger of things to come in North America? Perhaps.

The Burge family settled in Winnipeg, and we still have a number of relatives in that area. Grandpa's family was big, just like Grandma Freda's was, and he was born with what were considered to be significant disabilities at the time. He was left-handed, which seems silly to think of as a disability now, but at the time, a left-handed child was a liability, almost to the point of being against God the Almighty, right-handed King of heaven and earth. Which prompts the question, do angels ever sit at the left hand of God? This bias is the opposite of what my Ojibwe relatives believe about offering a spiritual gift to the earth or another living being. The Ojibwe traditional way is to hold the gift in your left hand, because that hand is closer to the heart. If Grandpa had been born into another belief system, perhaps he would have been spared the stigma of being different from others. He may have even been revered for the strength and efficacy of his prayers.

William, or Bill, in addition to favoring his left side, also inherited poor eyesight and was further cursed with a stutter, which made school lessons and speaking up for himself very difficult if not impossible. Aunt Lila had shared some of these details about her father's life with her daughter Lilean, who in turn shared what she knew with me. The sad family story is that Grandpa Bill was abused and tortured by his own mother as a very young child, something that was confirmed by my mother, who said, "[Grandma Burge] would tie his left hand behind his back from the time he was in a high chair" in an attempt to change his dominant left hand to a prevailing right hand. And when he brought home poor marks from school, he was sent to the attic and left there all alone, sometimes for days at a time. Being banished to the attic got to be more routine the older he got, and young William was essentially living as a prisoner in his own house. Grandpa wasn't one to share these kinds of stories with his own kids, and it's likely that Aunt Lila and others knew about it only because Grandma Freda told them about it later, after they grew up. Lilean recalled that Great-grandma Burge was a "very staunch English teacher . . . and she was ashamed of Grandpa."

Unable to withstand this very damaging constraint set upon him by his mother, Grandpa Burge left home at thirteen and crossed the border into the United States illegally to escape his situation. He was a refugee of sorts, coming to America to find safety and freedom. After he fled from Winnipeg, he was an outcast from the family for a long period of time. My mother, Aunt Lila, and my cousin Linda went to visit our Burge relatives in the 1980s, and while they were there my mother asked Grandpa's sister about their family life, in particular, Great-grandma Burge's cold disposition. My great-aunt denied that there was any bad family history to divulge. According to my mother she said, "No, I never felt anything but love from my mother." Perhaps she was blessed with right-handedness, or maybe she wasn't telling the whole truth.

There weren't a lot of warm feelings for Great-grandma Eliza, or "Lila," which was what everyone called her. As my mother recalled, when they were a bit older, she would come to Warba and stay for months at a time. Mom said that Grandpa Bill and Grandma Freda would give her their bedroom downstairs. According to Joyce, "Mom didn't like her being there. She always had to have hot water in the morning and one day she tried to accuse Grandma Freda of poisoning her. We had one radio and she had it in her bedroom; she would never let us listen to it, unless it was something she wanted us to listen to. She was old when I knew her—like with white hair. She was always really crabby to us. She wasn't loving—we never sat on her lap or anything like that. She also picked at Carol. Lila was named after her, so she liked that. My memory of her is that she was quite selfish."

Given that she tormented her own son, it's not hard to imagine why Great-grandma Burge chose to pick on Carol, because Carol almost always found herself in a bit of an upside down, downside up sort of predicament. For example, she got impetigo as a young girl and spent a year or more itching and scratching her skin into scabs. She also got ringworm all over her face and Grandma treated it with zinc oxide, so Aunt Carol had to walk around with a cartoonish white mask on her face for a week. According to Mom, "She was a mess as a kid." One time Carol infamously put a kernel of corn in her nose and it just festered up there, until it sprouted and started to stink. No one noticed that anything was amiss until Carol started to smell like a granary. It's not clear why she put that kernel up her nose, but I guess ours is not to reason why. As my mom said, "She just did everything other kids would not normally do. Mom was too busy to even notice that she was doing anything like that."

A lot of the time, it was "out of sight, out of mind" for the Burge kids. My mother said that in the summer they would play outside in a place she called "the Grove," where she and Carol would pretend to pickle dandelion blossoms in Mason jars and play house. When mom was five and Carol was seven, their sister Betty, who was eight, had a bad ankle, and so a lot of that summer, Carol and Joyce spent all of their days together, playing outside. She said with regret that "we were kind of mean to Betty too. You know kids." She and Carol slept in the same bed, and Betty finally had her own bed after the older kids left. Carol's difficulties in her waking life would also carry over into her unconscious world. She had the bizarre habit of sleepwalking and at times would get out of bed in a dream state and amble down the stairs to the first floor without waking up. Eventually a sibling or one of her parents would find her standing in the kitchen, eyes open, but fully asleep and say, "Go back to bed, Carol."

****

Farming is a mean life if you are sensitive about animals and the life-and-death cycle of things, and my mother is still somewhat traumatized by it. There was the weekly beheading of chickens, followed by the boiling and plucking of feathers. Mom still has a hard time with the smell of unseasoned boiled chicken. And it's important to know that it wasn't Grandpa holding the cleaver; it was Grandma Freda who did the killing. Mom would bear witness to her systematic butchering process that involved chasing a hen around the yard, grabbing it by the neck, forcing it onto a sturdy chopping block and whacking its head off. Afterward, the kids would watch the bloody chicken carcass reflexively run away from the killing stump. Yes, chickens keep moving even after their heads are cut off. She also said that they always had at least one cow and a dog, but the dogs were only allowed in the house if it was below zero, and if a dog made the mistake of chasing a cow or killing a chicken, the poor thing would unceremoniously "disappear," never to be seen again. I shudder to think about how the innocent Burge family farm dogs met their various endings. It's how life was, back on the farm.

This rugged lifestyle also applied to the daily upkeep of things when it came to personal hygiene and the amount of effort required to maintain some semblance of order at the farm. Mom said they didn't have baths a lot, but in the summer they all went swimming at Shallow Lake once a week. There was a nice beach there, and that's where she learned to swim. My mother has always been a strong swimmer, and those summers in Warba conditioned her to love being in the water. The family also had a big washtub and in between swimming days, Grandma or Aunt Faye would wash the little girls' hair. Carol and

Betty were both blonds when they were young, but my mom had dark-brown ringlets when she was a kid.

Uncle George was thirteen years older than my mom, and after he left home, he worked at a bottling company in Bovey to help pay for his college tuition. My mother explained that "once a week he'd come home and bring us grape or orange pop. That was a real treat." She, like Aunt Betty, has very fond memories of George: "When I was really little, he would hold me in his lap and sing 'Clementine' to me. He was always good to me." She added, "I don't know if he was nice to Carol too. Pete was meaner to Carol than he was to me." My mother's theory as to why Pete was mean to Carol stems from the idea that Carol "would have been cute if she hadn't pulled her eyelashes out."

* * * * * * *

Auntie Carol's angst as a young girl went a lot deeper than anyone really knew. Aunt Betty and my mother both remember seeing their sister ritualistically pull out her own eyelashes and put them in her mouth. I wondered if Carol also suffered from obsessive-compulsive disorder like my mother did, which is, of course, passed along genetically in families. Her compulsion to pluck out her eyelashes, and once they were gone, move on to her eyebrows, was definitely an indication that something was amiss. Kids sometimes develop destructive habits and eventually grow out of it. I remember being in junior high and biting down hard on my tongue to ensure that I wouldn't start yelling uncontrollably during class. A compulsion that I eventually grew out of, thankfully. But if the behavior lingers over many years, it's likely that someone is experiencing symptoms of a brain disorder—a systemic illness that won't go away without treatment. This may have been the case with Carol, whose bad thoughts were manifesting themselves in destructive ways. It could have been OCD, but it also could have been a direct response to some kind of personal trauma she experienced during life on the farm. This possibility might also explain her tendency to sleepwalk at night—her subconscious attempts to get away from whatever terrible reality she was forced to face as a young girl.

Trichotillomania is a disorder that is caused by "a combination of genetic, biological and behavioral factors."[1] It affects roughly 2 percent of the global population, which means that about 150 million people in the world compulsively pull hairs out of their scalp, eyebrows, eyelashes or from another part of the body. It is often miscategorized as symptomatic of obsessive-compulsive disorder, and historically it has "has never been taken seriously enough."[2] Interestingly, females who suffer from trichotillomania outnumber males four to one. Doctors associate the disorder with the onset of puberty, having high intelligence, experiencing anxiety, or, in extreme cases, as a reaction to a traumatic incident. It's a coping mechanism that gives an initial feeling of release, followed by long-term negative effects like shame, embarrassment, baldness, and low self-esteem.

Poor Auntie Carol. It turned out that her eyelashes and eyebrows never grew back, and so she lived most of her life looking a bit odd. My mother said it "made her look stark." In her teenage and adult years, Carol penciled in her eyebrows, and she could have fit right into a 1950s Elvis movie starring Ann-Margret. Suffering from trichotillomania may help explain her behavior, but there is no clear or justifiable explanation for why Grandma or Grandpa didn't do anything to help her, or at least try to figure out why their second youngest daughter was ritualistically maiming herself. It's not sufficient to say that it was a matter of too many kids and not enough money, but that was certainly part of it. Once again, the morbidity of motherhood proved to be overwhelming and problematic, resulting in the creation of more children, but not necessarily healthier children. Like a mother bird with seven chicks and only one beak, Grandma's ability to nurture sometimes fell short. And so, the older kids stepped in as needed and did the best they could.

As Aunt Betty has said, Faye ended up doing a lot of the mothering at their house when Betty, Carol, and Joyce were young. My mother clarified the role her oldest sister played in their upbringing: "Faye was a bright spot for us—she did all she could to take care of us three girls. She was our mother figure for sure, all our lives. Not our 'mother' so much, but our mother figure."

****

When my mom was two, Grandpa Burge went through the naturalization process to become an American citizen. The instructor, Veronica Hall, prepared students for the test, which was administered in Grand Rapids. Grandpa was very proud that he passed, and my mother remembers that "he was so happy" whenever he talked about it. His Social Security card is in the Burge box of treasures. It was issued December 29, 1936. Grandpa was thirty-five years old when he was given the rights of citizenship and was able to vote. My uncle Pete said that Grandma and Grandpa had always admired Democrats, and President Franklin D. Roosevelt in particular. So, when FDR died and Harry Truman became president, Grandpa was empowered to help decide the direction of our country during the nuclear age and ahead of the Korean War. I imagine that this was a great honor for him, since he was a "man without a country" from the age of thirteen to thirty-five. But I think it's important to add some counterbalance to Grandpa Burge's achievement.

Back in his home province of Manitoba, First Nations people were not allowed to vote in federal elections until 1960, unless they agreed to relinquish their tribal status.[3] In the United States, the women's suffrage movement had secured the vote for white women in 1920, but most Native American women were not granted the right to vote until 1924. In the states of Arizona and New Mexico, Native American men and women were not allowed to vote until 1948, and in some states like Maine and Utah, Native American people were not given the vote until the mid-1950s. On the Drouillard side of the family, Grandpa Fred would have been fourteen years old when his own mother was granted voting status. Women of Asian descent in the United States were not made eligible to vote until 1952, and, obviously because of the civil rights movement, Black women and men born in the United States were finally granted legal voting status in 1965. Grandpa Burge wasn't born in this country but was still able to study hard, answer a series of questions on paper, and be given the full rights of citizenship, almost thirty years before Black Americans who were born here (most of whom were the descendants of people who were forced to come here against their will) were allowed the rights of full citizenship. Grandpa's experience is a good example of how equal rights and equal protection under the law continue to welcome people with white, Anglo-Saxon backgrounds, even if they sneaked into the country as refugees from harm.

The men who worked with Grandpa at the mine often called him

"Canada Bill," making their own distinctions clear about his country of origin. Aunt Betty described her Canadian grandmother as "very stern. Very into school and being very serious." Apparently, her manner of speaking was proper, and Betty reported that "once Carol asked her, 'Grandma, do you talk English?'" Betty giggled at that, remembering how her silly sister would just blurt out things that got her in trouble.

Carol and Betty were in the same class in school, owing to Betty's missing first grade because of her nearsightedness. The two sisters stuck together from one school to the next all across the Iron Range, starting with middle school in Grand Rapids. My mom said, "We all hated Grand Rapids school. We were from Warba and they treated us bad." School in general was not a great experience for any of the Burges, except maybe Uncle George, who was the only one to go to college. My mom was a few grades behind her sisters, but they all attended the same schools, no matter what town the family was living in at the time. Aunt Betty told me how they ended up temporarily moving to Keewatin, about twenty-six miles away, which forced them to transfer once again to a new school: "One day Dad came home and said that he had a job in Keewatin and we were going to move. I remember all three of us going for a walk down by the barn. We were very quiet and we cried and were very upset about it. Carol and I were in tenth or eleventh grade. Joyce was in eighth grade."

The relocation was particularly hard on Joyce, the youngest sister. As Aunt Betty said, "There was a mean teacher [in Keewatin] and Joyce would come down to my locker crying. It was her English teacher. She cried and said, 'She's so mean to me.' Her name was Miss Ryan. She had hair like George Washington."

Joyce would ask her sister, "Why does she single me out?"

And Betty told her, "I think it's because you are so cute and pretty." Betty continued on: "So, we lived in Keewatin for two years. Carol was skinny there. I was fatter, but I had lost a little weight. In Keewatin there were three hundred to four hundred kids in the school. Those kids were snots. I didn't have the money to get my sewing material and there was one girl that was so mean about it. But the teacher was nice about it and she helped me."

* * * * * * *

I think it's very telling that Aunt Betty associated certain times of her life with whether she was "fatter" or "skinny." This kind of relational body talk is very common in the Burge family and I've grown to be very sensitive about it, having been exposed to it my whole life. My imaginary word for it is **fat·throw·er.** *Noun:* 1. A person who considers body weight a primary measure of life experience. 2. One who incorporates positive, negative, or neutral body observations into unrelated instances. 3. Someone who makes unsolicited, negative comments about their weight or another person's weight. *See also: Fatbully. Use:* "A notorious fatthrower, Boris's brother always made him feel anxious at mealtimes." *Also:* "It made her sad to hear that as a young girl, Carol experienced fatthrowing at the hands of her older sister."

The Burge family fatthrowing started before Auntie Faye's wedding and continues each time we're together, in almost any incarnation. The complicated relationship that most women have with their bodies is exacerbated by our growing-up kid words, and then later, our adult words. Many, many books have been written on the subjects of how women's bodies are unmercifully subjected to society's narrow views on beauty, the expectation to conform to an unrealistic ideal (see chronic femininity), and how capitalism exploits women's bodies to make men rich. And even though there are all these books intended to help us break free of this very unhealthy pattern, we continue to judge ourselves and other people based on what shape our bodies are in, instead of what we have to say, how smart or funny we are, or what's inside our hearts.

Fatthrowing is not necessarily about being "fat" or "skinny"; it's (primarily) about women's tendency to get together and talk about our bodies—how fat we were, how skinny I was, how I thought I was fat, how skinny I wish I was, and on and on into the deep pits of therapy sessions and compulsive eating binges everywhere. The amount of time that smart women spend on fat-phobic, body-shaming rhetoric while socializing, eating lunch together, passing around cake at an office birthday party, or pretty much anywhere that women gather, is time on this earth that none of us will ever get back. All of the Burge family, including my uncles, have either struggled with their weight or been obsessed by fat. We are all fatthrowers, and I wish to Holy Grandma Freda above that we were all healthier and would learn to love ourselves as we are, and not feel like we have to apologize for being fat, or not fat, as the case may be.

When Aunt Betty, Cindy, Mom, Dawn, and I drove to California to visit Aunt Carol and her family, I was at the formative age of thirteen. When we left home for sunny Los Angeles, I had never been so far away from Minnesota, or been in such a big city, with so many different people and a completely foreign lifestyle, so different from how we did things in our tiny town of Grand Marais. I had sixty-five kids in my class at school and in L.A. our cousins, Ronny and Brian, went to schools that were known for their ridiculously overcrowded conditions, sometimes with double that many kids in one math classroom. While we were there visiting, Aunt Carol let Ronny and Brian stay home from school so that they could go on adventures with us. Aunt Carol piled everyone into an enormous white Ford Econoline van with a navy-blue stripe down the side, and she drove us all over Los Angeles. And it was quite a load, with the five of us, plus Grandma Burge, Carol, Ronny and Brian, and of course, Uncle Lloyd, our surprise addition to the trip. She took us to Disneyland, where my sister and my cousin Cindy rode on the Mad Tea Party cups about a hundred times; we marveled at the It's a Small World fantasy ride, dodged skeletons with the Pirates of the Caribbean, and got scared out of our wits in the Haunted Mansion, including Mom, who mistook an actual person on the elevator for a hologram ghost and then screamed her brains out when the person said "BOO!" right in her face. Aunt Carol played our tour guide at all of these vacation hot spots, including Knott's Berry Farm, where a goat ate the daily pass off my belt loop while I stood passively by, which everyone thought was hilarious.

The weather wasn't great the day we went to the beach. It was unseasonably cold, so no one was really up for swimming. Aunt Carol, Mom, Aunt Betty, Uncle Lloyd, and Grandma were all sitting or lying down on beach blankets while us kids picked up shells and other exotic mementos. I was close enough to hear a group of teenage boys say something really mean about my Aunt Carol's weight. I'm not going to quote them here, because their fatbullying doesn't deserve to be in print. I sincerely hope Aunt Carol was oblivious and that the sound of the waves protected her from what they said. But I heard it as clear as day, and ever since then, bullyish words about people's appearance or weight will hit me like a rogue Pacific wave. Fatthrowing and fatbullying go hand in hand in terms of the amount of damage they can cause. One is set upon the world more thoughtlessly or seemingly thoughtlessly, because we're so used to women talking about our bodies, and one is just purposely mean and intended to cause harm to someone. The ways that we, as human beings, use hurtful names, barbed words, and insensitive comments to wound and slowly kill each other (and ourselves) are exclusive to humankind. We are the animal species with the most nuanced form of communication, and the words and languages we have created to express ourselves are loaded with the ability to assert power, to belittle, to shame or even gouge out a pound of flesh, if it suits us. We put these words in our mouths, and we have the ability to pull them out like rotten molars. It's our conscious choice.

A few years ago, while fishing in Grand Marais harbor I experienced exactly what happened to Aunt Carol. We were out enjoying the day, hoping for a coho salmon to bite on a lure. My line was looking good, and just then, some teenage boys standing on the break wall unleashed the very same words on me that the mean kids on the beach in California unleashed on Aunt Carol. The EXACT same words. Almost simultaneously, a salmon took my line down and I reeled it in— a keeper. I should have been happy, but my entire day was ruined by the mean and careless words of total strangers. And so, every time my aunties or my mother have talked about how they are "fat" or feel the need to point out that "you've lost weight," lying silently in the inverse is, "you've gained weight" or "you're still fat." No matter what I do to prepare myself, it's always difficult to recover from the assault.

Fatthrowing is the result of many, many years of conditioning designed to make us believe that our value depends on whether or not we fit society's expectations of women as pretty things to look at. Inextricably connected to chronic femininity, fatthrowing is another aspect of intergenerational trauma that needs to be confronted before we will be able to move beyond it. Joy Harjo has said, "The ritual of the storytelling allows us to move through the pain of the past" because "we are tired of going around it."[4]

Mean and self-loathing words and phrases are one of the ways that patriarchal societies take charge of women's bodies without ever touching us physically. The spatial, spiritual bodies of girls, women, aunties, grandmas have ceaselessly been occupied against our will by the words, bodies, and actions of men who feel it is their right to usurp space that doesn't belong to them. Cruel and insensitive words are like small land claims across the surface of our bodies and minds, just as unwanted physical intrusions are. Sometimes girls and women are the fatbullies, but mostly, it's men who use careless and cruel words to diminish the power of girls and women. The incident on the beach with the mean teenagers was just one of the formative things that happened while we were visiting Aunt Carol in California.

****

One of my new "California" outfits was a terrycloth shorts and camisole set—white with orange piping along the seams. Los Angeles was much warmer than anywhere I had ever visited, and I hoped to get a nice tan while I was there. At thirteen, I was just getting used to my own body, and as a kid who lived in her head most of the time, mind–body awareness has never come naturally to me. Some of it is my personality, being fairly shy and reserved. And some of it is because of David Peterson, our principal at Sawtooth Elementary, who made me feel like his special helper until the day he asked if he could take pictures of me in my bathing suit. I was in fifth grade and it was when our family was struggling to survive Mom's mental health crisis. "Don't tell anyone I asked you that," he whispered. And so, I didn't tell anyone. And it nearly ate me alive. Even years later, when it was discovered that he was molesting other kids, I still didn't tell. If I had been given the tools of empowerment that all children should be granted as soon as they are able to talk, I would have felt safe enough to tell my teacher, or one of my aunties or my grandma, what he said. He tried to steal ownership of my body that day, and what he did affected me in ways that are deeply engrained and have long stifled me. He used just a few words, which was all it took. I didn't tell back then, but I'm tired of going around it, so I'm telling it now. At thirteen, most girls have never experienced being subjected to a sexualized male gaze. This is something that usually only happens later, if you are lucky. I wasn't one of the lucky ones.

I was in the street outside my aunt Carol's house, on the frontage road next to the eight-lane freeway. It was a beautiful sunny day, and I was trying to get my head around the idea of skateboarding. Our long-haired California cousins were really into their skateboards, particularly back in the late 1970s and early '80s, when Los Angeles was known as its birthplace. I was in my new outfit, which provided much more coverage than a swimming suit, but much less than what I normally wore, being from Minnesota and all. As far as I knew, I was invisible to the outside world and was just focusing on how to get on the board and ride it, and not much of anything else. And then a car roared up right next to me, squealed on the brakes, and four or five young men started calling out parts of my body and trying to lure me into the car with them. I froze, one foot on the skateboard, the other on the pavement. Time sort of slowed down and it seemed like one of the men was about to get out of the car. I ran as fast as I could into the house, leaving the skateboard in the middle of the road in front of my Aunt Carol's house.

I didn't tell my mother or anyone else about what happened, but it is something that has stayed with me my whole life, and there's a part of me that still freezes inside when I think back to how I felt that day. The reality is that women of all shapes and sizes learn at some point in our lives that our bodies are spaces that can be taken over and inhabited by others, whether we want to make room for them or not. Sometimes we are ransacked by words, sometimes it's an outright physical takeover, and sometimes it's a combination of both. There is old pain that stays inside us and resurfaces as physical or mental anxiety in the bodies and minds of those who are burdened with it. If I could give a healing gift to my aunties, it would be the removal of this old pain. If I could give a healing gift to all the girls and boys who are in pain because of the words and deeds of people who took advantage of them, it would be the elimination of this lingering torment.

My mother was very honest about how the collective pain of the Burge family manifested itself in her and her sisters: "We all had that feeling that we weren't good enough, so we bought into it." Low self-worth is the source of bad decision-making and poor health, and these things are in turn learned and inherited by the generations that come after, unless we can confront the pain and move through it, using the right words to fill us up, instead of the wrong ones.

* * * * * * *

When Aunt Carol was a teenager, she always was lugging kids and dogs and cats around. My mom said, "She loved little kids, and they just loved her—always did her whole life." A softhearted animal lover, Carol loved cats but they weren't allowed to have animals in the house because Faye was allergic and Grandma didn't believe in having pets inside. So, any dogs or cats lived in the barn, which was down the hill, quite far from the main house. Uncle Pete used to work for Archie Hall, who lived down the road and had a big garden and farm operation. Aunt Betty said, "One time, Pete stuck a cat in his shirt from the Halls' farm and brought it home to Carol. I can still picture her with that cat." As a sensitive girl, Aunt Carol found solace in the innocence of kittens and animals on the farm, and it makes me feel very tender toward her and that younger version of Carol, who felt better if she had something more vulnerable than she was to care for and carry around in her protective arms.

Betty described Carol as "kind of a tomboy" when she was a young girl. She spent a lot of time in the barn where the animals were, much more than her sisters did. She was blond when she was younger, but her hair got darker as she grew into being a teenager. My mom shared that Carol was sent to live with a relative for a whole summer when she was about sixteen. Aunt Etta was either Grandma Freda's or Grandpa Bill's cousin—my mom couldn't recall. She lived in Edina, Minnesota, and had a son everyone called "Pudge" (yes, I know); they were well-off financially. My mom didn't know how they made their money, but she remembers Etta as "a nice old lady . . . we liked her." Carol went to stay with her and, according to Mom, "was like her flunky," helping with the cooking, cleaning, and gardening. Aunt Etta would occasionally visit the Burge farm, but she would never stay very long. Joyce remembers that "Mom would go all out and cook her the best food when she came."

* * * * * * *

The workings of extended family are different for everyone. For both the Burges and the Drouillards, the aunts took everyone in as part of a big, motherly, family effort. This is how we all grew up, with kids being sent to this aunt's house for a summer, these sisters going to live with that family relative, and this cousin or that one moving in for a short time to help with childcare. It's the way we all learned how to be in the world outside our own nuclear families. Some of this was out of necessity due to the sheer number of children who needed to be tended to. Some of it is cultural, the way our aunties learn to be surrogate parents for their brothers' and sisters' children. And some of it comes from desperation, which was the case for Aunt Carol and Aunt Betty as they grew into adulthood and motherhood together.

With only twenty dollars in their pockets, the two of them stayed with Uncle George and Aunt Elna for a while, as part of this extended-family tradition. George and Elna had kids of their own, but it was the family way to take in your sisters' and brothers' kids when they needed help. It wasn't hard for them to find work: Aunt Betty got hired as a phone operator at the Grain Belt Brewery and Aunt Carol worked at the Flame Bar and Café. My mother was still in high school, and she remembers spending a summer with Carol and Betty at their apartment. The sisters took Minneapolis by storm in some ways, and Mom has bittersweet memories of Carol getting too drunk and then ending up on the stairs, crying her eyes out about one thing or another. Life was still hard for her, even if she was far away from the terrors of the farm. She and Betty had made fast friends with two other young women, Kitty and Patty. They all lived together for a while in Minneapolis, scraping by and learning about getting and keeping a job. Aunt Carol had a pretty exciting gig waiting tables at the Flame, a downtown Minneapolis icon that had been a jazz club in its early days; Dizzy Gillespie, Gene Krupa, Sarah Vaughn, and Buddy Rich played on the big stage. In the late 1950s, when Carol worked there, it had changed into a country and western bar, complete with dancing girls dressed in very little except glitter and cowboy boots. Big country and western stars performed there regularly, and so Betty, Kitty, and Patty would hang out there when Carol was working, trying to rub elbows with the stars of the day. Jean Shepard, Wanda Jackson, The Carl Perkins Trio, Tex Ritter, and many more performed there in 1956–57, when Aunt Carol was working at the bar. My mom described Carol as "a good worker" and laughed when she said, "but when one of those girls quit, they would all quit!"

When the four of them got tired of chasing down jobs in Minneapolis, Patty and Carol made the big decision to move to Seattle; Betty and Kitty chose Chicago as their next adventure. My mom said Carol did have a few boyfriends when she was in her teens, but not serious ones. In Seattle she fell in love, for real, with a man in the navy. They had a fling, but he was on active duty and had to leave the area. According to my mom, "She didn't run into him for a long time." Carol had a rough go of it in Seattle, and during that time she sent the following letter to my mom, who was living in Grand Marais and engaged to be married:

OCT. 11, 1956

Dear Joyce,

Bet you're surprised I'm writing again. Found a real good job as secretary and starting at $285.00 a month. But you know what, I don't get paid for 3 weeks. If you've got about $15.00 you can borrow me, I'll send it right back, if you can I'd really appreciate it and I'll send it right away when I get paid. If you haven't got it, don't worry about it. Joyce, please don't tell the folks or Red or anybody I asked you, but maybe I can do you a big favor someday. Boy, I'm really broke. I thought my money would go further. How are you and Pooty doing? Do you see him very much? All there is down here is sailors. Real nice huh? Boy I wish you were out here with us. You'd really have fun. But, of course you've got something I haven't got—"love." Well Joyce I hope to hear from you real, real soon and I promise to pay you back right away. THANKS.

Loads of Love,
Carol

My mom did send her the money and she didn't tell "the folks" about it. I don't know if Aunt Carol ever paid Mom back, but it doesn't really matter that much. It was sisters taking care of sisters. Carol left Seattle after a short time and moved back to Chicago, where she lived with her oldest sister, Faye. After she made the move Carol started seeing a man named Ray, and their romance resulted in a baby boy. She was just twenty years old. One of Carol's friends at the restaurant where she worked had a car dealership, and Betty was able to buy a car from him so that she could go home to Warba for Christmas. She said Carol didn't go with her because she was pregnant, and she was very afraid of what her parents would say or think about her getting pregnant without having a husband. Here's my mother's assessment of the situation: "They sure made a beautiful child. They dated for quite a while, but I think there was a lot of drinking that went on then. She told me his name, but she didn't care about him that much. When she got pregnant, he was gone."

* * * * * * *

I asked Mom if she and her sisters knew anything about preventing pregnancy or had any kind of access to birth control in the late 1950s in Chicago, and she said it simply was not available. She said, "Doctors wouldn't give it out." And then she cited the underlying principle of the morbidity of motherhood, which is that "women were put on earth to have children." So, then I asked her specifically, "You knew that if you had sex you could get pregnant, right?" She said, "Yes—they had the information, but they didn't think it would happen to them. I don't know. But we knew, yes, you would get pregnant if you had sex."

And so, Auntie Carol had Ricky in Chicago and Aunt Betty went right to the hospital with her, sitting anxiously in the maternity waiting room right along with all the expectant fathers. She was there for her sister through it all, because that's what they grew up learning how to do. Here is what Betty had to say about that time in their lives: "I was with her when she was pregnant. I don't know where Ray went, but Carol worked at the BBM restaurant in Chicago at the time. She had a really good friend who worked there, and the owners were really supportive of her. She worked almost right up to the day Rick was born." And then she added, "Burges are very strong willed and very independent."

As if Aunt Betty needed to tell me that. She went on to say about Carol's new little baby: "I took the day off when she brought Ricky home. He was so cute. She hired babysitters for him. I would watch him at night when she was working."

According to Betty, Carol always had "expensive taste" in clothes. "She made pretty good tips. She liked nice things," she went on to say.

And after that, she said how "attractive" Carol was, using plenty of quantitative words about Carol's body and bust size at the time. Aunt Betty thought these were primary to the story of her sister, but if I had another chance to talk to her about Carol's life, I would have asked her instead to tell me more stories about the funny things her sister used to say and what Chicago was like, back then, for two single women with a lot on their minds.

As my mother tells it, when Ricky was born, Grandpa Burge didn't want anything to do with Carol, because "being unmarried with a baby was the worst thing in the world." When Ricky was a tiny baby, Auntie Faye's husband, Bob, died and all of the Burge family made plans to meet in Minneapolis for the funeral. Given that Aunt Carol had always had a fraught relationship with her father, the thought of showing up at the funeral with a newborn baby was crippling for her. Betty, her dutiful sister, wrote a faux letter to Grandma and Grandpa in Warba, and Carol copied it in her own hand and mailed it—to let them know about their new grandson.

And so, at the funeral, there they all were. Grandma Freda was holding Ricky and "oohing and ahhing" over him and she said enticingly to Grandpa, "Oh, come and look at this beautiful baby!" And because of the magic of Freda, he softened his view on the matter of Ricky that day. My mother's thoughts are that "he would never do anything to damage his relationship with Ma and she had to lead him into seeing that Ricky was loved and accepted." Betty's memory was that "when Dad saw Ricky, he didn't pay attention. But Ma would never leave her—she would always be there to protect Carol."

Eventually Carol and Ricky lived with her parents and her sister Faye in Warba so that Carol could get on her feet financially. Faye was suffering the loss of her husband and the pain of losing Jimmy and Johnny, and so she went to Warba for a while, too. Grandma Freda would babysit Ricky in Warba while Carol worked, and everyone doted on him and loved him. Aunt Betty helped them move and said, "We warmed up Rick's bottle on the heater of the car on the way to Warba!"

****

A little while after Aunt Carol had Ricky, she and Betty were back living in Chicago and the navy man from her past came looking for her. He was originally from the South, and he claimed he was still in love with Carol and wanted to marry her, but he told her that she would have to leave Ricky behind because his family wouldn't accept her having another man's baby. My mother said that "Betty offered to take Ricky and raise him, but Carol couldn't ever do that. She was too softhearted." So, she put her little son Ricky first over the option of getting married to her past love. Of course that was what she decided to do. It was the only choice for a young woman who used to walk around with a kitten in her arms all day.

I asked my mother what she thought it was like for Carol to have a baby outside of marriage in the 1950s, and she said that at the time, it was considered "worse than murder." She then told the story of a neighbor girl, "down the road in Warba, who had a baby. To hear Mom and Grace [the neighbor lady] talk about it—it was the worst thing you could do." She reiterated, "You could have murdered someone and it was just a bit worse than having a baby outside of marriage."

Being part of the next generation of women who benefited and learned from the hard-earned wisdom, foibles, and struggles of our mothers and aunties, I'm still left wondering why it was always considered the woman's fault when she got pregnant without being married, or why society punished young women more than men for not following the timeline they were expected to adhere to. And in a world ruled by the morbidity of motherhood, why were some babies considered to be a magical cure-all, and others were scandalous if the mother wasn't married to the father of the child? After all, Carol wasn't the only Burge daughter to get pregnant without being married. This societal conundrum is related to the Christian, patriarchal view that women are the property of men—that our bodies and minds are put on earth to fulfill the morbidity of motherhood cycle, which can only be validated by having a husband. Carol's happiness was never considered, nor was her strong sense of motherality, a strength she exhibited on the day she chose Ricky over a marriage proposal. The truth is that only women are blessed with the burden and beauty of pregnancy, the ability to give birth, and the physical means to nurse a baby into a healthy life. This is not something Carol should have been punished for. She should have been celebrated for it.

Even into adulthood, the Burge girls were all treated differently by their parents. From my mother's perspective, their dad's bias against Carol was confirmed when she brought her little boy into the family. As my mom said, "It was Dad who always thought she wouldn't amount to anything, so he was more down on her. It's like he used it to convince himself she was no good."

I then asked my mother what she thought their parents' expectations were for Carol and the rest of her sisters and brothers. She said, "I don't think they had expectations—they just wanted us out of the house. The boys were made to think they were capable, but not the girls. They put a lot of expectations on George. And Lila disappointed them too. But Lila was Dad's favorite, so he didn't treat her the same as Carol."

For Auntie Carol, being a single mother was something she had to figure out mostly on her own, but she also had a lot of support from her sisters. Because of Faye's sad circumstances and Carol's own predicament, the two sisters started on a lifelong journey to take care of each other. Aunt Betty also took care of her sisters, but as things changed in her life, she was not there to help as much. My mother was still in school, and what remained of the Burges lived at Taconite Harbor on the North Shore.

****

When Ricky was a baby, a number of the Burges moved back to Milwaukee, which is where Grandpa had cataract surgery that resulted in permanent damage to his vision. Faye, Carol, and Ricky were also in Milwaukee at the time, and it was in Milwaukee that Aunt Carol met a man named Earl Hagdon. My mother said they initially met at a bar, where Earl had been unkind to Carol. He felt bad about it, so the next time he saw her, he apologized for his bad behavior. Carol accepted his apology and the two of them started dating, and pretty soon there was a wedding. They named their first son Earl, after his dad, and everyone knew him as "Little Earl." The Hagdons moved back to Minneapolis, where Earl's family was originally from. Faye and Jeannie also went to live with them, and for a short time the whole Garner family was there, too, with Carol, Earl, Little Earl, and Ricky, all in the same house in Minneapolis. Lilean was about five years old and remembers that "we rented a house with Aunt Carol and Uncle Earl in Minneapolis. I remember Aunt Carol with great big bosoms, playing Elvis songs and dancing with Ricky. He crawled under the table and she couldn't get at him." The Garners lived there only a few months before moving back to Grand Rapids.

Aunt Betty explained that "Earl adopted Ricky after they got together." And within a few years or so, Carol and Earl had three boys, Ricky, Little Earl, and Ronny. In Minneapolis, Faye met George Lindley, who had a connection to Uncle Earl, and after that, she and her sister Carol never lived very far away from each other.

The Hagdons moved across the country to Los Angeles in the early 1960s. They rented a house first, before buying the house next to the freeway. Quite a few years after Ronny was born, the Hagdons brought a fourth little boy into the world whose name was Brian. Of course, Carol loved him with all of her heart. My mother said that "Earl was a good provider for them," because he had a stable job at Owens Glass Company. For the first time in her life, Aunt Carol didn't have to worry so much about having enough money to pay their bills. She and Earl raised their four boys at a very wild time, and in a very wild place, at least that was my impression of it. One time everyone was abuzz because Carol had called and said that she and her friend were going to be on *The Price Is Right*, the TV game show hosted by Bob Barker in the 1970s. She let everyone know that we needed to tune in on a certain day so that we could see it for ourselves. Sure enough, there was Bob Barker yelling her friend's name: "Faye Spicer, come on down!" Aunt Carol was only visible for a few seconds and her friend didn't actually win the "Showcase Showdown" or get to join Bob on stage, but it was exciting for us nonetheless.

Despite the Hollywood glamour of it all, kids could get into all kinds of trouble in L.A. so Aunt Carol often worried about her boys being safe and making good decisions. They are some of the cousins I don't really know very well, but they are family just the same. When we were visiting them in Los Angeles, Ricky had long moved out of the house, as had Little Earl. Ronny and Brian were still at home, and I remember Ronny being really nice and patient with his strange northern relatives, and Brian was a good kid who got along really well with his cousin Cindy, who was the same age. Ronny and Brian seemed to love their mom a lot. They were sort of exotic to me, boys with long blond hair who skateboarded really fast and got to go to the beach every weekend. Meeting them was part of what made our trip out west so memorable, for good reasons and not bad.

I don't remember much about leaving California or our drive back home, but there were certainly a few more vanilla milkshakes at Stuckey's, or Stuckey's, or Stuckey's—your choice—at least until we got back to the Midwest. In a show of protest, the muffler of the station wagon fell off right in front of Aunt Betty's house as soon as we got back to Grand Marais. Uncle Lloyd was already home, of course, being the jet-set guy full of surprises that he was. We pulled into their driveway, they unloaded their stuff, we backed out onto County Road 7, and then the rusty thing fell off. We dragged it all the way back home, with sparks flying in every direction. It was a fitting end to a road trip that would help shape who I was as a person, and who I am now, the niece of seven aunts.

****

My mother always stayed in close touch with Auntie Carol, even though she was so far away. She told me, "I talked to her at least once a week. Especially after she had Brian. She worried about her kids and drugs out in L.A. Because if you don't get off drugs, you die from them." She said proudly that "Carol was on top of it—she always had to protect her kids."

Protecting her oldest son, Ricky, was particularly challenging. In pictures, Ricky came across like a movie star. He was stunningly handsome, and everyone would say so. A surfer who lived on the beach, he was in the thick of Los Angeles culture, where you could get any drug you wanted and test the limits of almost anything you wanted to do. Ricky's story isn't mine to tell because I didn't know him, I only knew of him. Based on what my mom and Aunt Betty have said, Carol had her hands full as a mother, and she had the ability to love her kids through a lot of ups and downs. My mom put it simply: "She would have died for any one of her kids . . . She was worried to death about Ricky. She knew he was in trouble and worried about him all the time."

In the springtime, after we had visited Grandma and Grandpa Burge at their trailer in Tucson, they decided they wanted to be closer to the bulk of their kids and grandkids, so they bought a cute little one-story house in Grand Marais, just four doors up from the Garners' house on First Avenue. Their plan was to spend summers on the North Shore and go back to Tucson in the winter. This was in 1981, when I was fourteen and my sister was ten. Grandma had Grandpa really busy after they moved in, fixing up this little thing, or adding that little thing to their new house. She still had some of Great-uncle Martin's inheritance money left, so they used that as a down payment. There was general excitement about them being back with all of us, and early on, they had a lot of visitors. Grandma seemed really happy to be there, with a view of Lake Superior out the front window and a small yard where she could plant flowers. A few months after they made the move, Grandma asked Grandpa to add a paper towel holder above the sink in their kitchen. He didn't have the right tools, so he walked the grassy alley down to Uncle Leroy's garage, which was about half a block away. Uncle Pete happened to be there visiting, so he and Grandpa walked down the hill to visit with Uncle Leroy and see if he had what they needed. They walked back up the hill and installed the paper towel holder, just where grandma wanted it. Grandpa wanted to return Leroy's tools right away, and he and Pete headed for the Garners' a second time, but just a little way down the hill, Grandpa collapsed on the ground. Uncle Pete tried to resuscitate him, but Grandpa's heart had given up for good. Grandpa had finished his final task on earth, ensuring that Grandma's kitchen was complete, and with that neatly buttoned up, he died, leaving Grandma alone in their new house.

My parents were at Isle Royale for a fishing trip that weekend. We were staying at Aunt Betty's, so when she and Dad came off the lake, Mom called Aunt Betty from Grand Portage, and Betty told her that Grandpa Burge had passed away. Uncle George, Aunt Faye, and Aunt Carol all drove to Grand Marais together for the funeral. Aunt Betty remembered that "Carol didn't have money at the time . . . she was so good-hearted she would have given her life for anybody."

Grandpa's funeral was at the Congregational church and I remember being in Grandma's new kitchen and all of my aunts and uncles were there, standing in a big circle around Grandma. Aunt Lila was crying and I'm sure other people were too. Grandma seemed kind of stunned and my dad said to her, "How are you doing, little Ma?" Triggered by tenderness, she gave up any facade or veneer of stoic German fortitude, sank into my dad's arms, and cried with deep sobs.

Here's a letter Grandma wrote to Grandpa in 1925, a year after they were married. He was working in Chicago and she and Uncle George, a newborn baby, made the trip to Weyauwega on the train for a long visit with her parents:

> Our darling Daddie, we got here just fine. Georgie was very good during the train ride, only he fussed a little when we changed at Rubbish Junction, as it was his feeding time, and I did not want to nurse him till I got on the train, but otherwise he slept most of the time . . . Mother thinks Georgie is too sweet for anything and she says he is a regular little Billie. There is a compliment for you. He gave Grandmother a smile, almost as soon as I got here. Oh, darling, the folks have a lovely little home, only the lawn is not as nice as at Bloomer. Mother and I sat out on the porch tonite, we could see right out to the lake and there are pretty trees near here and all of a sudden, we hear a Whippoorwill. I was wishing and in fact, I am wishing it all the time that you would be with Georgie and me. Mother was saying that a beach was near here too, won't that be lovely? So, don't forget your bathing suit and bring mine too, won't you dear? And do you know that I forgot my curling irons and my pearls, if you come bring them too, it will not be necessary to send it as I will buy a ten-cent curling iron . . . Oh darling you just must come, fishing season is now open except for bass and that will be open the fifteenth of June. I just went in to look at Georgie, he is going to sleep with me till the carriage comes. He looks so sweet, it makes tears come to my eyes when I look at him and think our darling daddie is not with us. The folks have gone to bed, it is after nine o'clock and I am tired too. Goodnite, hugs and kisses from Georgie & Maw.

Grandma had a strong desire to be close to her husband, but there was perhaps an equal or even stronger desire for her to take her baby son home to meet her mother. Bringing the babies home was medicine for her, and for Great-grandma Pauline, just as it would be for Aunt Carol when she brought Ricky "home," at the risk of what her father would do or say. It was Grandma Freda who took him in her arms and administered the cure of bringing a beautiful child home to mother. I like to think Grandma knew very well what she was doing—bringing the babies home was what she had done seven times, and it would have been eight, if her second child, Mark, had not died in infancy. This might be an indication of why Aunt Carol was so protective of Ricky in particular. His existence in this world had somehow made up for the fact that she had disappointed her parents, and the hope that comes along with a new baby would serve as a balm between her and her father, at least for a little while.

* * * * * * *

I call Grandma Freda my "Rose Grandma," not just because she smelled like roses but also because her skin was soft like rose petals and she often wore rose-colored blouses, pants, sweaters, scarves, and coats. From the pale, delicate pink of wild roses to the bold fuchsias found on heirloom rose bushes all over the Midwest, Grandma wore it well. She stayed in her house in Grand Marais for a few years after Grandpa died, and those were the years that I got to know her the best. I was now in my midteens, trying to navigate the minefields of high school, and the best part of my day was often spent hanging out with my grandma. Instead of having lunch in the rank and unappetizing school cafeteria, I would walk one block down the street to have lunch with Grandma instead. This became our ritual for a time. She would make me lunch, or I would eat my bag lunch there with her at her kitchen table, and then go back to school. It was completely beautiful, being able to spend that time with her. She once made a wild blueberry buckle, one of her specialties, with berries Aunt Betty had picked that summer. It was oozing with perfectly sweet and tart blueberries and topped with buttery crumble, and she had just pulled it out of the oven as I was walking in the door. She and I had that for lunch together, with ice cream. It was one of the best things I have ever tasted in my life, because my grandma had made it especially for me.

Grandma's house became a kind of Grand Central Station for us. I remember her, Aunt Lila, Aunt Betty, and my mom sitting at her kitchen table playing partners cribbage and getting into hooting and

Freda Burge on her front porch in Grand Marais, 1976. This is a rare photograph, because Grandma Freda notoriously hid her face whenever there was a camera around.

hollering matches, shouting at and laughing with one another, depending on how a particular game was going. And I don't want anyone to think Grandma was perfectly sweet and innocent about everything, because she was a known cheat at cards and would literally sit on aces or fives, which she would pull out when she needed a 15 or 31. This was a point of hilarity for her daughters, who were helpless against their mother's tricks.

It was good she was there, so close to three of her daughters when Grandpa died, because she had never lived alone, and I'm sure she struggled mightily with that. Winter was too much for her, being there all by herself, so Grandma sold the trailer in Tucson and bought a trailer up in Banning, California, where her son George and daughter Faye were living. They helped Grandma get things done, and her Minnesota family didn't get to see her very often after that.

It was when she was in Banning that Grandma got sick. She had been treated for precancerous cervical cells earlier in her life. These bad cells came back as ovarian cancer, and her body couldn't survive it. It's not fair for anyone to die of cancer, and it's especially grievous when you are eighty-five and have gone through as much as Grandma did in her life. Dying of cancer in a strange hospital, far away from the green grass and whip-poor-will calls of Weyauwega, doesn't even come close to the kind of dignified death she deserved.

When Grandma got sick, Auntie Faye's life was a mess. She had suffered her own health problems and during that time, the utter ugliness of George Lindley hovered like a specter over her life. Aunt Carol was Grandma's primary caretaker when she was ill, and when Grandma died, Carol was the person who was there to identify the body she left behind. According to my mom, "When there was a crisis, Carol was always the one who took charge of things, and I think her son Earl has taken over that role now."

Bodies ultimately fail us, and Auntie Faye's body failed her just one year after Grandma Burge's did. My mother told me that "after she died, my sister Carol had to identify her body, just like she had to identify Mom when she died. Carol told me, 'I can't do it again.' But she did."

* * * * * * *

Carol and Faye had taken turns caring for each other throughout most of their lives on earth, and while Auntie Faye was never known to be someone who divulged her secrets to others, I suspect Aunt Carol knew everything. She grew up as a sensitive girl who continued to be tender and careful as a mother, sister, and grandma. I asked my mom if Aunt Carol ever talked about her grandkids and she said, "She did know them, yes." One of her granddaughters is named after her. And before Carol got injured, her son Ron would drive her up the coast and into Oregon to see her son Earl's family—his wife, Carmen, and their daughters, Carol and Christie. Ron has his own son and Ricky has two, all of them grandmothered by Carol. Mom says, "She loved them, all of her grandchildren."

My mother doesn't know how it happened, but Aunt Carol injured her back badly sometime around 2000 or 2001, and it changed her quality of life forever. Mom said, "She went to some surgeon out there that was supposed to be like God," but it turns out that he (or she) wasn't a god, and the surgery just made things worse. Carol was in such pain and she lived that way for an inconceivable amount of time. As the pain persisted, she and her husband, Earl, sold their house and moved into a trailer. Earl stayed with her throughout the agony of chronic pain and everything that goes along with it. When your body isn't functioning, it's very hard to do anything but focus on the minute-by-minute urgency of finding relief from the pain. This, of course, took a toll on everything else in Aunt Carol's life, including her and Earl's relationship. Her doctors had prescribed hydrocodone for her pain, and Carol grew reliant on it. The drug made her pain better for a short time but made the rest of her life much more difficult. Mom said that sometimes she would call and "would be slurring her words and everything."

Her three sons kindly took care of their mother during her time of need, and at some point, she ended up going to the hospital for treatment and never left. Little Earl, Ronny, and Brian all listened to her when she said she couldn't go home. She had to stay in the hospital, where the pain continued to be unbearable, but for reasons only Aunt Carol knows, it was better at the hospital than being at home. Perhaps she didn't want to be a burden on Earl and her sons, but we'll never really know the reasons why she chose to stay there.

Aunt Carol was hospitalized when her son Ricky died. The other boys came and told her he had been killed in a bicycle accident in Hawaii, where he was living. Losing Ricky was devastating for her, and she was powerless over it. My mother said, "I talked to her a lot. She feared the worst and didn't know how he died. It really bothered her." So, Mom helped Carol get a copy of his death certificate from Hawaii. The cause of death was deemed to be accidental and related to alcohol intoxication. Carol was finally able to get a bit of peace, because she knew the truth about how Ricky died, instead of fearing the worst. And fear, whether it's caused by actually losing a child or involves living in fear that you might lose a child, is its own acute form of pain, something Great-grandma Pauline, Grandma Freda, and Auntie Faye felt, and now Aunt Carol knew what it felt like too.

Living with physical and emotional pain was not new for Auntie Carol. She showed symptoms and signs of being in pain her whole life. In my mother's experience, "She always seemed troubled. We'd laugh and giggle and things, but I think mentally she was troubled." And then she shared some of her thoughts about why Carol had such a hard time, both in her young life and later, when her role as a sister sometimes blurred the lines of motherhood: "Each one of us were different. Faye was more like a mother to us than anything. Especially Carol and me. After Faye had her breakdown, she came home and would have presents for us. That continued through Carol's whole life, and vice versa. I think Carol almost got in the spot that she was taking care of Faye. Ricky was little, and Faye and Betty babysat Ricky so Carol could work. So, then Carol felt like she couldn't leave Faye after Faye's mental breakdown."

Sisterhood blurring the lines into motherhood was a survival mechanism for the two of them, each taking turns at mothering the other, depending on the circumstances in their lives. But after a certain point, perhaps Aunt Faye's life reached the point of no return, and no amount of mothersistering could save her.

The family dynamics were shaped by Grandpa's own traumatic childhood and what I've come to see as a deeply dysfunctional relationship with his own children because he himself never got the love and acceptance he needed from his own mother. When he fell in love with Freda back in 1924, she was the first person to really love him and make him feel worthy of being loved. My mother, in all her hard-earned wisdom, sees it like this: "I think he loved Mother so much, he saw us kids being in the way. And they would pick sides. I was trying to please both of them. Carol got the worst of it somehow, I think. I was cute, so I got tolerated more than her. She always had something going on, breakouts on her face, corn up her nose [laughs]. Carol would tell me, 'Joyce, Mom, and Grace would always talk about how beautiful you were!' Carol told me that, but I never believed I was." And then she admits, "I got by with more than Betty or Carol."

Auntie Carol was smart, sensitive, and funny, and if you knew her at all, you knew it was easy to love her. Her life was complicated by the relationship she had with her father, and the perceived or actual absence of love at the most formative time in her life. And love is something that everyone is entitled to, even if you have corn sprouting up your nose. My mother's insights into her sister Carol's life are that "she always wanted to be loved, you know. I think she probably slept with guys right away. She always wanted a man to like her, because of her relationship to Grandpa Burge."

While Aunt Carol was in the hospital my mother and she talked a lot and during that time my mom read every single love letter from the Burge box of history out loud to Aunt Carol over the phone. This seemed to help her work out some of her old hurts, from the days when she was afraid to walk past Grandpa's chair. Mom said, "After I read her those letters, she had a better understanding of their relationship." Acknowledging the very real challenges Grandma and Grandpa faced as young parents with seven children, who were under financial pressure most of their lives, and on top of it all, suffering through their own emotional traumas, my mother was willing to give them grace by saying that "they did better than I would have ever done under those circumstances. It had to be tough. I have no bad feelings, but Carol still had bad feelings about Dad even when she died. She never resolved it."

****

Human beings are not that different from the animals we forcibly cage—digging their beds into the snow or the straw and just trying to keep warm and stay dry. When an animal is in pain or suffering there are always clear signs of distress. Some animals pace or chew the fur off their bodies, or furiously rub up against trees, trying to rid themselves of irritants or placate the anguish of being trapped in a pen that's too small. As a kid, Aunt Carol did show clear signs of being in pain that went ignored, or worse, resulted in her being punished for exhibiting signs of weakness. Some human beings are so smart and sensitive that the perils of life on earth are too much for them. If a child suffers trauma at the hands of another person, whether it's emotional or physical trauma, it's going to show up on the surface somewhere because it doesn't just go away, it pops up in another place and will eventually spread to one's relationships with others.

The day Aunt Carol unintentionally wore her fuzzy pink slippers to the store and playacted like she was an injured animal so that other people wouldn't think she was a crazy lady, has a funny sort of irony about it, knowing how much actual pain she experienced and survived throughout her life. The antidote to pain is of course, healing, and in order to heal from the hurts that hobble us, we have to be brave enough to see, speak, and hear the truth about things. It's like walking in the woods and finding the remnants of an abandoned car—if you open the door, what will you find inside? There could definitely be something wild with teeth in there, but maybe it's just a whole new ecosystem of plants and creatures who are taking advantage of a safe place to live and grow. We just won't know until we open the door.

And in fact, Aunt Carol was very brave. While she was in the hospital, Auntie Carol would tease the nurses and say funny things that would make them laugh, and she always told my mother that she was being treated well. The initial injury and then the botched surgery left her unable to walk, move, sit, stand, or sleep. Sometimes when she would call our house on Eighth Avenue to talk to Mom, I would answer the phone. I remember hearing the pain in her voice, which was always quiet, a bit husky sounding and always very loving. "Your mom is so proud of you, honey." She would say, and it makes me cry, knowing just how much pain she lived through and yet still had plenty of loving and kind words left in her heart for others.

My mom said she misses her sister's sense of humor the most. "We talked about everything when we talked on the phone. We tried to resolve things together. She understood just about anything because of what she had been through. She was a good sister."

Mom was able to visit Aunt Carol in person while she was in the hospital in Los Angeles. This time, it wasn't Mom or Carol driving all over L.A.; it was my sister, Dawn, who played chauffeur. Mom said, "I'm glad I went to visit her in L.A. We drove up there to the hospital and there she was. Oh, she was happy to see us. We went to lunch with Earl. He stuck by her all those years. We went back and visited a little while longer."

I recently found a picture of my mom that was taken in Carol's room on the day they visited with her. Mom is leaning over her sister in a tender way, her eyes are closed, and she's smiling, and so is Aunt Carol.

In 2013 Carol's good friend Elizabeth went to visit her, something she did regularly. My mom didn't know it, but Carol was in the late stages of dying. Based on conversations she had with Carol, my mother knew that "she didn't want to die. She was terrified of dying. She came so close so many times, but they always brought her back." My mother talked to Elizabeth on the phone not long afterward, and Elizabeth told Mom that she had been visiting Carol a lot lately, but "it was different this time." Aunt Carol's pain ended later that day, not long after her friend had come to visit her.

****

About six years ago a number of Burges got together to honor Aunt Carol and put some of her ashes in the ground at the Maple Hill Cemetery in Grand Marais. My mother put a sprig of cedar inside the wooden box that my dad had made, along with some of Carol's ashes, and we had a small ceremony. Her ashes were placed close to where Grandma and Grandpa Burge are buried. Great-uncle Martin, who to my knowledge never set foot in Grand Marais, is also nearby. Grandma wanted him to be close to her, and so he is. Uncle Leroy and Aunt Lila are there, too, and there's always a flag on Leroy's grave to honor his service during World War II. Uncle Lloyd also has a little flag near his headstone, and Auntie Betty can be honored there too. Some of Auntie Faye's ashes are next to Grandma and Grandpa, even though she never formally lived here. Every Memorial Day Mom makes sure their graves are swept off and tidied up. She often brings little bouquets of cedar for her sisters and her parents, and I am getting ready to take on that responsibility once Mom is no longer able to do it.

As the great Burge migration transpired from Winnipeg and Milwaukee to Weyauwega and Warba, the fact that all four of my Burge aunties ended up together again here on the North Shore is a real comfort to me. This is because families are supposed to stick together and take care of each other, no matter what—which is something Grandma Freda and all my aunties taught me, even before I could speak their names or knew the happy sounds of them laughing together at something funny Aunt Carol had just said.

Sensitive Girls: A Poem for Carol

Sometimes life is too much
for sensitive girls,
the ones who cry
when life is mean.
Sensitive girls are often
funny girls,
the ones who see
the ridiculousness
of life, when laughing
is easier than crying.
Because everyone
loves to laugh
but no one
loves to cry.

All my love,
Diane

Diane

WHEN I WAS A LITTLE GIRL, I thought my Aunt Diane was the most beautiful woman in the world. She used to spend a full hour getting ready for her bartender shift at the Kove—a big, dark, and cavernous restaurant and bar that was built just a few feet away from where Great-grandmother Anakwad's house used to be, on the East Bay in Grand Marais. Aunt Diane's house was just three blocks away, a yellow two-story right on the lake side of Highway 61 that used to overlook Dick Eckle's old fish house. The house is still there and it's still yellow, although no one lives there anymore because it's been converted into the North House Folk School's store. Back when it was still Aunt Diane's house, I have a clear memory of being in her tiny, cramped bathroom, sitting on the toilet with the lid closed and watching her get ready for work. She and I were talking to each other about something, I don't remember what, while she meticulously painted sticky, tar-black mascara onto her top and bottom lashes. Then, using a wicked-looking metal tool, she would squeeze her top lashes upward in a gentle swoop, and then move on to her lower lashes, training them to swoop the other way, like a gardener trains plants to follow a trellis. Once her eyes were·"done," she would uncap a tube of deep-red Revlon lipstick and paint it within the beautifully defined lines of her upper lip, and then use it to expertly fill in the curve of her bottom lip. The shade she chose wasn't a cartoonish red, but deep and dramatic, like the color of a ruby. This rich color set off her dark eyes and helped to balance the midnight color of her hair, which she always left in rollers until she was fully dressed. Within my young and burgeoning perceptions about femininity and beauty, Aunt Diane never looked overdone or ostentatious. Hers was a mysterious and exotic beauty, which is the opposite of how the 1970s television culture wanted me and other girls to formulate our impressions of feminine beauty. When you grow up thinking of your auntie this way, there's not a lot that can mar your opinion of her, no matter what other people think.

My lovely auntie is memorialized in her high school graduation picture, which was taken around 1957. She is wearing a scalloped-collared sweater with a soft bow that mimics the curve of her mouth. Her face was the kind of beautiful that caused people to stare—because of the perfect symmetry of her features, but also because there was always a smoky haze of intrigue about her. In her yearbook photo, she is not posing or acting for the camera; she is simply sitting still and gazing slightly off-center—not acknowledging the viewer in any way or giving even a whiff of attention to any of the people who were caught staring at her.

Aunt Diane most often kept her hair short, and in the 1950s she wore it in subtle curls that framed her face like a pretty bell. Later on, in the 1960s, she favored a high bouffant, with big, wide curls on top of her head, which she doused heavily with Aqua Net hair spray to keep the whole "do" in place. There was always a big purple can of it on the porcelain shelf at the back of her toilet. Aqua Net—the ozone-layer–depleting, aerosol beauty tool, not to be confused with "Anakwad," another seven-letter word with a similar sound. Anakwad is the name of our Anishinaabe family relatives and means "cloud" in Ojibwemowin. And while Aqua Net has now been proved to destroy clouds, at least the ones inside the ozone layer, anakwadoon might be used to describe the puff of lofty curls Diane used to elevate her petite stature. Whenever she was getting ready to go to work, or go out on the town, she always saved the care of her luxurious curls for last, adding yet one more layer of drama on top of all the others. This whole ritual was for me, a girl of eight or nine, a theatrical show of femininity unlike anything I had ever experienced before, and I was fascinated by it. Aunt Diane possessed a unique kind of femaleness that wasn't at all like the Farrah Fawcett brand of chronic femininity that plagued me as a teenager. Hers was much more interesting. She had a tough sense of independence about her, and no one ever looked quite like she did. When I was in my twenties and struggling to put my own face "on," so to speak, I would reach for my own dark shade of red lipstick and apply it just like she used to do—top lip first, and then the bottom. I wore it like a shield, or calling card, and I wonder if that's also what she was aiming for every day when she put her lipstick on.

My auntie was always sweet to me, and that's also what I remember best about her. The image that was reflected in her bathroom mirror didn't divulge any secrets or clues about her past, nor did her outward image give any indication of what her inner life was really like. She left people speculating, and that was a part of her beauty. She is the aunt who still retains the most mystery when it comes to knowing the big events of her life and understanding what made her tick. But even so, she is the auntie whom I feel the most aligned with in a lot of ways. I may have even known this when I was there in her bathroom, breathing in clouds of Aqua Net and watching her get ready for work.

****

When she was living in the yellow house, Aunt Diane worked nights until 1:30 a.m. serving highballs and lowballs to people she probably saw every damn night. She still felt it was important to put her best face forward, because you never know when a stranger from out of town might sit down at the bar and have something new to say. That was back when drinking in bars was the primary source of grown-up entertainment, at least in terms of how the adults in town chose to spend their pre- and post-dinner hours. Happy Hour at the Kove was always "double bubble," and I remember seeing the parking lot overrun with cars as soon as the clock hit 5:00 p.m.

My mom worked there, too, as a waitress out front and also as a bartender. We spent a lot of time there as kids—not so much in the bar but in a booth in the dining room overlooking Lake Superior. If we were lucky, Mom would order us grilled cheeseburgers and hand-cut French fries for an early dinner. The last school bell rang at 3:10, and so my sister and I would sometimes walk down the hill from school to the Kove and wait for mom to get off work at 4:30. The bar was usually empty at 3:00, but as it began to fill up with customers, it felt off-limits to us. I do remember watching Aunt Diane working the bar under dim lights on some of these evenings. It was a "lounge" in the true sense, with low ceilings, red swivel chairs, globe candles on each table, and a piano in the corner, which was often played by E. J. Croft, the old-timer who used to hammer out old songs while wearing his chopper mittens. And sometimes it would be Frank Gillis on the bench, a local, well-known jazz pianist who played there during Happy Hour, or on Saturday nights, when the whole place would be full of diners and drinkers.

The Kove was just one of many bars in town—albeit somewhat fancier than the others. You could get a blended grasshopper or a proper martini, which didn't happen at other places back then. The Legion downtown was another hot spot, and while we were growing up, we heard a lot of stories about how, back in the day, the small-town cops would look the other way when a local husband and father got plastered at the bar before dinner and proceeded to drive himself and his truck right through a signpost. In fact, back then, the local cops really didn't care how much you drank as long as you were able to get yourself home in one piece without hurting yourself or someone else. That's what it used to be like in our very tiny, rural Minnesota town where everyone knew each other, they knew what you liked to drink, and they most likely knew a lot of your secrets too. Some of that has changed, but some of it is still the same. DWIs are no longer tolerated, but the local 'tender still knows your drink, and the secrets still run rampant, that's for sure.

With the consequences very different back then, the job of a bartender was to get everyone nice and drunk and listen to their secrets. In Aunt Diane's case, she did all that and looked glamorous doing it. I imagine she pretty much saw and heard it all from behind the dark-stained wood of the Kove bar. A fast bartender who made drinks four at a time, she likely made hundreds of dollars in tips every night. And I'm sure she had to handle plenty of pickup lines and not-so-subtle innuendos from flirtatious customers. Aunt Diane was beautiful, but she was also darkly funny and had a hoarse giggle—an engaging trait that added yet another layer of intrigue. Her way of speaking and laughing was similar to the way Uncle Stormy and Uncle Bruce talked, because the three of them spent the most time together when they

were little. Uncle Bruce was most particularly known for his ability
to summarize a ridiculous situation by delivering a sharp and funny
one-liner, but really, all my Drouillard uncles and aunts, as well as my
dad, have a gift for making people laugh. Theirs is a uniquely Drouillard way of forming words and making jokes, which is a reflection of
when, where, and how they grew up.

****

The youngest of seven, Diane was born at home in the woods outside
Grand Marais, on the same September day that her mother almost
died bringing her into the world. Lola Drouillard had delivered all
six of her other children at home with the help of a niece or a family friend such as Lucy Caribou. These were the circumstances when
all of my father's other brothers and sisters were born, but in 1939,
when Grandma Lola's seventh and final baby was ready to be born, it
was clear that this delivery was going to be different for her. It was in
early September, less than two years after their next youngest child,
Stormy (Gale), was born. Uncle Stormy was named "Gale" because
there was a big storm on Lake Superior the day he was born. But he
never liked the name Gale (he thought it was girly), so everyone called
him Stormy.

Grandma Lola was thirty years old when Diane was born. She
was always a very small woman, barely five-foot-one, and yet her
diminutive but able body had already brought six healthy babies into
the world—all of them born without major complications. There was
no hospital or clinic back then, and the business of delivering babies
was considered to reside firmly within the realm of women's work,
especially if you were one of the Anishinaabe families who couldn't
rely on the help of town doctors or nurses to make house calls. So,
Grandma Lola was reliant on the help of relatives and Ojibwe mid-
wives who knew a lot about delivering babies and traditional medicines. On the day Grandma went into labor, it's likely that Lucy Caribou, their neighbor and friend, was called on to help with the delivery,
since she had been there to bring a number of the Drouillard babies
into the world. On this seventh occasion, Fred and Lola's new baby
daughter was born into the hands of family, washed in warm water,
and then wrapped tightly in a blanket. But after the baby came Fred

knew something was wrong. By the time Grandma Lola started hemorrhaging, Grandpa did the only thing he could do, and that was to go and find help. He left Grandma there with her attendants, six kids and their newborn baby daughter, and he headed up the hill to Mike and Sophie Powell's house, which was about half a mile through the woods.

Mike and Sophie's son Milt, a longtime friend of our family, recalled the visit, and told me that there was a knock at the door that night and "it was your grandpa." According to Milt, his dad took Grandpa Fred out in the woods surrounding their house and dug up a certain kind of root. And then Mike Powell told Grandpa Fred to go home and make a strong tea with the root, instructing him to "have Lola drink a cup of it." He said, "It would taste like the devil, but have her drink it all." Grandpa Fred did what Mike told him to do, and the medicine she drank caused Grandma Lola's bleeding to stop. As Milt put it, "She cleared up."

I've often wondered if Aunt Diane knew this story, or if it was kept hidden away from her and the rest of the family. At that time, using traditional medicine was considered taboo by the non-Native, mainstream medical doctors, and so maybe Grandpa didn't tell anyone how close Grandma had come to dying. But the fact that a common root, dug out of the clay soil in northern Minnesota and made into tea was used to save Grandma Lola's life, is an extraordinary part of Aunt Diane's story. That magical root, and Mike Powell's knowledge of it, literally changed the trajectory of life for everyone in the Drouillard family, especially for Aunt Diane. In some ways, her existence on earth was formulated at that moment, when her mother didn't die on the day she was born. The earthly magic that saved her own mother's life would always be present in Diane's after that.

Based on what I know about her, and some of the conversations we've had over the years, I believe Aunt Diane was a very insightful person who was highly sensitive to her surroundings, and she believed in the power of intangible things—particularly the magic of the woods. Raised in the forest, she knew certain things about birds and other animals, and about trees that only a kid raised in northern Minnesota would know. And as she got older and discovered that people will oftentimes let you down—it would be the wild things in life that could reliably bring her joy and satisfaction. This is another thing she and I have in common. I recognized this in her, and she saw it in me. She loved animals of any sort, and almost always had at least one dog, sometimes more. For a brief period of her life, she also had horses. That was when she lived in Monticello in southern Minnesota. The one and only time we visited her there, I remember seeing the horses behind their fences, and meeting a three-legged German shepherd for the first time—which left a big impression on me, because I had never known a dog missing one leg or been around a dog that was so big. And no matter where she lived, she liked to feed the birds in the winter, and in the summer, she would put out hummingbird feeders full of sugar water. She especially loved hummingbirds, our seasonal miracles—which in my opinion are the embodiment of supreme design and magic on earth.

As the seventh child, Diane was the baby of the family, and like my mother's experience as the youngest of the Burges, Diane benefited from the attention of her older siblings and to some extent her parents, Fred and Lola. But this was true only to a point, because she was born in 1939, at the height of the Chik-Wauk Lodge days, when Grandpa and Grandma Drouillard spent their summers on Saganaga Lake at the end of the Gunflint Trail. So, like her siblings, Diane was also forced to learn how to be independent at a young age, because her parents would leave her at home all summer with her older sisters or a family friend while they were away. Aunt Diane, unlike my dad, never assigned any romantic notions to the fact that the kids were left to fend for themselves a lot of the time. Never afraid to call things by name, she was always really good at clearing the air, and once when I was visiting her, she said to me, "If that were to happen today the parents would be put in jail for child abuse." And that could very well be.

* * * * * * *

The Drouillard family has always been built on the idea that work was primary to everything else—including family or creating a safe and coherent life for your kids. This was framed in rough-cut timber by Grandpa Fred, who was guiding moose hunters in Canada when he was ten, and Grandma Lola, who worked every damn day of her life, even with seven kids at home. When she was little, all of Diane's older brothers and sisters already had their own jobs working in restaurants downtown, or they were sent up the trail to Chik-Wauk, where many of them learned how to cook in the kitchen or, in the case of the boys, work on the dock alongside their dad, who took guests out on daylong fishing excursions. Saganaga is a really big lake. Before he set off, he needed his sons' help to gas up the fishing boats and get minnows from traps they had set the day before on a tiny lake just north of Chik-Wauk. Later the sons helped to clean the daily catch of trout or walleye before it was sent into the kitchen, where Grandma Lola and one of the girls would prepare it for the guests' dinner entrées.

I've been really lucky to be able to spend a lot of time on Saganaga Lake as an adult, camping and fishing with my family. It's now part of the Boundary Waters Canoe Area Wilderness, and with the establishment of the BWCAW in 1978, the old resort culture came to a forced (and somewhat bitter) end. Many of the old buildings and resorts are gone now, and the days of guided fishing and big walleye dinners have changed from a resort-based economy to one that supports independent guides and towboat service for canoeists who want to avoid having to paddle the big part of the lake, which can be dangerous even for small motorboats. The waters of Saganaga can be life threatening, especially when the waves are whipped into a frothy chop out of the northwest. The translation of the Ojibwe name is "twisting lake with many islands," and it's the channels between the islands that are the most dangerous when the wind is up.

Outfitters and guides are still making a living on the lake, but the old tradition of booking a log cabin and employing an Anishinaabe guide to take you out on the lake for the day has now dried up. This way of life on the upper Gunflint Trail is stored away within the memories of old-timers who used to patronize a number of lodges and resorts along the Sag Corridor, or on the Canadian side of the lake. The rules are different in Canada, and so a good number of people are able to maintain summer homes and cabins that are built past the invisible international border, which stretches across the lake from east to west. This is somewhat hilarious to people like my dad who grew up knowing the old way of life on Sag, where boating into Canada was never much trouble, and it was just as common for him to motor into

Betsy Powell's place on the Canadian side as it was for him to head west past American Point, which is now strictly enforced as a "canoe only" waterway.

In these times, I'm just one of many thousands of summer visitors who gain access to campsites and good fishing by getting a permit and following the rules put in place by the U.S. Forest Service, which oversees it as a federal wilderness area. I love it on Saganaga, not just because of our family connection, which is very meaningful, but also because of its history as *Anishinaabewaki* (meaning "Anishinaabe lands" or "Anishinaabe earth")—the primary route from Lake Superior to Lac La Croix and beyond. I feel at home there, as if it's in my blood, because it is. It's one of the good things we inherited from Grandpa Fred, and every time our boat hugs the rock wall at the Narrows, I put some tobacco in the water for him, and for Grandma Lola, and my dad, too, because they all went through that channel hundreds of times, in work and in play. But mostly the wilderness was the place that provided for them and their family—it was the reason they were able to put food on the table, and shoes on their kids' feet. This is not something that was ever taken for granted by the Drouillards, who worked very hard at a time when things were pretty bad for other off-reservation families and the families who lived on the reservation at Grand Portage.

This tradition of work is one of the debts owed to the Indigenous families who showed the first European settlers how to survive in a wild and, at times, unforgiving place. Perhaps Grandpa's pride and his own strong work ethic was rooted in this history—knowing that he could survive off the land and had the tools and skills required to provide for his family, no matter what the white men threw at him. This sense of pride was ingrained in his kids, and so all of them knew what it was like to work very hard, and at various times in their lives, all of them would travel back to Chik-Wauk and Saganaga as formative places in their minds and hearts, even though most of them never went back to Saganaga after Chik-Wauk and the other lodges closed down. When the Boundary Waters Canoe Area Wilderness Act was passed in 1978, it was a lesser-known fact that tribal members with a tribal ID card didn't need a permit to access the lakes and rivers within the BWCAW. Even my dad didn't know this until much later. It felt off-limits to him, and so, he just stopped going there, even though it was such a big part of his life.

The family history and strong work ethic helped define each of my Drouillard aunts and shaped their lives in profound ways. In my attempts to learn more about Aunt Diane's life, I reached out to Larry Krause, an old friend of hers who was in the same class in school and shares a longtime connection to Saganaga Lake. Larry had some astute observations about the Drouillard family, beginning our conversation with, "Your family were all good workers . . . They had a tough life. Every one of 'em—the whole family. I thought they were all nice people. They had a tough life."

It pains me now to think about how hard my grandma and grandpa worked and how little they had to show for it in the end. Particularly Grandma Lola, whose cooking and baking made a lot of people rich, while she worked for an hourly wage and took leftovers home in order to feed her own kids. My dad and his sisters and brothers were raised to believe that work and chores came before anything else, including playing basketball or going to school. And in spite of their labors, sometimes even the most monumental efforts fell short, and they and their kids had to go without. In a candid admission, my aunt Gloria, Diane's next oldest sister, shared that "when I was really, really young and in grade school I used to feel bad because we didn't have clothes. We had to wear those old, brown stockings, you know, and I had mine rolled down around my ankles. They were too big and they wouldn't stay up around my legs."

There were many times when the family reached dire straits, and that would mean more hours for Grandma at the El Ray or Mabel's Café, and a scramble on Grandpa's part to make extra money at a time when jobs were scarce. He infamously turned to bootlegging to turn some cash, and sometimes he took more furs than he was allowed to, because it was the difference between his kids having socks to wear to keep the cold air from getting through the holes in their shoes. It also kept the game wardens on his trail, at a time when tribal rights to hunt, fish, and gather on ceded territory were not routinely communicated to band members. My dad once told me, "Your grandpa didn't even know that it was within his rights to go moose hunting."

In fact, it wasn't until the 1854 Treaty Authority was established in 1988 that Grand Portage tribal members had a formal organization in place that worked to preserve their rights to hunt, fish, and gather within the land base ceded to the U.S. government in 1854.[1] Being cut off from his way of life and way of making a living was a bitter pill to swallow for someone who had been guiding non-Native moose hunters through the forests of Canada and northern Minnesota since he was a boy.

* * * * * * *

Hunting and fishing were Grandpa's work, but when it came to shopping for new socks or washing the dirty ones, that was Grandma Lola's job, sometimes Aunt Doreen's and, later, Auntie Gloria's. They all watched Grandma Lola work her fingers to the bone, just trying to keep everyone fed, and socks on all eighteen of their feet. When Aunt Diane was born in 1939, it was the women in their family who were charged with taking care of the babies and everything inside the house. The cooking and cleaning and mending and pampering were the job of the women. Men's and boy's responsibilities involved doing things outside the house, like cutting firewood or hunting to put meat on the table. The men were also charged with doing whatever it would take to pay the bills, although Grandma Lola certainly did her share of that work too. This way of functioning (or not functioning) as a family reflected the overarching patriarchal norms of the time, which would have been very different from the way Grandpa Fred was raised by his Anishinaabe mother. She and her immediate relatives lived as part of large extended family group in Chippewa City in the 1880s, concurrent with the era when Anishinaabe men's and women's traditional roles had begun to change.

   This shift from a totemic/family way of subsisting to an individualistic, independent way of getting by was something that defined Grandpa Fred's own approach to raising a family. He was a pioneer, given that he was the first generation of the Anakwad Ojibwe to live sandwiched between the old ways and the new ways. It's also an expectation the first six Drouillard children would try to conform to. Doreen and Gloria very much tried to stay in their sanctioned "lane" when it came to women's roles in the family—and it put terrible pressure on them. I think they both tried to find ways to escape it, sometimes at their peril. And certainly, all the boys were put to the test when it came to their woodsmanship—often being forced to prove themselves in the ways of the masculine stereotypes of the time. They had to teach themselves how to survive in the woods, because that's what their father had to do. In my dad's case, he had help from Philomene Evans, an elderly Ojibwe woman he lived with over the summers of his eighth and ninth years. It was Philomene, not his father, who taught him how to snare rabbits, fish for brook trout, and shoot a gun. So early on, with Philomene as a role model, my dad and his brothers and sisters were brought up with mixed messages about men's and women's roles in the 1930s and early '40s—mixed messages for a mixed-blood family. That's how it was.

What I've learned in thinking through all this history is that Aunt Diane was really the only one to break free of the mixed-up expectations placed on her as a young woman. She resisted the morbidity-of-motherhood doctrine (with a vengeance), and she sank the ridiculously narrow definition of womanhood, as dictated by chronic femininity, in the deepest part of Saganaga Lake. This emancipation from expectation would create her life, for both good and bad. And in doing this, she was the only Drouillard auntie to reclaim some of the older, more traditional female roles that were put in place back when women ran the wigwams but also the seasonal ricing and sugaring camps, as well as did the kind of work that was seen through mainstream eyes as being within the realm of men, not women. It's not something she was ever given a lot of credit for. With that in mind, I'd like to say, I see you, Aunt Diane-iban! I see what you accomplished and what the odds were against you. You were up against a lot, because the monumental shift between what we are trained to see as "women's work" versus what we are conditioned to see as "men's work" has everything to do with the prevailing culture's attempts to assimilate Indigenous people into the mainstream institutions of American society. These institutions are white and patriarchal at their core.

****

In the mid- to late 1800s, when Great-grandma Anakwad was born, the gradual shift from matriarchal or egalitarian societies to patriarchal or paternalistic ways of organizing everyday life was already underway. This shift put a lot of pressure on Anishinaabe men like Grandpa Fred, because it required him to take "manly" control of his household and, subsequently, all the people in it. Anyone familiar with Indigenous history knows that assimilation was unleashed as forced and coerced religious, educational, and/or linguistic conversion, but it's also important to recognize how mainstream society's views on masculinity and the role of women were also part of the process of assimilation. This happened both blatantly and subtly over time.

In her wonderfully researched book *Holding Our World Together*, Brenda J. Child writes about how during the Great Depression and in the years leading up to World War II, the government had the power to impose changes on the traditional Anishinaabe way of dividing work. This was when patriarchal society began to infiltrate what was traditionally a more egalitarian approach to making a living. "When the Great Depression struck in the United States, American Indians were among the first to lose jobs and wages, and this additionally burdened a convergence of colonial circumstances that had undermined Ojibwe life since the creation of reservations. Land loss, cultural assimilation, environmental degradation, and the denial of treaty rights had already created squalor and misery in Ojibwe Country before the unemployment and poverty of the 1930s."[2]

On June 19, 1933, the Bureau of Indian Affairs within the Department of the Interior established the Civilian Conservation Corps-Indian Division. Created by President Roosevelt, the CCC-ID focused on Minnesota's Native American population, and the program was administered by the Bureau of Indian Affairs. "In line with the Indian Reorganization Act of 1934, many CCC-ID projects focused on preservation of Ojibwe and Dakota culture, including management of wild rice habitat and teaching modern methods of maple sugaring. These men also built roads and cleared diseased trees in local forests."[3]

The CCC and its counterpart, the Works Progress Administration (WPA), often further disrupted families by removing young husbands and fathers, as well as boys in their teenage years, from their home reservations and sending them to work on government projects on other tribally held reservation lands. This taught them that labor, rather than family, came first. CCC cultural preservation efforts on

2

62 / *Diane*

the North Shore included completion of the first major fur-trade-era archaeological study at Grand Portage, upgrades to the historic Grand Portage Trail, and work on the reconstruction of the North West Company Fur Post site located on Grand Portage Bay on Lake Superior. To be clear, these are all good things that continue to benefit a lot of people, but as infrastructure projects, they were enacted at the expense of Ojibwe family life.

In the fall, when the wild rice was ripe and ready to harvest, a lot of men would leave the CCC encampments and go back to their home reservations to help their families move to the ricing grounds for the harvest. Manoomin (wild rice), an irreplaceable food staple in Ojibwe Country, was critical for families who were preparing for winter and already struggling to get by. Rather than discourage the men from leaving camp, the government CCC supervisors decided to permit the men to leave and, Child writes, "took the further step of taking charge of and 'improving' the indigenous harvest." According to Child, these non-Native, male government managers "were unaware of the fact that harvesting wild rice was a predominantly female enterprise, and because the work was conducted outdoors and very labor intensive, it fit within their own cultural categories of men's work." This was the point in history at which harvesting manoomin and other kinds of outdoor work became "gender neutral," with white supervisors introducing "their own culture's notions of masculinity, physical labor, and the work ethic."[4]

The CCC and WPA went as far as creating "Indian rice camp" operations at various locations around the Great Lakes, where men were paid to work the harvest and women were sidelined. The CCC-ID handbook specifically "suggested subordinate roles for Indian women in poverty relief programs, saying they could serve camp matrons or assist in 'recreation and leisure-time activity as will make camp life attractive.'"[5]

****

Dismissing Anishinaabe women from the important work of harvesting manoomin or overseeing the harvest of maple sap in the spring, another important task traditionally considered to be the responsibility of women, was the government's way of pushing women out and pulling men in, without regard for the way things had always been done. Women were in the lead back in the days when totemic family groups would move from winter hunting grounds to spring maple sugar encampments, an annual event that happened like clockwork, except without a clock. Pushing women out was another way of ensuring that Anishinaabe people would essentially become more like white people, where a woman's place was inside the home and not outside boiling sap over a fire, teaching her daughters and granddaughters when the sap was ready, and when it had gone too far.

Going to sugarbush was firmly within the realm of our Anakwad ancestors. All three Ankawad sisters would head up the hill every spring in March, when the days got warm and the nights were still cold, and oversee the harvest. In one family story, Great-grandma Anakwad stubbornly marched herself and all of her children into a spring blizzard because the sap wouldn't wait. The Drouillards' neighbor Lucy Caribou used to go to her own family sugarbush, and she would give Aunt Gloria and the other kids maple candy as a treat when they were really little. Aunt Gloria said, "I remember getting maple sugar candy and she would only give us a small piece because you could choke on it." Just little pieces for little kids, and larger pieces as they got bigger. Something that is so simple, but so telling, about the relationship they had with Lucy.

With their parents away at work, the Drouillard girls would stay with Lucy, who was their closest neighbor and family friend. They all grew up knowing that it was the women who were in charge of the sugarbush, and it was also the women who took care of their own children and those of others, if circumstances warranted it. It was a way of keeping the circle going, even though people lived far apart from one another. This is how the women held our extended families together, even while they had to work outside jobs, make things to sell to tourists—or in the case of the girls, learn how to take care of things inside the house, be in charge of watching your little brothers and sisters, make supper and clean up afterward, and then, only after those duties were all taken care of, try to get your schoolwork done. This is what sets large poor families apart from rich ones, and the conditions my Drouillard relatives survived in are offered as a real and primary example of why building wealth in America is much different from earning wages in America. It also explains why consistent access to education goes hand in hand with a young American's ability to build wealth, especially for Black and Indigenous people of color.

Going to school was an added burden for Doreen and Gloria, who never quite made it through, but Diane had an easier time of it, because she was the youngest and there was no one coming up after her that she had to take care of. So, being the youngest was lucky for her in some ways. And being a student was something she was good at it. Her old friend Larry says, "I knew her from school. She was always real quiet but she knew her school lessons. She was friendly, but real quiet, you know?"

The Grand Marais school used to be on First Street and Broadway. It was a multistory, cinder-block behemoth of a building, with tall ceilings, big windows, and inlaid oak floors. All the classes were housed there, from kindergarten to twelfth grade. In 2018, after Aunt Diane died, Larry gave me a copy of a photograph from his personal collection that was taken of their school class in 1948, when Aunt Diane was about nine years old. She's in the next to last row, sitting primly in her desk, amid a tidy row of other students. It's springtime and she is wearing a short-sleeved white dress with brown loafers and cotton anklets in an off-white shade. They don't look new, neither the socks nor the shoes, but at least they aren't the long stockings that got baggy at the ankles, like the ones that used to embarrass Aunt Gloria when she was little. Diane is smiling for the camera, showing the signs of a sunny day on her cheeks, which are flushed and rosy. Her wavy black hair touches her shoulders, and she has a cute little barrette in her hair. The teacher has written on the board: "Signs of spring: Crows, Wrens, Grackles, Woodpeckers, Chickadees," along with other birds who emerge once the snowpack recedes. In the photograph, Aunt Diane seems to embody her friend Larry's memories of her as a schoolgirl: "She was always a very tidy person and quiet. Never called much attention to herself."

* * * * * * *

Knowing that my aunt Diane always held back, staying quiet and being an observer, reminds me of how my mom used to keep quiet and try to "be perfect" so that she wouldn't garner any negative attention from her dad. I'm guessing that's what life was like for Aunt Diane too. Both she and my mom were the babies of the family, and they both were conditioned to keep their heads down, stay quiet, and not ruffle anyone's feathers. They let their older siblings test the waters and watched closely what happened when the older kids got in trouble. Neither of them wanted any part of that, so they tried to be invisible.

Diane did what she was told, both at home and in school. It was how she survived the many chaotic and frightening situations she witnessed growing up. Aunt Diane was only eleven when her next oldest sister, Gloria, got married and moved to California. Diane was the only girl left at home, along with three older brothers. She also was ill when she was a little girl, which made her even more isolated. I wish I could have asked her what that was like—when it was just the four of them at home. My guess is that it must have felt lonely for her. As the littlest of seven, she put her head down and put her best face forward, just like she did when she got older. I understand what it's like to be reserved and shy, and this is yet another thing that my auntie and I have in common. My seventh-grade teacher once told my mom, "Staci doesn't ever raise her hand, but when called on, she always knows the answer." My auntie didn't call attention to herself either, but she always knew exactly what was going on. I completely understand this way of being in the world, and it makes me love her even more.

When Diane was sixteen, going on seventeen, Grandma Lola was in the midst of her attempt to leave Grandpa Fred, and she and Diane went to live in a little cabin next to Great-aunt Ida's house in downtown Grand Marais. While Grandpa was trying to woo Grandma back by dangling a whole restaurant in front of her, like a castle with a fancy gas stove, Aunt Diane was still in school, with one year left before graduation. It's not clear if Fred and Lola's apartment in Duluth above their new restaurant wasn't big enough for three, or if Aunt Diane made the decision on her own to stay in Grand Marais and finish school, but that's what she did. She spent some time living with my parents, who were newlyweds at the time, but she also stayed at her old school friend's house on Good Harbor Hill, a safe place for her to live while she tried to stay focused on her schoolwork. As Larry Krause explained, "Diane wanted to finish school. We always got along good. She was really cute, and everyone kind of had a crush on her. She must have asked my dad—when she wanted to finish her senior year. So, she lived with us in the farmhouse with me and four stepbrothers. (Larry's mom died when he was six.) I think she had the front bedroom. I was working—I only went to school four hours a day. We used to ride the bus to school, down County Road 7."

When she lived with them at the farmhouse, Larry wasn't home much. He said, "So, I'm trying to remember how long she stayed there. He went to work early and came home late at night. I was making a dollar an hour at the Co-op store, and I made $2,900 that year."

I asked Larry what happened to Aunt Diane after the got her diploma and he said, "I can't remember—I'm sure she left as soon as she graduated."

Larry didn't see Diane very much after that. He did hear things about her, such as the news that she had gotten married. He said, "I knew she had gotten married, and I didn't know him, but I knew who he was."

****

Aunt Diane married a man named Jim Johnson, who was a friend of her brother Bruce. They met in Minneapolis, which is where Bruce was living at the time. Uncle Bruce was married to Marietta, and they introduced Diane to the only man she would marry. Diane and Bruce ended up living pretty close to each other in southern Minnesota—she in Monticello and he in Faribault. When my cousin Cathy was eighteen and pregnant with her son Jason, she was sent to live with Aunt Diane for several weeks. She recalls that "Diane was beautiful. Her husband was crazy about her. She was the most fortunate of the three girls because she was the baby. I kind of think of her as 'the one that got away' from their childhood past. I always wanted to have her life and be at her house."

Cathy was just starting to "show" when she lived with Diane that summer. Grandpa Fred was sick and in the final stages of his life, and her mom, Gloria, was a single parent, soon to be a grandmother. She remembers that Diane and Jim's sons, Cody and Lance, had collected a number of garter snakes from the field outside and put them in a terrarium inside the house. It wasn't snake proof, and the critters escaped and crawled into Jim Johnson's shoes near the door. Cathy remembers Jim screaming when he put his foot into a shoe and was surprised by a mass of sleepy, curled-up garter snakes. Cathy said Aunt Diane took good care of her while she lived there and didn't make her feel bad about her situation—being unmarried and pregnant. She said, "I had vowed I wouldn't do what [my mom] did. And then most of us girls did." Diane didn't place any judgment on her, which is just what I would have expected. Cathy added, "It was then that Aunt Diane told me a lot of family truths. Aunt Diane knew a lot." According to Cathy, Diane "didn't drink like her sisters did when they were young. She was a good mother to the boys when they were little. But her husband Jim Johnson drank."

When I was eight or nine, we visited her at their house in Monticello. I distinctly remember arriving there and witnessing most of the adults get very drunk around her kitchen table. It's what we kids were used to back then, especially on the rare occasions when all the Drouillard aunts and uncles got together. I recall most of the adults slamming loudly out of the house, most likely on their way to a downtown bar. My mother stayed behind with us kids, which included me, my sister, and a number of cousins. Aunt Diane's three-legged German shepherd was also there and made my mother very nervous. This was right around the time she was having her own mental health crisis, and in retrospect, it's easy to see why big changes had to be made for the sake of her own health and the health of our family. She stayed there in a strange house with other people's kids and a dog she was afraid of, while her husband and his family were oblivious to everything but their own need to commune together, which always coalesced around drinking.

It's a distinct feeling, being in an unfamiliar house and witnessing your dad and your aunts and uncles all feed off the same family sickness that had terrorized them as kids—and now their own kids were watching it happen and it was as if we didn't matter at all to them. It's as if they had forgotten what it felt like to be young and forced to play second chair to a bottle of whiskey. I'm not really sure what the occasion was, but I know most of the Drouillard siblings were there: Doreen, Gloria, Diane, Stormy, Bruce, and my Dad. It could have been because Uncle Stormy was visiting from California, which would have been a big event, since he didn't come home very often. That night, after they all returned from the bar, they proceeded to get in a fight about something someone said (or because they were all drunk and hadn't eaten a damn thing). I knew my mother was upset by the circumstances and while I don't remember many details, I am able to connect with how I felt at that moment, watching all of their demons come together, like long-lost cronies, and witnessing how alcohol took over their physical bodies right there in the kitchen. They became like strangers standing in a sloppy circle on the clean, white tile floor, their faces reflected by the harsh florescent lights on the ceiling, yelling at each other while their kids pretended to sleep. I remember Aunt Diane's three-legged dog whining at the door, begging to get out, and I sympathized with it, because that kitchen was no place to be.

****

I'm tired now of writing about how alcohol dependency destroys the people we love. But there are still some things that need to be said about it. Aunt Diane, being an astute observer of all things, didn't drink alcohol as a young woman. It wasn't until after her marriage to Jim Johnson broke up that she started to use alcohol. Where there is pain, there is often addiction and self-destructive patterns. More often than not, we end up doing the same damn thing our parents did, just like my cousin Cathy admitted.

Jim had a reputation of being a "good guy." I never met him, or if I did, he left no impression on me, either good or bad. Marriages are complicated, and so are people, which is an absolute certainly in life, even though we are taught to believe maidens are rescued by handsome princes, and men and women are supposed to live in "holy matrimony" forever and ever, amen. But that didn't work out for Aunt Diane, and it doesn't work out for lot of us. It's just another lie women are told to keep the status quo. My own made-up, imaginary word for women who lose themselves inside the disappointments of marriage is **wi·drown.** Noun: A variation of "widow," referring to a married woman's loss of individualism. Use: "Under pressure to choose marriage over college, the young woman was at risk of becoming a widrown and sacrificing her dreams of becoming a doctor." Verb form: wi·drowned. The act of self-destruction as it relates to marriage. Use:

"Widrowned and suffering inside a bad marriage, Diane was left with no choice other than to file for a divorce."

Some women float; widrowns sink. And if the man you are married to is abusive, an addict, or hates himself, you are in danger of going down with the ship. Aunt Diane didn't do that. She left, and she floated. At least she tried to. And floating is its own kind of peril, but at least you have a chance of swimming to safety or reaching land eventually, and it's under your own power, not someone else's. Aunt Diane was no one's widrown.

There is also the complicated nature of insightful women who aren't easily placed into a recognizable mold. We aren't Jell-O, after all. Aunt Diane was also this kind of woman. Her sexuality was that of a two-spirited person—something that she talked about fairly openly, especially when she was a lot older and had seen a lot more life. My cousin Cathy said that it wasn't much of a secret that, when her marriage with Jim Johnson started to crumble, she left him for a "florist named Nancy." If my auntie were still here on earth, I would ask her about this, and she would tell me about it, because she didn't usually hide from things like that. And if she were still here, I could tell her about my own life and being two-spirited myself. It's yet another thing that she and I have in common.

* * * * * * *

In the Anishinaabe way, being born two-spirited is seen differently than it is by most patriarchal God-man worshipping societies that view men and women through the lens of an omnipotent male God. When Anton Treuer wrote about the life of Bagone-giizhig, or Hole in the Day, he included some specific history about men's and women's roles in traditional Anishinaabe society, before the realm of the God-man worshippers infiltrated Anishinaabewaki. He wrote specifically about the sociopolitical leaders of the time, who were usually men, but not always. Gaagige-ogimaansikwe (Forever Queen) was a highly respected leader of the Pembina Band in the Red River region of Minnesota and North Dakota.[6] Treuer writes that "women leaders in this sphere were usually, but not always, lesbian. Though female, they functioned as men socially and politically, took other women as wives, hunted, and engaged in war."

Treuer also wrote that it was considered taboo for women fighters who were at war to use anything that would pierce an enemy's body, such as arrows or bullets. So, women were allowed into battle, but only with blunt objects like clubs or stones. And counter to the prevalent and strictly patriarchal forms of society, the traditional Ojibwe culture readily "accepted variation" when it came to who actually did the men's and women's work—with men sometimes acting as women, and vice versa. As Treuer explained, "Men who chose to function as women were called ikwekaazo, meaning 'one who endeavors to be like a woman.' Women who functioned as men were called ininiikaazo, meaning 'one who endeavors to be like a man.'"

The role of two-spirited people in Anishinaabe society was considered sacred, "often because they assumed their roles based on spiritual dreams or visions." And they were "always honored, especially during ceremonies." If my aunt Diane had been born 250 years earlier, she would have been upheld as a powerful person whose life on earth was considered to be medicine for her people. She would have been honored with the ability to save and protect lives, much like the medicinal root that Mike Powell and Grandpa dug out of the ground on the day she was born. And perhaps her dreams and visions would have been honored instead of diminished.

But it was the 1960s, not the 1690s, and Aunt Diane's love affair with the florist didn't last very long. For reasons known only to her, Aunt Diane left her husband and Monticello behind, and moved back to her hometown, Grand Marais. It's not clear why she and our cousins Cody and Lance ended up living in our basement for a little while, but it really wasn't that unusual, because our Drouillard aunties were always a big part of our extended family, and this is how we did things. It seems like our aunties and cousins were always flowing in and out of our house on Eighth Avenue. Sometimes Aunt Gloria's daughters would come and stay for a week, and Thomasena would babysit us while our parents were out. I remember Bridgette, Tommy, and Melissa all staying at our house at certain times. And Aunt Doreen's kids were at our house a lot too. Sue mostly babysat us, but our cousin Tina was there all the time, which makes her more like our sister than a first cousin. So, when Aunt Diane moved into the basement for the summer, it seemed normal, because Grandma Lola had lived down there, and we were used to having someone pop in or come up from the basement for supper or breakfast—it didn't really matter who or when.

* * * * * * *

After Grandpa died in 1972, Grandma Lola lived with Aunt Gloria and her kids in Duluth for a while. Grandma Lola used to smoke a lot of cigarettes, and back then people smoked at will, in the house or the car. It's not like it is now. And so, wherever Grandma Lola was, there was also cigarette smoke, and usually a cup of strong, black coffee. She was tiny, but I never thought of her that way, because I used to watch her heft gigantic commercial mixer bowls of dough up onto the counter at the Harbor Inn Restaurant, which must have weighed about one-third of what she did.

Not long after Grandpa was gone, Lola's daughters Gloria and Doreen took her shopping for clothes and she got all kinds of new things, just for herself. I don't ever remember seeing her wear skirts or dresses—she favored stretchy pants and button-down blouses. When she went on her shopping spree, she picked out several new polyester suits that had matching pants and jackets. I remember her wearing a dark brown one in particular. It had decorative white stitching on it, and she looked so cute in it, my little grandma. Everyone loved Grandma Lola a lot, and she loved everyone back, times ten. Gloria's daughter, Cathy, who lived at home with her mom and grandma at that time, said that Grandma "finally had shoes that weren't those white cook shoes. And she got a new coat!"

A woman who had survived marriage to a man whose mood was as unpredictable as a woodland firestorm, Grandma deserved new shoes, a new coat, and a lot more. This is the time of her life when her kids took turns having her live with them, and she lived with Aunt Gloria for a while, and in our basement. My dad had spruced it up for her by adding a closet in one corner of her "apartment," which was really just the whole side of our basement that had the woodstove in it. She had her little batch of things down there: a bed, an old-fashioned rolltop desk, and lots of pulp fiction novels and true crime stories to read, which is an interesting look inside her mind. Crossword puzzles and word games were also her thing, and there was always a stack of magazines with word games in them next to her bed.

She still worked part-time as the morning baker at the Harbor Inn. Mom or Dad would give her a lift downtown, and she would do her work, making fresh bread, rolls, caramel rolls, and cinnamon loaves for the diners at the restaurant. Her niece Lois, her sister Ida's daughter, worked there, too, and so did my mom. Lois was always a very funny person, and Mom remembers her "talking stupid" and making Grandma Lola laugh so much that she would have to sit down on a crate of potatoes to avoid peeing her pants. I remember the two of them coming home after their shifts at the restaurant, which occasionally involved having a few drinks at the Legion. Neither of the two were skilled at drinking—in fact, they were ridiculously bad at it. So, they would come in the back entryway of our basement level, giggling and making a bunch of racket, and then they would fire up Grandma's turntable and play country music, dancing and laughing together the whole time like sisters, instead of an auntie and her niece. Oh, the things they knew and saw back then! We would peer at their dance party through the heating grate in the living room and it left quite an impression on me—watching Grandma and Lois totally cut loose, like they didn't have a care in the world.

****

Four months after Grandpa died our family drove to Florida to visit Uncle Monty and his family. Grandma Lola went along, and so did our cousin Sue Ellen, Aunt Doreen's daughter, who was sixteen at the time. I was five and my sister, Dawn, was just barely two. The six of us packed up into the family station wagon—the one with the wooden side panels—and headed out in the middle of February. This was the same car my mother drove to California, except it was five or six years newer and there was no danger of the muffler falling off. Five is just about the age where I started to form vivid, childhood memories that really stuck, and so I clearly remember sitting next to Grandma Lola in the wide back seat of the car most of the way to Florida. Dawn was in a car seat, and Sue Ellen rode in the jump seat, all the way in the back. There was a dramatic moment when Dad, misjudging the route through Chicago, ended up driving us straight down Wacker Drive and under the L train, a stunning moment for a kid who had never been farther away from home than Duluth, a comparatively tiny metropolis.

It was somewhere between downtown Chicago and Nashville that Grandma Lola taught me how to tie my shoes. There is a picture of the two of us, taken at Uncle Monty's house in Homestead, Florida. We're sitting side by side at the picnic table in his backyard. She has a cigarette in her right hand, and she's lightly resting her head on that same hand, while looking intently at the camera. I'm mimicking her posture exactly, in reverse, my left elbow propped on the table and resting the side of my own head lightly on my hand. I don't have a cigarette, of course, and my hair was long and dark, while hers was always cut into a pixie. But other than that, we are cookies cut from the same roll of dough.

Grandma was also the person who taught me the multiplication tables when I was in third grade. She was living in the basement, and she and I would sit at our dining room table and practice them together until I had every configuration memorized. It's a wonderful thing, to be able to say that your grandma loved you that much. I feel fortunate that she lived with us back then, because otherwise I may never have learned the solution to 8 x 7, or that bread rises when you put the pans on a warm heating grate, or that the perfect condition for yeast is "wrist temperature," which means that if the water feels too hot on your wrist, it's going to kill the yeast and your bread won't rise. These are just some of the things that she taught me in the little kitchen of our house on Eighth Avenue.

* * * * * * *

Grandma wasn't given very much time to laugh with Lois or live her own life after Grandpa died. There were about four years when she was healthy, and then the cigarettes finally got her. I hate cigarettes now because they took Grandma Lola away from us. She started to get sick in 1976, and she spent the last year of her life in a terrible state of pain and indescribable agony. I just don't understand how or why someone who went through everything she did in her life would be subjected to such a terrible death. She was shown no mercy and was given no reprieve. At first, she stayed with Aunt Doreen in Eveleth, and Doreen tried her best to take care of her. But pancreatic cancer is known as one of the most virulent and painful forms of cancer, and even now, medical research hasn't made much progress in learning how to save someone from that form of the disease.

When she was very sick, her kids made a plan to check her out of the hospital for an afternoon and bring her to our house. It was Christmas Eve, and knowing my family, there was likely some hope that she would be able to enjoy herself, even just for a little bit. I remember most of my aunts, uncles, and a lot of cousins were there, with the exception of Uncle Monty. There was some kind of potluck dinner planned, and everyone was concerned whether Grandma would be able to eat a little something. She was lying on the couch in our family room, wrapped up in blankets, and everyone was doing their best to put their best faces on for the sake of their matriarch.

My clearest memory of that terrible night was watching Grandma vomit into a bowl. Her family was standing helplessly by, and I remember that it was Aunt Diane who first started crying, which soon developed into her choking out terrible, sorrowful sobs. I don't remember anyone reaching out to comfort her, and though I'm sure the others were also crying over the state of Grandma Lola, the Drouillard sense of stoic resolve was on full view when it came to my dad. Men weren't supposed to cry, even when the saddest thing in the world is transpiring right in front of you. My ten-year-old self remembers that even in the sadness and darkness of that evening, my aunt Diane was brave enough to lead the way with her sorrow, and that she still looked beautiful to me, despite her tears that wouldn't stop.

When Grandma was in the late stages of her illness, she was in so much pain that nurses at the hospital had to tent the sheets around her little body, because it hurt to have fabric of any kind touch her skin. This fact makes it extremely difficult for me to understand or sympathize with the concept of "God's will," or belief in a divine plan that rains down on us lovingly from above. I stubbornly and resolutely refuse to believe that a merciful God or grandly designed spirit would intentionally put my little grandma through so much pain. And damn them if they did. When her torture finally came to an end, her funeral was at the Catholic church in Grand Marais and she was given

Lola Drouillard with her first four children, somewhere in the north woods. My father, Francis, is the baby, and next to him are Gloria, Doreen, and Monty. Grandma Lola was likely pregnant with her fifth child, Bruce, when this picture was taken in 1936.

a Catholic burial, just as Grandpa Fred would have dictated, had he still been on earth. She was laid to rest next to him, and their shared headstone is now close to Aunt Doreen's. It's also where we buried some of Uncle Bruce's ashes because his infant son is buried nearby at the edge of the cemetery.

Knowing that Grandma Lola used to teach Sunday school at the Congregational church, and that she converted to Catholicism because Grandpa asked her to might be construed as something she did for love, but what if her decision was based on fear instead? What if it was just another way for her husband, Fred, to control her in life, and now in death? On her daughter Diane's birthday—the day Grandma Lola almost died, it was earth magic that saved her life. That, and the human magic of the old ones, who knew what was needed and where to dig it up. When prayers and symbolic devotion failed, it was the earth that saved her, not the Catholic or Christian gods, who would have let her die that day. Because of the old ways of knowing, she lived for another thirty years, and was here to teach me to tie my shoes and when to brush melted butter on the top of a loaf of bread when it still has a few more minutes left in the oven. That to me is the work of heaven on earth. And behold! It came in the shape of Grandma Lola, who was saved by a simple root that grows in the forest—the church that surrounds us in Anishinaabewaki.

****

After Grandma died, our basement sat mostly empty until Aunt Diane and her boys moved in. My cousins Cody and Lance are five or six years older than me, and they were at our house most days, unless they were out on their bikes or rambling around with older kids whom I didn't know. Aunt Diane must have been in a rough place at that time, essentially homeless and forced to feel grateful to have three rollaway beds for her two kids and herself. Our house had only a single tiny bathroom with one toilet and one shower, and our whole family (all four of us) and Aunt Diane, Cody, and Lance all had to use it. I can see how her long stints in the bathroom getting ready for her bartending shift may have become an irritant to my dad, who at that time suffered from cluster headaches, which were sometimes so terrible he would have to drape his head with a hot towel over a bathroom sink full of steaming water in order to relieve the pressure built up inside his skull. So, it may have been the bathroom situation that sent him over the edge, or maybe it was the fact that Aunt Diane would go to work in the afternoon and be gone for a few days at a time, leaving her preteen sons in the care of their aunt and uncle, who already had plenty of struggles of their own. In any case, the night Aunt Diane tried to creep into the basement in the middle of the night to retrieve something from her stash of belongings, my dad was waiting for her and yelled at her to "get out of his house."

What's sad is that Dad had placed conditions on Diane, and when she didn't meet whatever expectation he had, he gave up on her and kicked her out. This is a big thing for children of alcoholics who struggle to gain control over things that are impossible to control—like your younger sister, who in his eyes, had screwed up her marriage and wasn't doing what she was supposed to do according to the laws of Poot. This kind of conditional arrangement wasn't new to the Drouillard family. The children of alcoholic families will often fall into the classic, codependent roles that develop when kids don't feel safe, and need to either feel cared for or be someone who takes care of others. In Dad's case, his role as family caretaker was fully formed as soon as he was old enough to realize that his mom was at times in a very dangerous situation, and that he could help her by taking care of things around the house and taking care of her and his brothers and sisters.

One incident he has shared from his mixed-up childhood happened when he was about twelve. He was working his first job, which was washing dishes at a café downtown. He had saved up enough money to buy Grandma Lola her first refrigerator, and he was really proud of it. The fridge was meant to make her life and the lives of everyone in the house easier, and she was over the moon about it. Grandpa Fred came home later that night, and in a drunken rage, pulled the refrigerator out of the house and threw it outside, damaging it beyond repair. The message, of course, was one of jealousy, but also that Dad had to be punished for showing up his own father, who made it crystal clear that he was the only "man" of the house, and that he could take care of things just fine. It still makes me sad, thinking about how that must have damaged my dad's self-esteem, a twelve-year-old kid who was just trying to take care of his mother.

Even as a young boy, Dad was always trying to take care of people and make things right, which was his role in the extended family. He felt a responsibility to take care of Aunt Diane in her time of need, just like he did for his mother, and at times his other two sisters, Doreen and Gloria. When Aunt Diane ignored the conditions that he had set up in his own mind about how she should live, act, or be while in his care, it was grounds enough to send her packing, along with his two nephews. With shame and anger come a breakdown in communications, and Aunt Diane and my dad didn't talk to each other for a while after that. She was good at making herself scarce and even better at burning bridges. It was her way of clearing the air from afar.

This is when she moved into the yellow house downtown, the one with the Aqua Net on the back of the toilet. Cody and Lance attended school in Grand Marais for a while and she worked at the Kove, serving up drinks four at a time to the regulars at the bar. Things at our house were pretty confusing then. It was when Mom was at the hospital in Duluth, and later at Prescott, Wisconsin, and Dawn and

I were in the care of Aunt Betty and Aunt Lila for the better part of a year. It's hard to remember things about that time in our lives, and whatever memories are there seem foggy and disjointed. When Mom got better and came home, I remember that Aunt Diane still lived in Grand Marais but we didn't see her very much.

There was just one incident that sticks out and it has to do with our poodle that we raised as a puppy. His name was Beau Jacques and he was a really smart dog, but unpredictable, especially around strangers or kids with food. In retrospect, it was bad timing for us to have any sort of pet, since there were a lot of other things that needed to be taken care of. I think the dog suffered for it, and one day he bit one of our friends from the neighborhood in the face. It was a vicious bite, and I remember it so clearly, like you remember the feeling of a bad burn, even many years later. It's something that still haunts my mom, who was never all that fond of having animals in the house anyway. My dad took it out on the dog, and then, because meanness begets meanness, Beau Jacques bit the UPS man. My parents decided that we would have to say goodbye to our little poodle, which in code meant that they were going to have him killed. Aunt Diane offered to take him instead, being a friend to animals and having some experience working with beasts much bigger than he was. Sadly, Beau Jacques never stopped biting, and I was afraid to ask what happened to him after that. Another bad ending, at a confusing time and when everyone was barely afloat.

****

It was after she moved back to Grand Marais that Aunt Diane decided a bartender's life was not for her. She stopped floating and was determined to swim herself to shore. She independently worked with the Grand Portage Education Office and secured tribal funding to go to college to study criminology. Her brother Stormy was working as a prison guard in California, and she may have been inspired by his line of work when she sent herself back to school. Uncle Stormy had worked at the infamous Folsom Prison and at Tehachapi correctional facility. He also worked at Soledad, where he guarded Sirhan Sirhan, the man accused and convicted of gunning down Bobby Kennedy. Uncle Stormy's stories about working in these huge prisons were always tantalizing to us when we were kids. It seemed like an important and colorful job, but now, with a fully adult perspective, working as a guard in a maximum security prison must have been a stressful and at times terrifying job.

Aunt Diane was accepted into a program at St. Cloud State University, from which she graduated with a two-year degree in criminology. She and Uncle Monty were the only two Drouillard siblings to attend college, and Uncle Monty got his degree through the U.S. Army, not as a civilian like Aunt Diane did. Uncle Monty was a lifelong soldier who served on the USS *Nautilus*, the first nuclear-powered submarine in the world. When he was a young man he used to say, "I'll travel the world and find my true love in Crete." And just as he predicted, he met a woman named Lucretia, whose nickname was Creta. He had found his true love, except she lived in Grand Rapids, Minnesota, not in Greece. The two of them were married and stayed together until Aunt Creta died. Together they had a family of boys— our Florida cousins. Uncle Monty's accomplishments were never fully appreciated or even recognized by our family, and I feel bad about this. I also feel bad that Aunt Diane's status as the only Drouillard daughter to graduate from high school and complete a college degree was often diminished or ignored. It's that old propensity to try to keep all your fellow lobsters in the pot, even though the water is about to get really hot. In my opinion, what she did was a really big deal, and it set her life on a new course, which is always the hardest thing to do when you are in danger of going under.

Aunt Diane first got a job working at the Minnesota Correctional Facility in St. Cloud as a guard. A men's prison that was first built back in the late 1800s, when she worked there it housed men ages eighteen to thirty. This is where she was allegedly embroiled in a love affair with a prisoner. I never asked Diane about it, but Aunt Gloria knew the story, and when she told me about it, it was the kind of thing that isn't easily forgotten. It sends my imagination running wild—trying to piece together the circumstances of the relationship, how it began, and where it took place. I also marvel at how very dangerous it would have been for both of them if they had been caught. Eventually they were, and that was how her first job as a correctional officer came to an end. I shudder to think what happened to the prisoner she was involved with. It's the kind of thing you would read about in a novel or see exploited in a Hollywood movie.

She moved to Las Vegas after that and we heard she was working in law enforcement, though it's not clear if she was employed as a prison guard or was working as a police officer on the beat. It's possible that she worked both jobs while she lived there. Her good friend Marie Spry said that while Diane was working in Vegas, she befriended a homeless woman whom she took care of at times. As Marie described it, "She was in the police force out there. When she was in Vegas, there was a homeless woman—she'd take her off the street, clean her up, feed her, she really watched out for these homeless people. She'd get her a shower, get her some clothes. There were others, too, that she helped."

We got a Christmas card from her one year that included a color picture of her wearing deep-red lipstick and her prison uniform, complete with badge, nightstick, and holstered gun. She had rightfully earned her weapons of war and was sanctioned by the powers that be to use them, as she deemed necessary. It was a significant accomplishment for anyone, but especially for a self-educated woman in the 1970s. In the picture, Aunt Diane's eyebrows were shaped differently, thinner at the edges and darkened-in with eyebrow pencil. Her expression looked a little bit harder than I remember, but she was still lovely in a familiar way, and I remember missing her and wondering if I would ever see her again. Being in full uniform and armed with her unique brand of tough femininity, and she wore it well. It also must have felt good for her to send that picture to us, as a way of showing my dad that his youngest sister really didn't need anyone to take care of her, that she was perfectly capable of taking care of herself, and others too. It makes sense to learn that she took it upon herself to befriend and help a homeless woman and other people who lived on the streets of Las Vegas. It fits with my own experience of knowing her as an empathetic and kind person who wanted to make a difference in the world.

* * * * * * *

My auntie stayed in Las Vegas until she reached retirement age, and then she moved back to the North Shore in 1999. She was hired to be the caretaker of the Elders' apartment building in Grand Portage, and I went to see her a quite a few times while she was living there. According to her friend Marie, "She would keep hallways, laundry rooms, kitchen clean and everything, and I think she collected rent from the people too."

Her apartment was always really smoky, but there were lots of neat things to look at. She really liked antiques and even though the place was hazy, it was always pretty tidy and everything had its place. When she first moved to Grand Portage she was still driving, and so once in a while she would make the trek to my parents' former place about a mile east of Reservation River.

She wasn't taking very good care of herself then. In addition to heavy smoking, she had developed a daily drinking habit. I don't know how much she drank, and it doesn't really matter anymore. The disease followed her, like it did so many others in our family. No doubt she tried to escape it, like she had escaped some of the Drouillard family's dark past at least once before in her life. The more she drank, the harder she was to get along with. Her natural propensity was to clear the air and burn bridges, and sometimes she was hard to be around. She was never mean to me, but I've heard some stories. When you live in an apartment building with a lot of other people it isn't a good idea to make enemies, and I'm sure some people saw through her tough exterior, while others didn't. This is not to say that Aunt Diane alienated everyone. Two of her good friends, Marie and Shirley, stuck with her throughout her last days on earth. She and Marie met at an Elders' event around 2002. Aunt Diane was making a turkey for the crowd and Marie said that "she insisted I eat something." Like her mother and her sisters, Aunt Diane was also a wonderful cook, and Marie said it was Aunt Diane who taught her how to make gravy. In Marie's words, "She was a heck of a cook—she really showed me a lot of things to do. I had no idea [how] to make gravy. She always told me that the trick to making gravy is to let it simmer a long time. She worked downtown in Grand Marais as a cook at the El Ray Café [now the Blue Water]."

When Marie and I were talking about Aunt Diane's life I mentioned that Auntie loved to feed people, but then she wouldn't eat anything herself. She had emacifeeder tendencies, just like her mom and my aunt Doreen did. Marie concurred with that assessment, but then told this story about a time when she successfully got Aunt Diane to eat a big bowl of soup: "I made corn chowder for the first time—I took a bowl over to her. She said, 'You know, this is so good I would serve this in my supper club.'" Bless you, Marie, for making sure Aunt Diane was well fed and giving her a place at the table.

* * * * * * *

In spite of her unpredictable temperament, Aunt Diane stayed productive when it came to doing the things she enjoyed and loved. An avid gardener and houseplant enthusiast, she once made a special planting for her friend Marie's office when she was first elected to the tribal council. One of Diane's more amazing accomplishments was the creation of a perennial garden at the Elders' apartment complex in Grand Portage. It was her idea to build it and she followed through in a big way—a project that lasted many years. The Elders' Community Garden was big—about twenty feet deep by forty feet long. Marie described Aunt Diane's effort like this: "She had the biggest, most beautiful garden you've ever seen. The whole backwoods along the edge of the parking lot were just full of perennials in beautiful colors. Sunup 'til sundown, she'd work in that garden. She had to put a couple of hoses together to water it. She would pull them across the parking lot to get the water from the building, and the groundskeeper, one time he run over her hose and cut it in half in several places on purpose. She had a time of it. But people would come up there all the time to see her garden. She didn't have a lot of help—but sometimes kids from a church in Ham Lake would come and help her weed. It had been going for a few years before I met her. There was a [creek] that ran through it. She had a gazebo back there and everything. She had all of these creatures she put in it—frogs and things."

The garden even made the local paper, with a picture of Aunt Diane next to the sign. I clipped it and have it here in the Drouillard file, where you'll find everything from Diane's perennial garden to a police report about the time Great-uncle Charlie and Grandpa Fred got arrested for a dustup downtown. It's all in there.

Auntie suffered from rheumatoid arthritis that got worse and worse with age. The more pain she was in, the more she let things go. Invasive lupines started to take over her garden and according to

Marie, "People went up there and dug her perennials up—for years she had them up there, and they kept disappearing. Originally, she only had lupines that were red—and there were just a few—they were a rare color. One day we went up there and they were gone. Someone had dug them up."

I just can't get over the meanness of people sometimes. A love of gardens and flowers is an important gift, and all of Diane's hard work digging, planting, transplanting, weeding, and watering a garden for the community was disrespected by some people who were only concerned with themselves. It's yet another instance in her life where people took her love and care for granted and let her down mightily— this time at the cost of her carefully tended garden that took her years to cultivate.

There's a larger point to make about Aunt Diane's need and desire to grow things. To be a successful gardener requires space, and taking up space and the use of land, especially if the land is designated for a community garden, should have been honored and respected by others. But I suppose that because she was sometimes hard to get along with, people felt justified in running over her garden hose or digging up her plants. It was their way of trying to keep her in her place, a particularly disappointing outcome, because breaking free of other people's expectations was something she struggled with her whole life. She more than deserved to take up space in this world, and the spaces she inhabited were uniquely hers—because there was no one quite like her.

Besides her work in the garden, Aunt Diane also volunteered to cook for holiday events at her apartment complex, and she would occasionally fry trout fingers at the Elders' booth during the annual Rendezvous Days and Celebration Pow-Wow. I stopped in to see her one time and was amazed to watch her in action at the fryer—her fingers were painfully swollen and gnarled with arthritis, but she was still able to expertly fry trout pieces to a perfectly golden brown. I swoon just thinking about how delicious the trout chunks were that day.

One terrible afternoon Aunt Diane was in her garden, and she tripped and fell, hurting herself pretty badly. She was sent to the hospital in Duluth and after she got a bit better, she came back to her apartment in Grand Portage. A medical doctor in Duluth prescribed morphine for her arthritis, which she got hooked on "for years." As Marie described it, "She had [doses] in two different sizes—big ones and smaller ones."

Whoever this doctor was ignored the holistic approach to help-ing Aunt Diane as a person, and instead prescribed a life-threatening opiate to an elderly woman who was a known alcoholic. This tragically misguided mistake, by a person who should have known much better, would be the catalyst that set Aunt Diane on a course from which she would never fully recover. Still drinking, smoking, and now taking daily doses of morphine, her quality of life got very strange. She still owned a Blazer SUV, but she was not well enough to drive it, and she eventually lost her license. My independent and tough auntie's life was now ruled by health problems, including her addiction to vodka, which was finding its way into her coffee mug early in the day. This is when she reached a new state of vulnerability, and things were very precarious for her. Once in a while there would be a snippet of a police report in the local paper that went something like this: *Grand Portage, Wednesday, 7:26 p.m.—caller reports seeing a man in uniform staring at them from the woods at the edge of the parking lot. Officers responding found no sign of an intruder.*

Although those small-town police reports never name anyone, I always had the sneaking suspicion that the call came from Aunt Diane, who was hallucinating things from the bottom of her empty coffee cup, and that she must have felt terrified and alone when she made the call. This makes me feel melancholy, knowing that the para-noia exhibited by her father in his old age had overtaken her body and mind similar to the invasive lupines in her garden, and that no amount of willpower or medical help would be enough to change the troubling genetics she inherited from her father. The odds were never in her favor when it came to escaping the same fate, and it just doesn't seem fair to her, or to her kids or anyone else.

****

Around this time, her younger son moved in with her at her apart-ment, which broke the rules of Elders' housing. The two of them then moved into a two-bedroom house on Upper Road. I never visited them there, but Aunt Diane's friend Marie stayed in touch with her throughout this difficult time in her life. It was Thanksgiving and as Marie tells it, "The one time when she was living in the brown house, I went down there with Thanksgiving dinner for her and she didn't answer the door. I couldn't get in, so I called law enforcement. At the time I was on the ambulance squad and the deputy broke the window and she was inside, laying on the floor in the bedroom and she was freezing cold. They took her in an ambulance to the hospital in Duluth."

Her caregivers in Duluth got her through the worst of her withdrawal, and then she was transferred to the hospital in Grand Marais, where her primary doctor carefully and diligently worked to wean her off the addictive pills she had been given, seemingly without regard, by another doctor. I went to visit her when she was recovering from this bout of illness, and the first thing she said to me after "Hello, dear" was "I'm teaching everyone to say 'fuck' around here."

We laughed really hard at this, and I knew then that the Aunt Diane I used to know and love was back. I sat with her for quite a while as she explained that she was feeling better, and that she was keeping the staff well entertained, including her primary care doctor, who knew just how to talk with her to make her feel like she was being heard. She was getting a lot of B-complex vitamins and she was eating food, and they had reversed the dehydrated state she was in when she was first admitted. And thankfully, she was off morphine, which may have been the very worst thing she could ever have ingested. She survived it, and now here she was teaching everyone to swear like a prison guard, including the innocent nurses who came in to check on her after breakfast. She told me she was planning to "get the hell out of here" and that her friend Marie would be coming to pick her up to take her home. And I believed her because she had once again taken charge of herself—something she had been doing her entire life.

True to her word, Aunt Diane sprang herself out and fired her well-meaning doctor, who was trying to keep her admitted and thereby safe from harm. According to Marie, "I think she fired him a couple of times." The day Aunt Diane checked herself out, Marie said, "she was at the Care Center and she called me. She told me, 'I'm going to get out of here, and I expect you to come and get me.' So I did. And there she was sitting out on the curb with all her stuff."

She discharged herself, kicked the doctor off her lawn, and lived the rest of her life exactly as she wanted to. I would expect nothing less of her. My partner and I were traveling in Ireland when my dad made the international call to tell me Aunt Diane had died. I started crying immediately, because I loved her and I didn't get to say goodbye. Hearing the news, I felt the loss of her in my heart, as if a bright little spark of light had moved through it and now it was gone.

Some people might say that Aunt Diane lived her life at the edge of a dark woods, but I only see her in the light of the sun. When she passed out of this world, her friends Marie and Shirley were there, and her son Lance. A dear friend of mine who worked at the Care Center was also there with her. She was very fond of Aunt Diane and saw some of the same things in her that I always did. She was there when the Catholic priest was called to deliver last rites, and then my auntie was gone. My friend said that when Aunt Diane left the pain and trouble of this world behind, "the room was full." She had come into the world blessed with earthly magic and insisted on following her own path through the forest. She knew how to behave but also had the courage to break all the rules; she succumbed to outside pressures but ultimately took charge of her own life; she fired her doctor twice and swore with abandon, like a lipsticked beat cop on the streets of Las Vegas. On the night she left, the room full of spirits swirled around her life, got her ready to travel, and opened their arms to make her feel welcome.

****

It was a beautiful, sunny, fall day and I was relaxing on the deck when a ruffled youngster of a hummingbird buzzed in right next to me and set its little body down on a piece of driftwood very close by. Its mother or sister was drawing nectar out of our feeder, and from her vantage point on the driftwood, the miniature bird began to let out tiny little "cheeps." Its needle-sharp beak kept opening and closing with the most delicate of movements, as it talked to me in its hummingbird language. Perhaps it was a warning sound, or maybe she was trying to tell me they were all about to take their leave from the hill—but wanted to reassure me that they would be back.

I haven't seen Aunt Diane's oldest son, Cody, since I was a kid. He recently sent me a Facebook friend request, which I ruminated on for a while. Even though we were cousins, he didn't quite fit my informal "friend" criterion, which is: if we've never been in each other's kitchen, or we haven't shared a meal together, add this person with caution. He had been in our kitchen of course, and I in his, it was just a really, really long time ago. Thinking of Aunt Diane, I approved his friend request and I'm glad I did.

Just the other day, he posted, "If hummingbirds are gods on earth, then I just stared into the eyes of God."

This personal quip sort of opened Cody up to me as a person I didn't know but had some understanding of, because it reminded me of something his mother might say. I could just hear Aunt Diane revealing this wisdom while she refilled her hummingbird feeder, which always hung on the outside wall of her apartment building in Grand Portage, just next to the sliding glass door that opened out onto the patio. I can so easily see her straining up to reach the hook, cigarette burning in an ashtray on a wooden bench. This is where she would sit and smoke when the weather was warm and drink her coffee throughout the day. The ashtray was overflowing with Marlboro butts, some with lipstick traces and some burned right down to the filter. At some point later in the day, she would switch from coffee to vodka, and if you were able to visit with her before the vodka took over, she would often be full of stories, tell some bawdy jokes, or occasionally deliver a philosophical musing that would hit you like a revelation.

"Staci Lola," she would say in her dark and husky voice, "did you know that hummingbirds are close to God?"

Cody's question really gets at why I don't care what Aunt Diane did or didn't do in her life. In some ways, I got the feeling she was the closest person to "God" I've ever known. And not because she liked to go to mass, or lived her life as a Christian or Catholic, which she did to a certain extent. Nor is it because she viewed life as an Ojibwe traditionalist who believed in earth magic and intangible things, which she also did. She was never very exact about any of that. It's because she was wickedly observant and would at times pass along her nuggets of divine wisdom in the form of an acute observation about the way things are according to Diane. The reverence she held for wild birds, horses, dogs (three-legged or otherwise), her lovingly created garden in Grand Portage, or the creatures of the woods that she had

known as a little girl, is something I have always known and understood. Aunt Diane was a deep person in a lot of ways. And she was
just as likely to commune with the earthly spirits as she was with the
denizens of the heavens. This is the place of the hummingbird—the
little being that brings medicine and healing to people who are sick or
suffering. I personally believe that it was the presence of those little,
winged spirits, and other earthly magical beings that visited her at various points in her life, that brought her through the very difficult, and
at times, deathly, self-destructive moments of her life here on earth.

That little bird today felt like it was speaking to me because it
knew I was missing someone. It was not afraid of being close by, and
its tiny, sweet voice carried with it the immense power of gods and
goddesses here on earth. I cried, thinking of how these birds travel for
thousands of miles twice a year. Every spring when they come back to
our yard in the hills along Lake Superior, I am completely humbled by
their divine presence. And so, today, when the male rubythroats have
already started their migration south, I felt so honored that I was able
to share the company of this beautiful young female before it takes off
for the next world. I want to explain everything. To tell it where I come
from and describe all the places that I want to go. My heart is full of
messages I'd like to send—one for each of my aunties. I want to tell
them how much I miss them and thank them for being mine. I open
my mouth to speak, and the little bird releases its hold on the earth,
hovers at eye level for a few seconds, and flies away.

Perhaps it's returning to the Yucatán, Costa Rica, Jamaica, or
back to an elderly Mexican woman's patio on the outskirts of Oax-
aca—a warm and sunny place where she has lovingly filled a feeder
with sugar water and hung it on the wall outside her little apartment.
This is where she'll sit, smoking a cigarette in the shade and waiting
for the face of God to return to her for the long winter. She has been
judiciously saving up her words, because she and the hummingbird
will have an awful lot to talk about.

Spirits: A Poem for Diane

Which came first,
hummingbirds or flowers?
Spirits in rare colors,
a flash of light
like a laugh,
the most profane part
of our human language.
Which came first,
hummingbirds or flowers?
Spirits in endless shapes,
a sweet voice
like a prayer,
the universal nectar
of our ancient language.

Seven Lessons

Bring the babies home. Modern research has proven that the presence of a maternal grandmother in a baby's life can increase child survival rates and overall health more than the presence of a biological father.[1] Grandma Freda knew this without knowing it.

Empower our girls to tell. There is freedom to live, freedom to roam, when everyone knows and understands the realm of truth.

Allow girls and women to embody ourselves fully. Teach the littlest ones to walk with their feet solidly on the earth. Those who walk with their feet fully planted are much harder for others to steal away.

Use words to nourish, not starve. Think of words as if they are a banquet, or a feast. Let the table be full and put out your very best dishes.

Invest in our women and girls as if life depends on them. Because it does. What, then, is the value of life? Acknowledge the high price of paucity and begin to pay it forward.

Stop the record from skipping.

Listen.

ACKNOWLEDGMENTS

Breathing Them In

How do you thank someone for saving your life? For accepting you as you are? For being an inextricable part of you, from beginning to end? My seven aunts are as close to me as the air in my lungs and yet as far away as the moon. I breathe them in and say their names: Faye, Lila, Doreen, Gloria, Betty, Carol, Diane. I keep their names quiet so I don't disturb them. This is for them and also for all of the people who miss them dearly. To my cousins on both sides—I love you all. There is nothing comparable to the shared experience of family, and I'm thankful for you.

Several cousins helped me directly with the chapters, sharing family stories, confirming historical facts, and doing the very brave work of reminiscing, which can at times be a terribly sad and painful process. Jeannie Miller, thank you for bringing your hope and truth to Auntie Faye's chapter. Linda Garner Hartman, Lilean Sedlacek, Lori Garner Hallfrisch, and Lisa Gomoll—thank you for reading the chapter about Aunt Lila, sharing her history, and helping me through it. I miss her so much. Sue Smith and Tina Voce—miigwech for your honest and helpful interviews and for sharing more about Aunt Doreen. You are my sisters. To Auntie Gloria's family—especially Cathy Ann Firth, Thomasena Pelkey, Bridgette Angelos, and Cameron McClure—thank you for your bravery, love, strength, good humor, and tears. I'm so proud of you all. Cindy Carol and Andrea Larsen, thanks for reading the chapter about Aunt Betty and, mostly, "thanks for being you." Ron Hagdon, I appreciate your review of Aunt Carol's chapter. I know you miss her a lot. To Cody Johnson—the hummingbirds return every year, bringing news from faraway places. They do know things, and I hope you hear from them in the spring. To Marie Spry and Larry Krause—thank you for loving Aunt Diane and for sharing your insight into her life. To my cousin Bob Swanson, miigwech for helping to fill in Hank Amyotte's military history and for your good work in documenting our family story.

Erik Anderson, Rachel Moeller, Laura Westlund, Mary Byers, Catherine Casalino, and everyone at the University of Minnesota Press—you make this seem like magic, which is an art in itself. Thank you for your time, careful thought, and close attention to your craft. I'm amazed by the work you do.

To Cathy Quinn—you bring riches to my life and to our family. Thank you for . . . everything. Francis Trout Endrizzi, I'm so proud to be your auntie. Thank you for your easygoing spirit and for thinking I'm funny. And none of these words matter very much without the love, beauty, and support of my mother, Joyce Alice Drouillard, who took me through the Burge family history and was willing to share the lives of her sisters with me, an act of faith and generosity. You continue to teach us how to do really difficult things, all the while maintaining your ridiculous sense of humor. To my Pa, Francis "Pooty" Drouillard, someone who has shown an awe-inspiring ability to evolve and change for the sake of your family, thank you for breaking the cycle. And to my sister, Dawn, who read every chapter and lived it right alongside me: Giza gi'in, I love you.

ηotes

FAYE

Interviews with Betty Larsen (2016), Joyce Drouillard (2020), Ray (Pete) Burge (2020), and Lilean Garner Sedlacek (2021); phone conversation with Jeannie Miller (2021); and Burge family letters contributed to this chapter. The photograph of Faye Palmer and the Burge children is from the George Burge photograph collection.

1. The Ojibwe Nation's traditional homelands are centered around the Great Lakes area. Ojibwemowin is the language of the Ojibwe people.

2. Leo Trunt, *"Prosper, Can You Tell Me More?": The History of Acropolis, Ball Bluff, Blackberry, Bruce Siding, Feeley, Goodland, Island Farm, Jacobson, Leipold, Sago, Swan River, Warba and Wawina, Minnesota* (Baltimore: Gateway Press, 1993).

3. Case 267 Wis. 272, *Supreme Court of Wisconsin, In re Adoption of Tschudy*, June 8, 1954. It should be noted that the widow in this case attempted to flee from Madison, Wisconsin, with the boy, rather than return him to the care of the state. The state then issued a warrant for her arrest, and she eventually surrendered the child. She had the resources to hire a lawyer and sued her home county for custody of the boy. Ultimately, the Wisconsin Supreme Court reversed the ruling of the lower court and issued the opinion that "following the death of petitioner's husband, the child was left in the care of responsible people, and that he suffered no ill effects during Dorothy Tschudy's absence while she was engaged in employment; that the bond of love and affection between the child and the petitioner was close, normal, and satisfactory; that the best interest and general welfare of the child will be promoted through the prompt return of the child to the petitioner. That such return will tend to avoid injury to his mental health; that placing him in a foster home and into another home on a year's trial basis before adoption will not be for the child's

welfare; that while a father for an adoptive family is desirable, it is not essential that there be such father for the bringing up of a boy."

LILA

Written notes by Lilean Garner Sedlacek (2021), Lori Garner Hallfrisch (2021), and Lisa Garner Gomoll (2021); interviews with Lila Garner (courtesy of Lisa Garner Gomoll), Lilean Garner Sedlacek (2020), and Joyce Drouillard (2020); Burge family letters; a memory from Aunt Lila's funeral, as shared by Linda Garner-Hartman (2021); and a phone conversation with Linda Garner-Hartman (2021) contributed to this chapter. The photograph of Lila Garner is from the author.

1. Joy Harjo, "Listening, Allowing and Creation," presentation, Collective Trauma Summit 2020, the Pocket Project.

DOREEN

Interviews with Sue Smith (2020), Tina Voce (2020), Gloria Martineau (2021), and Cathy Ann Firth (2021); as well as written notes from Tina Voce (2021) contributed to this chapter. Photograph of Doreen Voce is from Gloria Martineau's photograph collection, with thanks to Cathy Firth.

1. While "Ojibwe" and "Anishinaabe" are sometimes used interchangeably, the definition of each word carries a different connotation. Ojibwe is the name of the tribe of Indigenous people who live in a large area surrounding the Great Lakes, including the Ojibwe Bands in Minnesota, Wisconsin, Michigan, and North Dakota, as well as the Ojibwe First Nations in Ontario. The term Anishinaabe is often used in a traditional sense to mean "spontaneous man" or "first man," and in some cases the word is used to describe all human beings. In an interview with Erik Redix for the radio series *Anishinaabe Bizindamoo Makak*, Fond du Lac language specialist Dr. Gordon Jourdain explained that "we are all Anishinaabe people, we just speak different languages" (WTIP Community Radio, November 2021).

2. Sue was visited by a fourteen-point buck and a pileated woodpecker during our interview.

3. Anton Treuer, *Everything You Wanted to Know about Indians but Were Afraid to Ask* (St. Paul, Minn.: Borealis Books, 2012), 118.

4. Brenda Child, *Holding Our World Together: Ojibwe Women and the Survival of Community* (New York: Penguin, 2010), 41–42.

5. Bill Amyotte, Grand Portage, interview by Karissa White and Brian Horrigan, 2006, Minnesota Historical Society, St. Paul. The racial slur "Jap" appears as it was recorded in the original interview. The author recognizes its use in a historical context and does not condone racist language.

GLORIA

Interviews with Cathy Ann Firth and Cameron McClure (2021) and Gloria Drouillard Martineau (2001) contributed to this chapter. Photograph of Gloria Martineau is courtesy of Cathy Ann Firth.

1. I think Auntie was referring to the Latin prayer "Gloria Patri, et Filio, et Spiritui Sancto. Sicut erat in principio, et nunc, et semper, et in saecula saeculorum" (Glory to the Father, and to the Son, and to the Holy Spirit. As it was in the beginning, is now, and ever shall be, world without end).

2. John Drouillard and Elizabeth Anakwad were never legally married in a Catholic ceremony. This may be because he never divorced his first wife, Mary Bachand, in Bayfield. Divorce was not commonplace, and on a number of the baptismal records for their children, including Fred's, there is a note indicating that it was a "conditional baptism," because the parents were not married in the Catholic tradition.

3. Willie Drouillard was Grandpa Fred's brother.

4. http://www.native-languages.org/pukwudgie.htm.

5. Sarah Pruitt, "Does Hangar 18, Legendary Alien Warehouse, Exist? Crashed UFOs, Alien Autopsies and Government Cover-Ups—Untangling the Legend Surrounding Ohio's Wright-Patterson Air Force Base," January 17, 2020, https://www.history.com/news/hangar-18-ufos-aliens-wright-patterson.

BETTY

An interview with Betty Larsen (2016) and Burge family letters contributed to this chapter. Photograph of Betty Larsen is courtesy of Cindy Larsen.

1. https://en.wikipedia.org/wiki/List_of_religious_slurs.

2. John Kinville, *The Grey Eagles of Chippewa Falls: A Hidden History of a Women's Ku Klux Klan in Wisconsin* (Charleston, S.C.: History Press, 2020), 31.

3. Briana Novacek, "Terribly Close to Home: Women's KKK History in Chippewa Falls," review of *The Grey Eagles of Chippewa Falls*, by John Kinville, *Volume One*, January 22, 2020.

4. Patrick Hanks, ed., *Dictionary of American Family Names* (New York: Oxford University Press, 2003), 580.

5. According to Joyce Drouillard, Faye and Bud were never married. Faye needed Bob Palmer's Social Security payments as income, and marrying Bud would have ended those payments.

6. Joy Harjo, "Listening, Allowing and Creation," presentation, Collective Trauma Summit 2020, the Pocket Project.

CAROL

Interviews with Joyce Drouillard (2021), Lilean Garner Sedlacek (2020), and Betty Larsen (2016), as well as Burge family letters, contributed to this chapter. Photograph of Carol Hagdon is courtesy of Joyce Drouillard, and photograph of Freda Burge is from the photograph collection of Sandy Burge, with thanks to Janelle Zielinski.

1. Elizabeth Paton, "Lockdowns Magnify a Vexing Disorder," *New York Times*, May 24, 2020.

2. Paton, "Lockdowns."

3. https://www.thecanadianencyclopedia.ca/en/article/indigenous-suffrage.

4. Joy Harjo, "Listening, Allowing and Creation," presentation, Collective Trauma Summit 2020, the Pocket Project.

DIANE

Interviews with Milt Powell (2012), Larry Krause (2020), Gloria Martineau (2001), Cathy Ann Firth and Cameron McClure (2021), and Marie Spry (2021) contributed to this chapter. Photograph of Diane Johnson is courtesy of Joyce Drouillard, and photograph of Lola Drouillard and her children is from the Drouillard family photograph collection.

1. In 1854, the Lake Superior Ojibwe (Grand Portage, Bois Forte, and Fond du Lac Bands) entered into a treaty with the United States ceding approximately 5.5 million acres to the United States government. These lands are called "1854 ceded territory," which covers all, or portions, of six counties. While reserving usufructuary rights to hunt, fish, and gather resources in ceded territory, the 1854 Treaty also established several reservations in Minnesota, Wisconsin, and Michigan.

2. Brenda Child, *Holding Our World Together: Ojibwe Women and the Survival of Community* (New York: Viking Penguin, 2012), 105–6.

3. https://www.mnopedia.org/civilian-conservation-corps-minnesota-1933-1942.

4. Child, *Holding Our World Together*, 111, 112–13.

5. Child, 107.

6. This and related quotations are from Anton Treuer, *The Assassination of Hole in the Day* (St. Paul: Minnesota Historical Society Press, 2011), 26–28.

CODA

1. Abigail Tucker, "Whale Mothers Need Their Moms. So Do I," *New York Times*, May 2, 2021.

Staci Lola Drouillard lives and works in her hometown of Grand Marais on Minnesota's North Shore of Lake Superior. She is a direct descendant of the Grand Portage Band of Ojibwe and author of *Walking the Old Road: A People's History of Chippewa City and the Grand Marais Anishinaabe* (Minnesota, 2019), winner of the Hamlin Garland Prize from the Midwestern History Association and the Northeastern Minnesota Book Award for Nonfiction.